On Education

The Mother

On Education

Sri Aurobindo Ashram, Pondicherry

First edition 1978
Second edition 1999
Sixth impression 2016

Rs 260
ISBN 978-81-7058-554-1

© Sri Aurobindo Ashram Trust 1978, 1999
Published by Sri Aurobindo Ashram Publication Department
Pondicherry 605 002
Web http://www.sabda.in

Printed at Sri Aurobindo Ashram Press, Pondicherry
PRINTED IN INDIA

Publisher's Note

This volume is a compilation of the Mother's articles, messages, letters and conversations on education. Three dramas, written for the annual dramatic performance of the Sri Aurobindo International Centre of Education, are also included.

PART ONE. ARTICLES

The fifteen articles here were first published in the *Bulletin of Physical Education* (later renamed *Bulletin of Sri Aurobindo International Centre of Education*) between 1949 and 1955. The Mother wrote them in French and translated a few, entirely or in part, into English; in this volume, these translations have been retained. The original translations made by others have been revised or new translations made.

PART TWO. MESSAGES, LETTERS AND CONVERSATIONS

I. SRI AUROBINDO INTERNATIONAL CENTRE OF EDUCATION. This section consists mainly of the Mother's correspondence and conversations with the students and teachers of the Centre of Education. Some messages and letters to other institutions and individuals are also included. Most of the statements were originally in French. Some were first published in various Ashram books and journals; others are presented here for the first time.

Dated statements within a subsection are usually placed in chronological order, undated pieces where they best fit in. The symbol §, placed at the end of some pieces, indicates a spoken comment of the Mother which was noted down from memory by a listener and later approved by her for publication.

II. SRI AUROBINDO ASHRAM DEPARTMENT OF PHYSICAL EDUCATION. The nine short pieces introducing this section first appeared in the *Bulletin* between 1949 and 1950. The middle two subsections include written and tape-recorded messages to the participants in the competitions and the annual demonstration of physical culture organised by the Department of Physical Education. The penultimate subsection contains general messages, and letters to individuals. The final subsection, "To Women about Their Body", was first published as a pamphlet in September 1960.

III. THE NEW AGE ASSOCIATION. This collection of messages and comments is taken from *The New Age: Speeches at the Seminars and the Conferences of the New Age Association*, published in 1977 in the English original. The Mother gave, chose or approved the choice of the subject of discussion for the quarterly seminars and for two of the annual conferences. She commented on several of these subjects, either spontaneously or in answer to questions submitted to her. For three of the conferences she gave messages. The final piece is a reply concerning the purpose of participation in the seminars.

IV. GLIMPSES OF THE MOTHER'S WORK IN THE SCHOOL. These letters and notations of the Mother's spoken comments were given to a teacher of the Centre of Education between 1960 and 1972. The complete collection was first published in the original French and in English translation in the *Bulletin* issues of April and August 1978.

V. ANSWERS TO A MONITRESS. Written originally in French to a young captain of the Department of Physical Education, the seven "Sutras" first came out in the *Bulletin* of November 1959; the correspondence following them was first published in its entirety in 1975 in *Réponses de la Mère à une monitrice*. Some of the letters appeared earlier in Ashram journals, including a series in the *Bulletin* of February 1970. The original translations have been revised for this volume.

VI. ANSWERS TO A MONITOR. This section contains the letters specifically about education from the Mother's correspondence with a young captain of physical education. The complete correspondence was brought out in the French original, with an English translation, in the *Bulletin* between April 1973 and November 1975. The same translation is published here, with a few minor revisions.

VII. CONVERSATIONS. This section includes two conversations of 1967 and six of February-March 1973. The 1973 conversations, held with one or two teachers of the Centre of Education, are the Mother's final recorded statements on the subject of education. Some were published previously in Ashram publications; this more comprehensive collection first appeared in the French original, with a new English translation, in the *Bulletin* of August 1978.

PART THREE. DRAMAS

The Mother wrote three dramas in French for the dramatic performance held annually on December 1 by the students and teachers of the Centre of Education. *Towards the Future* was produced in 1949, *The Great Secret* in 1954 and *The Ascent to Truth* in 1957. Each play was issued as a booklet immediately after its performance, with the text in both French and English. For this volume, the original translations have been revised. For *The Great Secret*, the Mother wrote the parts of the Statesman, the Artist and the Unknown Man; the parts of the four other characters were written, in consultation with the Mother, by others. The parts of the Writer and the Athlete were written in English. A letter to the person who portrayed the Industrialist is included as an introduction to the drama.

Contents

Part One. Articles

Part Two. Messages, Letters and Conversations

Contents

Contents

On Education

Part One

Articles

In these articles I am trying to put into ordinary terms the whole yogic terminology, for these Bulletins *are meant more for people who lead an ordinary life, though also for students of yoga — I mean people who are primarily interested in a purely physical material life but who try to attain more perfection in their physical life than is usual in ordinary conditions. It is a very difficult task but it is a kind of yoga. These people call themselves "materialists" and they are apt to get agitated or irritated if yogic terms are used, so one must speak their language avoiding terms likely to shock them. But I have known in my life persons who called themselves "materialists" and yet followed a much severer discipline than those who claim to do yoga.*

What we want is that humanity should progress; whether it professes to lead a yogic life or not matters little, provided it makes the necessary effort for progress.[1]

25 December 1950   The Mother

---

[1] *Questions and Answers 1950-51*, Cent. Vol. 4, p. 7.

The Science of Living

To know oneself and to control oneself

A N AIMLESS life is always a miserable life.
Every one of you should have an aim. But do not forget
that on the quality of your aim will depend the quality
of your life.

Your aim should be high and wide, generous and disinterested; this will make your life precious to yourself and to others.

But whatever your ideal, it cannot be perfectly realised unless you have realised perfection in yourself.

To work for your perfection, the first step is to become conscious of yourself, of the different parts of your being and their respective activities. You must learn to distinguish these different parts one from another, so that you may become clearly aware of the origin of the movements that occur in you, the many impulses, reactions and conflicting wills that drive you to action. It is an assiduous study which demands much perseverance and sincerity. For man's nature, especially his mental nature, has a spontaneous tendency to give a favourable explanation for everything he thinks, feels, says and does. It is only by observing these movements with great care, by bringing them, as it were, before the tribunal of our highest ideal, with a sincere will to submit to its judgment, that we can hope to form in ourselves a discernment that never errs. For if we truly want to progress and acquire the capacity of knowing the truth of our being, that is to say, what we are truly created for, what we can call our mission upon earth, then we must, in a very regular and constant manner, reject from us or eliminate in us whatever contradicts the truth of our existence, whatever is opposed to it. In this way, little by little, all the parts, all the elements of our being can be organised into a homogeneous whole around our psychic centre. This work of unification requires much time to be brought to some degree of perfection. Therefore, in order to accomplish it, we must arm ourselves with patience and endurance, with a determination to prolong our life as long as necessary for the success of our endeavour. As you pursue this labour of purification and unification, you must at the same time take great care to perfect the external and instrumental part of your being. When the higher truth manifests, it must find in you a mind that is supple and rich enough to be able to give the idea that seeks to express itself a form of thought which preserves its force and clarity. This thought, again, when it seeks to clothe itself in words, must find in you a sufficient power of expression so that the words reveal the thought and do not deform it. And the formula in which you embody the truth should be manifested in all your feelings, all your acts of will, all your actions, in all the movements of your being. Finally, these movements themselves should, by constant effort, attain their highest perfection.

All this can be realised by means of a fourfold discipline, the general outline of which is given here. The four aspects of the discipline do not exclude each other, and can be followed at the same time; indeed, this is preferable. The starting-point is what can be called the psychic discipline. We give the name "psychic" to the psychological centre of our being, the seat within us of the highest truth of our existence, that which can know this truth and set it in movement. It is therefore of capital importance to become conscious of its presence in us, to concentrate on this presence until it becomes a living fact for us and we can identify ourselves with it.

In various times and places many methods have been prescribed for attaining this perception and ultimately achieving this identification. Some methods are psychological, some religious, some even mechanical. In reality, everyone has to find the one which suits him best, and if one has an ardent and steadfast aspiration, a persistent and dynamic will, one is sure to meet, in one way or another — outwardly through reading and study, inwardly through concentration, meditation, revelation and experience — the help one needs to reach the goal. Only one thing is absolutely indispensable: the will to discover and to realise. This discovery and realisation should be the primary preoccupation of our being, the pearl of great price which we must acquire at any cost. Whatever you do, whatever your occupations and activities, the will to find the truth of your being and to unite with it must be always living and present behind all that you do, all that you feel, all that you think.

To complement this movement of inner discovery, it would be good not to neglect the development of the mind. For the mental instrument can equally be a great help or a great hindrance. In its natural state the human mind is always limited in its vision, narrow in its understanding, rigid in its conceptions, and a constant effort is therefore needed to widen it, to make it more supple and profound. So it is very necessary to consider everything from as many points of view as possible. Towards this end, there is an exercise which gives great suppleness and elevation to the thought. It is as follows: a clearly formulated thesis is set; against it is opposed its antithesis, formulated with the same precision. Then by careful reflection the problem must be widened or transcended until a synthesis is found which unites the two contraries in a larger, higher and more comprehensive idea.

Many other exercises of the same kind can be undertaken; some have a beneficial effect on the character and so possess a double advantage: that of educating the mind and that of establishing control over the feelings and their consequences. For example, you must never allow your mind to judge things and people, for the mind is not an instrument of knowledge; it is incapable of finding knowledge, but it must be moved by knowledge. Knowledge belongs to a much higher domain than that of the human mind, far above the region of pure ideas. The mind has to be silent and attentive to receive knowledge from

5

above and manifest it. For it is an instrument of formation, of organisation and action, and it is in these functions that it attains its full value and real usefulness.

There is another practice which can be very helpful to the progress of the consciousness. Whenever there is a disagreement on any matter, such as a decision to be taken, or an action to be carried out, one must never remain closed up in one's own conception or point of view. On the contrary, one must make an effort to understand the other's point of view, to put oneself in his place and, instead of quarrelling or even fighting, find the solution which can reasonably satisfy both parties; there always is one for men of goodwill.

Here we must mention the discipline of the vital. The vital being in us is the seat of impulses and desires, of enthusiasm and violence, of dynamic energy and desperate depressions, of passions and revolts. It can set everything in motion, build and realise; but it can also destroy and mar everything. Thus it may be the most difficult part to discipline in the human being. It is a long and exacting labour requiring great patience and perfect sincerity, for without sincerity you will deceive yourself from the very outset, and all endeavour for progress will be in vain. With the collaboration of the vital no realisation seems impossible, no transformation impracticable. But the difficulty lies in securing this constant collaboration. The vital is a good worker, but most often it seeks its own satisfaction. If that is refused, totally or even partially, the vital gets vexed, sulks and goes on strike. Its energy disappears more or less completely and in its place leaves disgust for people and things, discouragement or revolt, depression and dissatisfaction. At such moments it is good to remain quiet and refuse to act; for these are the times when one does stupid things and in a few moments one can destroy or spoil the progress that has been made during months of regular effort. These crises are shorter and less dangerous for those who have established a contact with their psychic being which is sufficient to keep alive in them the flame of aspiration and the consciousness of the ideal to be realised. They can, with the help of this consciousness, deal with their vital as one deals with a rebellious child, with patience and perseverance, showing it the truth and light, endeavouring to convince it and awaken in it the goodwill which has been veiled for a time. By means of such patient intervention each crisis can be turned into a new progress, into one more step towards the goal. Progress may be slow, relapses may be frequent, but if a courageous will is maintained, one is sure to triumph one day and see all difficulties melt and vanish before the radiance of the truth-consciousness.

Lastly, by means of a rational and discerning physical education, we must make our body strong and supple enough to become a fit instrument in the material world for the truth-force which wants to manifest through us.

In fact, the body must not rule, it must obey. By its very nature it is a docile and faithful servant. Unfortunately, it rarely has the capacity of discernment it ought to have with regard to its masters, the mind and the vital. It obeys them blindly, at the cost of its own well-being. The mind with its dogmas, its rigid and arbitrary principles, the vital with its passions, its excesses and dissipations soon destroy the natural balance of the body and create in it fatigue, exhaustion and disease. It must be freed from this tyranny and this can be done only through a constant union with the psychic centre of the being. The body has a wonderful capacity of adaptation and endurance. It is able to do so many more things than one usually imagines. If, instead of the ignorant and despotic masters that now govern it, it is ruled by the central truth of the being, you will be amazed at what it is capable of doing. Calm and quiet, strong and poised, at every minute it will be able to put forth the effort that is demanded of it, for it will have learnt to find rest in action and to recuperate, through contact with the universal forces, the energies it expends consciously and usefully. In this sound and balanced life a new harmony will manifest in the body, reflecting the harmony of the higher regions, which will give it perfect proportions and ideal beauty of form. And this harmony will be progressive, for the truth of the being is never static; it is a perpetual unfolding of a growing perfection that is more and more total and comprehensive. As soon as the body has learnt to follow this movement of progressive harmony, it will be possible for it to escape, through a continuous process of transformation, from the necessity of disintegration and destruction. Thus the irrevocable law of death will no longer have any reason to exist.

When we reach this degree of perfection which is our goal, we shall perceive that the truth we seek is made up of four major aspects: Love, Knowledge, Power and Beauty. These four attributes of the Truth will express themselves spontaneously in our being. The psychic will be the vehicle of true and pure love, the mind will be the vehicle of infallible knowledge, the vital will manifest an invincible power and strength and the body will be the expression of a perfect beauty and harmony.

Bulletin, November 1950

Education

THE EDUCATION of a human being should begin at birth
and continue throughout his life. Indeed, if we want this education to have its maximum
result, it should begin even before birth; in this case it is the
mother herself who proceeds with this education by means of
a twofold action: first, upon herself for her own improvement,
and secondly, upon the child whom she is forming physically.
For it is certain that the nature of the child to be born depends
very much upon the mother who forms it, upon her aspiration
and will as well as upon the material surroundings in which she
lives. To see that her thoughts are always beautiful and pure,
her feelings always noble and fine, her material surroundings as
harmonious as possible and full of a great simplicity — this is
the part of education which should apply to the mother herself.
And if she has in addition a conscious and definite will to form
the child according to the highest ideal she can conceive, then
the very best conditions will be realised so that the child can
come into the world with his utmost potentialities. How many
difficult efforts and useless complications would be avoided in
this way!

Education to be complete must have five principal aspects
corresponding to the five principal activities of the human being:
the physical, the vital, the mental, the psychic and the spiritual.
Usually, these phases of education follow chronologically the
growth of the individual; this, however, does not mean that
one of them should replace another, but that all must continue,
completing one another until the end of his life.

We propose to study these five aspects of education one by
one and also their interrelationships. But before we enter into
the details of the subject, I wish to make a recommendation
to parents. Most parents, for various reasons, give very little

thought to the true education which should be imparted to children. When they have brought a child into the world, provided him with food, satisfied his various material needs and looked after his health more or less carefully, they think they have fully discharged their duty. Later on, they will send him to school and hand over to the teachers the responsibility for his education.

There are other parents who know that their children must be educated and who try to do what they can. But very few, even among those who are most serious and sincere, know that the first thing to do, in order to be able to educate a child, is to educate oneself, to become conscious and master of oneself so that one never sets a bad example to one's child. For it is above all through example that education becomes effective. To speak good words and to give wise advice to a child has very little effect if one does not oneself give him an example of what one teaches. Sincerity, honesty, straightforwardness, courage, disinterestedness, unselfishness, patience, endurance, perseverance, peace, calm, self-control are all things that are taught infinitely better by example than by beautiful speeches. Parents, have a high ideal and always act in accordance with it and you will see that little by little your child will reflect this ideal in himself and spontaneously manifest the qualities you would like to see expressed in his nature. Quite naturally a child has respect and admiration for his parents; unless they are quite unworthy, they will always appear to their child as demigods whom he will try to imitate as best he can.

With very few exceptions, parents are not aware of the disastrous influence that their own defects, impulses, weaknesses and lack of self-control have on their children. If you wish to be respected by a child, have respect for yourself and be worthy of respect at every moment. Never be authoritarian, despotic, impatient or ill-tempered. When your child asks you a question, do not give him a stupid or silly answer under the pretext that he cannot understand you. You can always make yourself understood if you take enough trouble; and in spite of the popular saying that it is not always good to tell the truth, I affirm that it is always good to tell the truth, but that the art consists in telling it in such a way as to make it accessible to the mind of the hearer. In early life, until he is twelve or fourteen, the child's mind is hardly open to abstract notions and general ideas. And yet you can train it to understand these things by using concrete images, symbols or parables. Up to quite an advanced age and for some who mentally always remain children, a narrative, a story, a tale well told teach much more than any number of theoretical explanations.

Another pitfall to avoid: do not scold your child without good reason and only when it is quite indispensable. A child who is too often scolded gets hardened to rebuke and no longer attaches much importance to words or severity of tone. And above all, take good care never to scold him for a fault which you yourself commit. Children are very keen and clear-sighted observers; they soon find out your weaknesses and note them without pity.

When a child has done something wrong, see that he confesses it to you spontaneously and frankly; and when he has confessed, with kindness and affection make him understand what was wrong in his movement so that he will not repeat it, but never scold him; a fault confessed must always be forgiven. You should not allow any fear to come between you and your child; fear is a pernicious means of education: it invariably gives birth to deceit and lying. Only a discerning affection that is firm yet gentle and an adequate practical knowledge will create the bonds of trust that are indispensable for you to be able to educate your child effectively. And do not forget that you have to control yourself constantly in order to be equal to your task and truly fulfil the duty which you owe your child by the mere fact of having brought him into the world.

Bulletin, February 1951

11

Physical Education

OF ALL the domains of human consciousness, the physical is the one most completely governed by method, order, discipline, process. The lack of plasticity and receptivity in matter has to be replaced by a detailed organisation that is both precise and comprehensive. In this organisation, one must not forget the interdependence and interpenetration of all the domains of the being. However, even a mental or vital impulse, to express itself physically, must submit to an exact process. That is why all education of the body, if it is to be effective, must be rigorous and detailed, far-sighted and methodical. This will be translated into habits; the body is a being of habits. But these habits should be controlled and disciplined, while remaining flexible enough to adapt themselves to circumstances and to the needs of the growth and development of the being.

All education of the body should begin at birth and continue throughout life. It is never too soon to begin nor too late to continue.

Physical education has three principal aspects: (1) control and discipline of the functioning of the body, (2) an integral, methodical and harmonious development of all the parts and movements of the body and (3) correction of any defects and deformities.

It may be said that from the very first days, even the first hours of his life, the child should undergo the first part of this programme as far as food, sleep, evacuation, etc. are concerned. If the child, from the very beginning of his existence, learns good habits, it will save him a good deal of trouble and inconvenience for the rest of his life; and besides, those who have the responsibility of caring for him during his first years will find their task very much easier.

Naturally, this education, if it is to be rational, enlightened and effective, must be based upon a minimum knowledge of the human body, of its structure and its functioning. As the child develops, he must gradually be taught to observe the functioning of his internal organs so that he may control them more and more, and see that this functioning remains normal and harmonious. As for positions, postures and movements, bad habits are formed very early and very rapidly, and these may have disastrous consequences for his whole life. Those who take the question of physical education seriously and wish to give their children the best conditions for normal development will easily find the necessary indications and instructions. The subject is being more and more thoroughly studied, and many books have appeared and are still appearing which give all the information and guidance needed.

It is not possible for me here to go into the details of the application, for each problem is different from every other and the solution should suit the individual case. The question of food has been studied at length and in detail; the diet that helps children in their growth is generally known and it may be very useful to follow it. But it is very important to remember that the instinct of the body, so long as it remains intact, is more reliable than any theory. Accordingly, those who want their child to develop normally should not force him to eat food which he finds distasteful, for most often the body possesses a sure instinct as to what is harmful to it, unless the child is particularly capricious.

The body in its normal state, that is to say, when there is no intervention of mental notions or vital impulses, also knows very well what is good and necessary for it; but for this to be effective in practice, one must educate the child with care and teach him to distinguish his desires from his needs. He should be helped to develop a taste for food that is simple and healthy, substantial and appetising, but free from any useless complications. In his daily food, all that merely stuffs and causes heaviness should be avoided; and above all, he must be taught to eat according to his hunger, neither more nor less, and not to make his meals an occasion to satisfy his greed or gluttony. From one's very childhood, one should know that one eats in order to give strength and health to the body and not to enjoy the pleasures of the palate. Children should be given food that suits their temperament, prepared in a way that ensures hygiene and cleanliness, that is pleasant to the taste and yet very simple. This food should be chosen and apportioned according to the age of the child and his regular activities. It should contain all the chemical and dynamic elements that are necessary for his development and the balanced growth of every part of his body.

Since the child will be given only the food that helps to keep him healthy and provide him with the energy he needs, one must be very careful not to use food as a means of coercion and punishment. The practice of telling a child, "You have not been a good boy, you won't get any dessert," etc., is most harmful. In this way you create in his little consciousness the impression that food is given to him chiefly to satisfy his greed and not because it is indispensable for the proper functioning of his body.

Another thing should be taught to a child from his early years: to enjoy cleanliness and observe hygienic habits. But, in obtaining this cleanliness and respect for the rules of hygiene from the child, one must take great care not to instil into him the fear of illness. Fear is the worst instrument of education and the surest way of attracting what is feared. Yet, while there should be no fear of illness, there should be no inclination for it either. There is a prevalent belief that brilliant minds are found in weak bodies. This is a delusion and has no basis. There was perhaps a time when a romantic and morbid taste for physical unbalance prevailed; but, fortunately, that tendency has disappeared. Nowadays a well-built, robust, muscular, strong and well-balanced body is appreciated at its true value. In any case, children should be taught to respect health and admire the healthy man whose vigorous body knows how to repel attacks of illness. Often a child feigns illness to avoid some troublesome obligation, a work that does not interest him, or simply to soften his parents' hearts and get them to satisfy some caprice. The child must be taught as early as possible that this does not work and that he does not become more interesting by being ill, but rather the contrary. The weak have a tendency to believe that their weakness makes them particularly interesting and to use this weakness and if necessary even illness as a means of attracting the attention and sympathy of the people around them. On no account should this pernicious tendency be encouraged. Children should therefore be taught that to be ill is a sign of weakness and inferiority, not of some virtue or sacrifice.

That is why, as soon as the child is able to make use of his limbs, some time should be devoted every day to the methodical and regular development of all the parts of his body. Every day some twenty or thirty minutes, preferably on waking, if possible, will be enough to ensure the proper functioning and balanced growth of his muscles while preventing any stiffening of the joints and of the spine, which occurs much sooner than one thinks. In the general programme of the child's education, sports and outdoor games should be given a prominent place; that, more than all the medicines in the world, will assure the child good health. An hour's moving about in the sun does more to cure weakness or even anaemia than a whole arsenal of tonics. My advice is that medicines should not be used unless it is absolutely impossible to avoid them; and this "absolutely impossible" should be very strict. In this programme of physical culture, although there are well-known general lines to be followed for the best development of the human body, still, if the method is to be fully effective in each case, it should be considered individually, if possible with the help of a competent person, or if not, by consulting the numerous manuals that have already been and are still being published on the subject.

But in any case a child, whatever his activities, should have a sufficient number of hours of sleep. The number will vary according to his age. In the cradle, the baby should sleep longer than he remains awake. The number of hours of sleep will diminish as the child grows. But until maturity it should not be less than eight hours, in a quiet, well-ventilated place. The child should never be made to stay up late for no reason. The hours before midnight are the best for resting the nerves. Even during the waking hours, relaxation is indispensable for all who want to maintain their nervous balance. To know how to relax the muscles and the nerves is an art which should be taught to children when they are very young. There are many parents who, on the contrary, push their child to constant activity. When the child remains quiet, they imagine that he is ill. There are even parents who have the bad habit of making their child do household work at the expense of his rest and relaxation. Nothing is worse for a developing nervous system, which cannot stand the strain of too continuous an effort or of an activity that is imposed upon it and not freely chosen. At the risk of going against many current ideas and ruffling many prejudices, I hold that it is not fair to demand service from a child, as if it were his duty to serve his parents. The contrary would be more true, and certainly it is natural that parents should serve their child or at least take great care of him. It is only if a child chooses freely to work for his family and does this work as play that the thing is admissible. And even then, one must be careful that it in no way diminishes the hours of rest that are absolutely indispensable for his body to function properly.

I have said that from a young age children should be taught to respect good health, physical strength and balance. The great importance of beauty must also be emphasised. A young child should aspire for beauty, not for the sake of pleasing others or winning their admiration, but for the love of beauty itself; for beauty is the ideal which all physical life must realise. Every human being has the possibility of establishing harmony among the different parts of his body and in the various movements of the body in action. Every human body that undergoes a rational method of culture from the very beginning of its existence can realise its own harmony and thus become fit to manifest beauty. When we speak of the other aspects of an integral education, we shall see what inner conditions are to be fulfilled so that this beauty can one day be manifested.

So far I have referred only to the education to be given to children; for a good many bodily defects can be rectified and many malformations avoided by an enlightened physical education given at the proper time. But if for any reason this physical education has not been given during childhood or even in youth, it can begin at any age and be pursued throughout life. But the later one begins, the more one must be prepared to meet bad habits that have to be corrected, rigidities to be made supple, malformations to be rectified. And this preparatory work will require much patience and perseverance before one can start on a constructive programme for the harmonisation of the form and its movements. But if you keep alive within you the ideal of beauty that is to be realised, sooner or later you are sure to reach the goal you have set yourself.

Bulletin, April 1951

Vital Education

OF ALL education, vital education is perhaps the most important, the most indispensable. Yet it is rarely taken up and pursued with discernment and method. There are several reasons for this: first, the human mind is in a state of great confusion about this particular subject; secondly, the undertaking is very difficult and to be successful in it one must have endless endurance and persistence and a will that no failure can weaken.

Indeed, the vital in man's nature is a despotic and exacting tyrant. Moreover, since it is the vital which holds power, energy, enthusiasm, effective dynamism, many have a feeling of timorous respect for it and always try to please it. But it is a master that nothing can satisfy and its demands are without limit. Two ideas which are very wide-spread, especially in the West, contribute towards making its domination more sovereign. One is that the chief aim of life is to be happy; the other that one is born with a certain character and that it is impossible to change it.

The first idea is a childish deformation of a very profound truth: that all existence is based upon delight of being and without delight of being there would be no life. But this delight of being, which is a quality of the Divine and therefore unconditioned, must not be confused with the pursuit of pleasure in life, which depends largely upon circumstances. The conviction that one has the right to be happy leads, as a matter of course, to the will to "live one's own life" at any cost. This attitude, by its obscure and aggressive egoism, leads to every kind of conflict and misery, disappointment and discouragement, and very often ends in catastrophe.

In the world as it is now the goal of life is not to secure personal happiness, but to awaken the individual progressively to the Truth-consciousness.

The second idea arises from the fact that a fundamental change of character demands an almost complete mastery over the subconscient and a very rigorous disciplining of whatever comes up from the inconscient, which, in ordinary natures, expresses itself as the effects of atavism and of the environment in which one was born. Only an almost abnormal growth of consciousness and the constant help of Grace can achieve this Herculean task. That is why this task has rarely been attempted and many famous teachers have declared it to be unrealisable and chimerical. Yet it is not unrealisable. The transformation of character has in fact been realised by means of a clear-sighted discipline and a perseverance so obstinate that nothing, not even the most persistent failures, can discourage it.

The indispensable starting-point is a detailed and discerning observation of the character to be transformed. In most cases, that itself is a difficult and often a very baffling task. But there is one fact which the old traditions knew and which can serve as the clue in the labyrinth of inner discovery. It is that everyone possesses in a large measure, and the exceptional individual in an increasing degree of precision, two opposite tendencies of character, in almost equal proportions, which are like the light and the shadow of the same thing. Thus someone who has the capacity of being exceptionally generous will suddenly find an obstinate avarice rising up in his nature, the courageous man will be a coward in some part of his being and the good man will suddenly have wicked impulses. In this way life seems to endow everyone not only with the possibility of expressing an ideal, but also with contrary elements representing in a concrete manner the battle he has to wage and the victory he has to win for the realisation to become possible. Consequently, all life is an education pursued more or less consciously, more or less willingly. In certain cases this education will encourage the movements that express the light, in others, on the contrary, those that express the shadow. If the circumstances and the environment are favourable, the light will grow at the expense of the shadow; otherwise the opposite will happen. And in this way the individual's character will crystallise according to the whims of Nature and the determinisms of material and vital life, unless a higher element comes in in time, a conscious will which, refusing to allow Nature to follow her whimsical ways, will replace them by a logical and clear-sighted discipline. This conscious will is what we mean by a rational method of education.

That is why it is of prime importance that the vital education of the child should begin as early as possible, indeed, as soon as he is able to use his senses. In this way many bad habits will be avoided and many harmful influences eliminated.

This vital education has two principal aspects, very different in their aims and methods, but both equally important. The first concerns the development and use of the sense organs. The second the progressing awareness and control of the character, culminating in its transformation.

The education of the senses, again, has several aspects, which are added to one another as the being grows; indeed it should never cease. The sense organs, if properly cultivated, can attain a precision and power of functioning far exceeding what is normally expected of them.

In some ancient initiations it was stated that the number of senses that man can develop is not five but seven and in certain special cases even twelve. Certain races at certain times have, out of necessity, developed more or less perfectly one or the other of these supplementary senses. With a proper discipline persistently followed, they are within the reach of all who are sincerely interested in this development and its results. Among the faculties that are often mentioned, there is, for example, the ability to widen the physical consciousness, project it out of oneself so as to concentrate it on a given point and thus obtain sight, hearing, smell, taste and even touch at a distance.

To this general education of the senses and their functioning there will be added, as early as possible, the cultivation of discrimination and of the aesthetic sense, the capacity to choose and adopt what is beautiful and harmonious, simple, healthy and pure. For there is a psychological health just as there is a physical health, a beauty and harmony of the sensations as of the body and its movements. As the capacity of understanding grows in the child, he should be taught, in the course of his education, to add artistic taste and refinement to power and precision. He should be shown, led to appreciate, taught to love beautiful, lofty, healthy and noble things, whether in Nature or in human creation. This should be a true aesthetic culture, which will protect him from degrading influences. For, in the wake of the last wars and the terrible nervous tension which they provoked, as a sign, perhaps, of the decline of civilisation and social decay, a growing vulgarity seems to have taken possession of human life, individual as well as collective, particularly in what concerns aesthetic life and the life of the senses. A methodical and enlightened cultivation of the senses can, little by little, eliminate from the child whatever is by contagion vulgar, commonplace and crude. This education will have very happy effects even on his character. For one who has developed a truly refined taste will, because of this very refinement, feel incapable of acting in a crude, brutal or vulgar manner. This refinement, if it is sincere, brings to the being a nobility and generosity which will spontaneously find expression in his behaviour and will protect him from many base and perverse movements.

And this brings us quite naturally to the second aspect of vital education which concerns the character and its transformation.

Generally, all disciplines dealing with the vital being, its purification and its control, proceed by coercion, suppression, abstinence and asceticism. This procedure is certainly easier and quicker, although less deeply enduring and effective, than a rigorous and detailed education. Besides, it eliminates all possibility of the intervention, help and collaboration of the vital. And yet this help is of the utmost importance if one wants the individual's growth and action to be complete.

To become conscious of the various movements in oneself and be aware of what one does and why one does it, is the indispensable starting-point. The child must be taught to observe, to note his reactions and impulses and their causes, to become a discerning witness of his desires, his movements of violence and passion, his instincts of possession and appropriation and domination and the background of vanity which supports them, together with their counterparts of weakness, discouragement, depression and despair.

Evidently, for this process to be useful, along with the growth of the power of observation the will for progress and perfection must also grow. This will should be instilled into the child as soon as he is capable of having a will, that is to say, at a much earlier age than is usually believed.

In order to awaken this will to surmount and conquer, different methods are appropriate in different cases; with certain individuals rational arguments are effective, for others their feelings and goodwill should be brought into play, with yet others the sense of dignity and self-respect. For all, the most powerful method is example constantly and sincerely shown.

Once the resolution has been firmly established, one has only to proceed rigorously and persistently and never to accept any defeat as final. To avoid all weakening and backsliding, there is one important point you must know and never forget: the will can be cultivated and developed just as the muscles can by methodical and progressive exercise. You must not shrink from demanding the maximum effort of your will even for a thing that seems of no importance, for it is through effort that its capacity grows, gradually acquiring the power to apply itself even to the most difficult things. What you have decided to do, you must do, whatever the cost, even if you have to renew your effort over and over again any number of times in order to do it. Your will will be strengthened by the effort and you will have only to choose with discernment the goal to which you will apply it.

To sum up: one must gain a full knowledge of one's character and then acquire control over one's movements in order to achieve perfect mastery and the transformation of all the elements that have to be transformed. Now all will depend upon the ideal which the effort for mastery and transformation seeks to achieve. The value of the effort and its result will depend upon the value of the ideal. This is the subject we shall deal with next, in connection with mental education.

Bulletin, August 1951

Mental Education

OF ALL lines of education, mental education is the most widely known and practised, yet except in a few rare cases there are gaps which make it something very incomplete and in the end quite insufficient.

Generally speaking, schooling is considered to be all the mental education that is necessary. And when a child has been made to undergo, for a number of years, a methodical training which is more like cramming than true schooling, it is considered that whatever is necessary for his mental development has been done. Nothing of the kind. Even conceding that the training is given with due measure and discrimination and does not permanently damage the brain, it cannot impart to the human mind the faculties it needs to become a good and useful instrument. The schooling that is usually given can, at the most, serve as a system of gymnastics to increase the suppleness of the brain. From this standpoint, each branch of human learning represents a special kind of mental gymnastics, and the verbal formulations given to these various branches each constitute a special and well-defined language.

A true mental education, which will prepare man for a higher life, has five principal phases. Normally these phases follow one after another, but in exceptional individuals they may alternate or even proceed simultaneously. These five phases, in brief, are:

(1) Development of the power of concentration, the capacity of attention.

(2) Development of the capacities of expansion, widening, complexity and richness.

(3) Organisation of one's ideas around a central idea, a higher ideal or a supremely luminous idea that will serve as a guide in life.

(4) Thought-control, rejection of undesirable thoughts, to become able to think only what one wants and when one wants.

(5) Development of mental silence, perfect calm and a more and more total receptivity to inspirations coming from the higher regions of the being.

It is not possible to give here all the details concerning the methods to be employed in the application of these five phases of education to different individuals. Still, a few explanations on points of detail can be given.

Undeniably, what most impedes mental progress in children is the constant dispersion of their thoughts. Their thoughts flutter hither and thither like butterflies and they have to make a great effort to fix them. Yet this capacity is latent in them, for when you succeed in arousing their interest, they are capable of a good deal of attention. By his ingenuity, therefore, the educator will gradually help the child to become capable of a sustained effort of attention and a faculty of more and more complete absorption in the work in hand. All methods that can develop this faculty of attention from games to rewards are good and can all be utilised according to the need and the circumstances. But it is the psychological action that is most important and the sovereign method is to arouse in the child an interest in what you want to teach him, a liking for work, a will to progress. To love to learn is the most precious gift that one can give to a child: to love to learn always and everywhere, so that all circumstances, all happenings in life may be constantly renewed opportunities for learning more and always more.

For that, to attention and concentration should be added observation, precise recording and faithfulness of memory. This faculty of observation can be developed by varied and spontaneous exercises, making use of every opportunity that presents itself to keep the child's thought wakeful, alert and prompt. The growth of the understanding should be stressed much more than that of memory. One knows well only what one has understood. Things learnt by heart, mechanically, fade away little by little and finally disappear; what is understood is never forgotten. Moreover, you must never refuse to explain to a child the how and the why of things. If you cannot do it yourself, you must direct the child to those who are qualified to answer or point out to him some books that deal with the question. In this way you will progressively awaken in the child the taste for true study and the habit of making a persistent effort to know.

This will bring us quite naturally to the second phase of development in which the mind should be widened and enriched.

You will gradually show the child that everything can become an interesting subject for study if it is approached in the right way. The life of every day, of every moment, is the best school of all, varied, complex, full of unexpected experiences, problems to be solved, clear and striking examples and obvious consequences. It is so easy to arouse healthy curiosity in children, if you answer with intelligence and clarity the numerous questions they ask. An interesting reply to one readily brings others in its train and so the attentive child learns without effort much more than he usually does in the classroom. By a choice made with care and insight, you should also teach him to enjoy good reading-matter which is both instructive and attractive. Do not be afraid of anything that awakens and pleases his imagination; imagination develops the creative mental faculty and through it study becomes living and the mind develops in joy.

In order to increase the suppleness and comprehensiveness of his mind, one should see not only that he studies many varied topics, but above all that a single subject is approached in various ways, so that the child understands in a practical manner that there are many ways of facing the same intellectual problem, of considering it and solving it. This will remove all rigidity from his brain and at the same time it will make his thinking richer and more supple and prepare it for a more complex and comprehensive synthesis. In this way also the child will be imbued with the sense of the extreme relativity of mental learning and, little by little, an aspiration for a truer source of knowledge will awaken in him.

Indeed, as the child grows older and progresses in his studies, his mind too ripens and becomes more and more capable of forming general ideas, and with them almost always comes a need for certitude, for a knowledge that is stable enough to form the basis of a mental construction which will permit all the diverse and scattered and often contradictory ideas accumulated in his brain to be organised and put in order. This ordering is indeed very necessary if one is to avoid chaos in one's thoughts. All contradictions can be transformed into complements, but for that one must discover the higher idea that will have the power to bring them harmoniously together. It is always good to consider every problem from all possible standpoints so as to avoid partiality and exclusiveness; but if the thought is to be active and creative, it must, in every case, be the natural and logical synthesis of all the points of view adopted. And if you want to make the totality of your thoughts into a dynamic and constructive force, you must also take great care as to the choice of the central idea of your mental synthesis; for upon that will depend the value of this synthesis. The higher and larger the central idea and the more universal it is, rising above time and space, the more numerous and the more complex will be the ideas, notions and thoughts which it will be able to organise and harmonise.

It goes without saying that this work of organisation cannot be done once and for all. The mind, if it is to keep its vigour and youth, must progress constantly, revise its notions in the light of new knowledge, enlarge its frame-work to include fresh notions and constantly reclassify and reorganise its thoughts, so that each of them may find its true place in relation to the others and the whole remain harmonious and orderly.

All that has just been said concerns the speculative mind, the mind that learns. But learning is only one aspect of mental activity; the other, which is at least equally important, is the constructive faculty, the capacity to form and thus prepare action. This very important part of mental activity has rarely been the subject of any special study or discipline. Only those who want, for some reason, to exercise a strict control over their mental activities think of observing and disciplining this faculty of formation; and as soon as they try it, they have to face difficulties so great that they appear almost insurmountable.

And yet control over this formative activity of the mind is one of the most important aspects of self-education; one can say that without it no mental mastery is possible. As far as study is concerned, all ideas are acceptable and should be included in the synthesis, whose very function is to become more and more rich and complex; but where action is concerned, it is just the opposite. The ideas that are accepted for translation into action should be strictly controlled and only those that agree with the general trend of the central idea forming the basis of the mental synthesis should be permitted to express themselves in action. This means that every thought entering the mental consciousness should be set before the central idea; if it finds a logical place among the thoughts already grouped, it will be admitted into the synthesis; if not, it will be rejected so that it can have no influence on the action. This work of mental purification should be done very regularly in order to secure a complete control over one's actions.

For this purpose, it is good to set apart some time every day when one can quietly go over one's thoughts and put one's synthesis in order. Once the habit is acquired, you can maintain control over your thoughts even during work and action, allowing only those which are useful for what you are doing to come to the surface. Particularly, if you have continued to cultivate the power of concentration and attention, only the thoughts that are needed will be allowed to enter the active external consciousness and they then become all the more dynamic and effective. And if, in the intensity of concentration, it becomes necessary not to think at all, all mental vibration can be stilled and an almost total silence secured. In this silence one can gradually open to the higher regions of the mind and learn to record the inspirations that come from there.

But even before reaching this point, silence in itself is supremely useful, because in most people who have a somewhat developed and active mind, the mind is never at rest. During the day, its activity is kept under a certain control, but at night, during the sleep of the body, the control of the waking state is almost completely removed and the mind indulges in activities which are sometimes excessive and often incoherent. This creates a great stress which leads to fatigue and the diminution of the intellectual faculties.

The fact is that like all the other parts of the human being, the mind too needs rest and it will not have this rest unless we know how to provide it. The art of resting one's mind is something to be acquired. Changing one's mental activity is certainly one way of resting; but the greatest possible rest is silence. And as far as the mental faculties are concerned a few minutes passed in the calm of silence are a more effective rest than hours of sleep.

When one has learned to silence the mind at will and to concentrate it in receptive silence, then there will be no problem that cannot be solved, no mental difficulty whose solution cannot be found. When it is agitated, thought becomes confused and impotent; in an attentive tranquillity, the light can manifest itself and open up new horizons to man's capacity.

Bulletin, November 1951

29

Psychic Education and
Spiritual Education

SO FAR we have dealt only with the education that can be given to all children born upon earth and which is concerned with purely human faculties. But one need not inevitably stop there. Every human being carries hidden within him the possibility of a greater consciousness which goes beyond the bounds of his present life and enables him to share in a higher and a vaster life. Indeed, in all exceptional beings it is always this consciousness that governs their lives and organises both the circumstances of their existence and their individual reaction to these circumstances. What the human mental consciousness does not know and cannot do, this consciousness knows and does. It is like a light that shines at the centre of the being, radiating through the thick coverings of the external consciousness. Some have a vague intimation of its presence; a good many children are under its influence, which shows itself very distinctly at times in their spontaneous actions and even in their words. Unfortunately, since parents most often do not know what it is and do not understand what is happening in their child, their reaction to these phenomena is not a good one and all their education consists in making the child as unconscious as possible in this domain and concentrating all his attention on external things, thus accustoming him to think that they are the only ones that matter. It is true that this concentration on external things is very useful, provided that it is done in the proper way. The three lines of education — physical, vital and mental — deal with that and could be defined as the means of building up the personality, raising the individual out of the amorphous subconscious mass and making him a well-defined self-conscious entity. With psychic education we come to the problem of the true motive of existence, the purpose of life on earth, the discovery to which this life must lead and the result of that discovery: the consecration of the individual to his eternal principle. Normally this discovery is associated with a mystic feeling, a religious life, because it is mainly the religions that have concerned themselves with this aspect of life. But it need not necessarily be so: the mystic notion of God may be replaced by the more philosophical notion of truth and still the discovery will remain essentially the same, but the road leading to it may be taken even by the most intransigent positivist. For mental notions and ideas have only a very secondary importance in preparing one for the psychic life. The important thing is to live the experience; that carries with it its own reality and force apart from any theory that may precede or accompany or follow it, for most often theories are no more than explanations that one gives to oneself in order to have, more or less, the illusion of knowledge. Man clothes the ideal or the absolute he seeks to attain with different names according to the environment in which he is born and the education he has received. The experience is essentially the same, if it is sincere; it is only the words and phrases in which it is formulated that differ according to the belief and the mental education of the one who has the experience. All formulation is thus only an approximation that should be progressive and grow in precision as the experience itself becomes more and more precise and co-ordinated. Still, to sketch a general outline of psychic education, we must give some idea, however relative it may be, of what we mean by the psychic being. One could say, for example, that the creation of an individual being is the result of the projection, in time and space, of one of the countless possibilities latent in the supreme origin of all manifestation which, through the medium of the one and universal consciousness, takes concrete form in the law or the truth of an individual and so, by a progressive development, becomes his soul or psychic being.

I must emphasise that what is stated briefly here does not claim to be a complete exposition of the reality and does not exhaust the subject — far from it. It is only a very summary explanation for a practical purpose, to serve as a basis for the education which we intend to consider now.

It is through this psychic presence that the truth of an individual being comes into contact with him and the circumstances of his life. In most cases the presence acts, so to say, from behind the veil, unrecognised and unknown; but in some, it is perceptible and its action recognisable and even, in a very few, the presence becomes tangible and its action fully effective. These go forward in life with an assurance and a certitude all their own; they are masters of their destiny. It is for the purpose of obtaining this mastery and becoming conscious of the psychic presence that psychic education should be practised. But for that there is need of a special factor, the personal will. For till now, the discovery of the psychic being and identification with it have not been among the recognised subjects of education, and although one can find in special treatises useful and practical hints on the subject, and although in exceptional cases one may have the good fortune of meeting someone who is capable of showing the way and giving the help that is needed to follow it, most often the attempt is left to one's own personal initiative. The discovery is a personal matter and a great determination, a strong will and an untiring perseverance are indispensable to reach the goal. Each one must, so to say, trace out his own path through his own difficulties. The goal is known to some extent, for most of those who have reached it have described it more or less clearly. But the supreme value of the discovery lies in its spontaneity, its ingenuousness, and that escapes all ordinary mental laws. And that is why anyone wanting to take up the adventure usually first seeks out some person who has successfully undertaken it and is able to sustain him and enlighten him on his way. Yet there are some solitary travellers and for them a few general indications may be useful.

The starting-point is to seek in yourself that which is independent of the body and the circumstances of life, which is not born of the mental formation that you have been given, the language you speak, the habits and customs of the environment in which you live, the country where you are born or the age to which you belong. You must find, in the depths of your being, that which carries in it a sense of universality, limitless expansion, unbroken continuity. Then you decentralise, extend and widen yourself; you begin to live in all things and in all beings; the barriers separating individuals from each other break down. You think in their thoughts, vibrate in their sensations, feel in their feelings, live in the life of all. What seemed inert suddenly becomes full of life, stones quicken, plants feel and will and suffer, animals speak in a language more or less inarticulate, but clear and expressive; everything is animated by a marvellous consciousness without time or limit. And this is only one aspect of the psychic realisation; there are others, many others. All help you to go beyond the barriers of your egoism, the walls of your external personality, the impotence of your reactions and the incapacity of your will.

But, as I have already said, the path to that realisation is long and difficult, strewn with snares and problems to be solved, which demand an unfailing determination. It is like the explorer's trek through virgin forest in quest of an unknown land, of some great discovery. The psychic being is also a great discovery which requires at least as much fortitude and endurance as the discovery of new continents. A few simple words of advice may be useful to one who has resolved to undertake it.

The first and perhaps the most important point is that the mind is incapable of judging spiritual things. All those who have written on this subject have said so; but very few are those who have put it into practice. And yet, in order to proceed on the path, it is absolutely indispensable to abstain from all mental opinion and reaction.

Give up all personal seeking for comfort, satisfaction, enjoyment or happiness. Be only a burning fire for progress, take whatever comes to you as an aid to your progress and immediately make whatever progress is required.

33

Try to take pleasure in all you do, but never do anything for the sake of pleasure.

Never get excited, nervous or agitated. Remain perfectly calm in the face of all circumstances. And yet be always alert to discover what progress you still have to make and lose no time in making it.

Never take physical happenings at their face value. They are always a clumsy attempt to express something else, the true thing which escapes our superficial understanding.

Never complain of the behaviour of anyone, unless you have the power to change in his nature what makes him act in this way; and if you have the power, change him instead of complaining.

Whatever you do, never forget the goal which you have set before you. There is nothing great or small once you have set out on this great discovery; all things are equally important and can either hasten or delay its success. Thus before you eat, concentrate a few seconds in the aspiration that the food you are about to eat may bring your body the substance it needs to serve as a solid basis for your effort towards the great discovery, and give it the energy for persistence and perseverance in the effort.

Before you go to sleep, concentrate a few seconds in the aspiration that the sleep may restore your fatigued nerves, bring calm and quietness to your brain so that on waking you may, with renewed vigour, begin again your journey on the path of the great discovery.

Before you act, concentrate in the will that your action may help or at least in no way hinder your march forward towards the great discovery.

When you speak, before the words come out of your mouth, concentrate just long enough to check your words and allow only those that are absolutely necessary to pass, only those that are not in any way harmful to your progress on the path of the great discovery.

To sum up, never forget the purpose and goal of your life.

The will for the great discovery should be always there above you, above what you do and what you are, like a huge bird of light dominating all the movements of your being.

Before the untiring persistence of your effort, an inner door will suddenly open and you will emerge into a dazzling splendour that will bring you the certitude of immortality, the concrete experience that you have always lived and always shall live, that external forms alone perish and that these forms are, in relation to what you are in reality, like clothes that are thrown away when worn out. Then you will stand erect, freed from all chains, and instead of advancing laboriously under the weight of circumstances imposed upon you by Nature, which you had to endure and bear if you did not want to be crushed by them, you will be able to walk on, straight and firm, conscious of your destiny, master of your life.

And yet this release from all slavery to the flesh, this liberation from all personal attachment is not the supreme fulfilment. There are other steps to climb before you reach the summit. And even these steps can and should be followed by others which will open the doors to the future. These following steps will form the object of what I call spiritual education.

But before we enter on this new stage and deal with the question in detail, an explanation is necessary. Why is a distinction made between the psychic education of which we have just spoken and the spiritual education of which we are about to speak now? Because the two are usually confused under the general term of "yogic discipline", although the goals they aim at are very different: for one it is a higher realisation upon earth, for the other an escape from all earthly manifestation, even from the whole universe, a return to the unmanifest.

So one can say that the psychic life is immortal life, endless time, limitless space, ever-progressive change, unbroken continuity in the universe of forms. The spiritual consciousness, on the other hand, means to live the infinite and the eternal, to be projected beyond all creation, beyond time and space. To become conscious of your psychic being and to live a psychic life you must abolish all egoism; but to live a spiritual life you must no longer have an ego.

Here also, in spiritual education, the goal you set before you will assume, in the mind's formulation of it, different names according to the environment in which you have been brought up, the path you have followed and the affinities of your temperament. Those who have a religious tendency will call it God and their spiritual effort will be towards identification with the transcendent God beyond all forms, as opposed to the immanent God dwelling in each form. Others will call it the Absolute, the Supreme Origin, others Nirvana; yet others, who view the world as an unreal illusion, will name it the Only Reality and to those who regard all manifestation as falsehood it will be the Sole Truth. And every one of these expressions contains an element of truth, but all are incomplete, expressing only one aspect of that which is. Here too, however, the mental formulation has no great importance and once you have passed through the intermediate stages, the experience is identical. In any case, the most effective starting-point, the swiftest method is total self-giving. Besides, no joy is more perfect than the joy of a total self-giving to whatever is the summit of your conception: for some it is the notion of God, for others that of Perfection. If this self-giving is made with persistence and ardour, a moment comes when you pass beyond the concept and arrive at an experience that escapes all description, but which is almost always identical in its effects. And as your self-giving becomes more and more perfect and integral, it will be accompanied by the aspiration for identification, a total fusion with That to which you have given yourself, and little by little this aspiration will overcome all differences and all resistances, especially if with the aspiration there is an intense and spontaneous love, for then nothing can stand in the way of its victorious drive.

There is an essential difference between this identification and the identification with the psychic being. The latter can be made more and more lasting and, in certain cases, it becomes permanent and never leaves the person who has realised it, whatever his outer activities may be. In other words, the identification is no longer realised only in meditation and concentration, but its effects are felt at every moment of one's life, in sleep as well as in waking.

On the other hand, liberation from all form and the identification with that which is beyond form cannot last in an absolute manner; for it would automatically bring about the dissolution of the material form. Certain traditions say that this dissolution happens inevitably within twenty days of the total identification. Yet it is not necessarily so; and even if the experience is only momentary, it produces in the consciousness results that are never obliterated and have repercussions on all states of the being, both internal and external. Moreover, once the identification has been realised, it can be renewed at will, provided that you know how to put yourself in the same conditions.

This merging into the formless is the supreme liberation sought by those who want to escape from an existence which no longer holds any attraction for them. It is not surprising that they are dissatisfied with the world in its present form. But a liberation that leaves the world as it is and in no way affects the conditions of life from which others suffer, cannot satisfy those who refuse to enjoy a boon which they are the only ones, or almost the only ones, to possess, those who dream of a world more worthy of the splendours that lie hidden behind its apparent disorder and wide-spread misery. They dream of sharing with others the wonders they have discovered in their inner exploration. And the means to do so is within their reach, now that they have arrived at the summit of their ascent.

From beyond the frontiers of form a new force can be evoked, a power of consciousness which is as yet unexpressed and which, by its emergence, will be able to change the course of things and give birth to a new world. For the true solution to the problem of suffering, ignorance and death is not an individual escape from earthly miseries by self-annihilation into the unmanifest, nor a problematical collective flight from universal suffering by an integral and final return of the creation to its creator, thus curing the universe by abolishing it, but a transformation, a total transfiguration of matter brought about by the logical continuation of Nature's ascending march in her progress towards perfection, by the creation of a new species that will be to man what man is to the animal and that will manifest upon earth a new force, a new consciousness and a new power. And so will begin a new education which can be called the supramental education; it will, by its all-powerful action, work not only upon the consciousness of individual beings, but upon the very substance of which they are built and upon the environment in which they live.

In contrast with the types of education we have mentioned previously, which progress from below upwards by an ascending movement of the various parts of the being, the supramental education will progress from above downwards, its influence spreading from one state of being to another until at last the physical is reached. This last transformation will only occur visibly when the inner states of being have already been considerably transformed. It is therefore quite unreasonable to try to recognise the presence of the supramental by physical appearances. For these will be the last to change and the supramental force can be at work in an individual long before anything of it becomes perceptible in his bodily life.

To sum up, one can say that the supramental education will result no longer in a progressive formation of human nature and an increasing development of its latent faculties, but in a transformation of the nature itself, a transfiguration of the being in its entirety, a new ascent of the species above and beyond man towards superman, leading in the end to the appearance of a divine race upon earth.

Bulletin, February 1952

An International University Centre

THE CONDITIONS in which men live on earth are the result of their state of consciousness. To seek to change these conditions without changing the consciousness is a vain chimera. Those who have been able to perceive what could and ought to be done to improve the situation in the various domains of human life — economic, political, social, financial, educational and sanitary — are individuals who have, to a greater or lesser extent, developed their consciousness in an exceptional way and put themselves in contact with higher planes of consciousness. But their ideas have remained more or less theoretical or, if an attempt has been made to realise them practically, it has always failed lamentably after a certain period of time; for no human organisation can change radically unless human consciousness itself changes. Prophets of a new humanity have followed one another; religions, spiritual or social, have been created; their beginnings have sometimes been promising, but as humanity has not been fundamentally transformed, the old errors arising from human nature itself have gradually reappeared and after some time we find ourselves almost back at the point we had started from with so much hope and enthusiasm. Also, in this effort to improve human conditions, there have always been two tendencies, which seem to be contrary but which ought to complement each other so that progress may be achieved. The first advocates a collective reorganisation, something which could lead to the effective unity of mankind. The other declares that all progress is made first by the individual and insists that the individual should be given the conditions in which he can progress freely. Both are equally true and necessary, and our effort should be directed along both these lines at once. For collective progress and individual progress are interdependent. Before the individual can take a leap forward, at least a little of the preceding progress must have been realised in the collectivity. A way must therefore be found so that these two types of progress may proceed side by side.

It is in answer to this urgent need that Sri Aurobindo conceived the scheme of his international university, in order to prepare the human élite who will be able to work for the progressive unification of mankind and be ready at the same time to embody the new force which is descending to transform the earth. A few broad ideas will serve as a basis for the organisation of this university centre and will govern its programme of studies. Most of them have already been presented in the various writings of Sri Aurobindo and in the series of articles on education in this *Bulletin*.

The most important idea is that the unity of the human race can be achieved neither by uniformity nor by domination and subjection. Only a synthetic organisation of all nations, each one occupying its true place according to its own genius and the part it has to play in the whole, can bring about a comprehensive and progressive unification which has any chance of enduring. And if this synthesis is to be a living one, the grouping should be effectuated around a central idea that is as wide and as high as possible, in which all tendencies, even the most contradictory, may find their respective places. This higher idea is to give men the conditions of life they need in order to be able to prepare themselves to manifest the new force that will create the race of tomorrow.

All impulsions of rivalry, all struggle for precedence and domination must disappear and give way to a will for harmonious organisation, for clear-sighted and effective collaboration.

To make this possible, the children should be accustomed from a very early age not merely to the idea itself, but to its practice. That is why the international university centre will be international; not because students from all countries will be admitted here, nor even because they will be taught in their own language, but above all because the cultures of the various parts of the world will be represented here so as to be accessible to all, not merely intellectually in ideas, theories, principles and language, but also vitally in habits and customs, art in all its forms — painting, sculpture, music, architecture, decoration — and physically through natural scenery, dress, games, sports, industries and food. A kind of permanent world-exhibition should be organised in which all countries will be represented in a concrete and living way. The ideal would be for every nation with a well-defined culture to have a pavilion representing that culture, built in a style that is most expressive of the customs of the country; it will exhibit the nation's most representative products, natural as well as manufactured, and also the best expressions of its intellectual and artistic genius and its spiritual tendencies. Each nation would thus have a very practical and concrete interest in this cultural synthesis and could collaborate in the work by taking responsibility for the pavilion that represents it. Living accommodation, large or small according to the need, could be attached, where students of the same nationality could stay and thus enjoy the true culture of their native country and at the same time receive at the university centre the education which will introduce them to all the other cultures that exist on earth. In this way, international education will not be merely theoretical, in the classroom, but practical in all the details of life.

Only a general idea of the organisation is given here; its detailed application will be presented little by little in this *Bulletin* as it is carried out.

The first aim will therefore be to help individuals to become aware of the fundamental genius of the nation to which they belong and at the same time to bring them into contact with the ways of life of other nations, so that they learn to know and respect equally the true spirit of all the countries of the world. For, in order to be real and workable, any world-organisation must be based on this mutual respect and understanding between nation and nation as well as between individual and individual. Only in order and collective organisation, in collaboration based on mutual goodwill, is there any possibility of lifting man out of the painful chaos in which he finds himself now. It is with this aim and in this spirit that all human problems will be studied at the university centre; and the solution to them will be given in the light of the supramental knowledge which Sri Aurobindo has revealed in his writings.

Bulletin, April 1952

2

Concerning the principles which will govern the education given at the Sri Aurobindo International University Centre, it has been mentioned that each nation must occupy its own place and play its part in the world concert.

This should not be taken to mean that each nation can choose its place arbitrarily, according to its own ambitions and cravings. A country's mission is not something which can be decided mentally with all the egoistic and ignorant preferences of the external consciousness, for in that case the field of conflict between nations might be shifted, but the conflict would continue, probably with even greater force.

Just as each individual has a psychic being which is his true self and which governs his destiny more or less overtly, so too each nation has a psychic being which is its true being and moulds its destiny from behind the veil: it is the soul of the country, the national genius, the spirit of the people, the centre of national aspiration, the fountainhead of all that is beautiful, noble, great and generous in the life of the country. True patriots feel its presence as a tangible reality. In India it has been made into an almost divine entity, and all who truly love their country call it "Mother India" (Bharat Mata) and offer her a daily prayer for the welfare of their country. It is she who symbolises and embodies the true ideal of the country, its true mission in the world.

The thinking élite in India even identifies her with one of the aspects of the universal Mother, as the following extract from the *Hymn to Durga* illustrates:

"Mother Durga! Rider on the lion, giver of all strength,... we, born from thy parts of Power, we the youth of India, are seated here in thy temple. Listen, O Mother, descend upon earth, make thyself manifest in this land of India.

"Mother Durga! Giver of force and love and knowledge, terrible art thou in thy own self of might, Mother beautiful and fierce. In the battle of life, in India's battle, we are warriors commissioned by thee; Mother, give to our heart and mind a titan's energy, to our soul and intelligence a god's character and knowledge.

"Mother Durga! India, world's noblest race, lay whelmed in darkness. Mother, thou risest on the eastern horizon, the dawn comes with the glow of thy divine limbs scattering the darkness. Spread thy light, Mother, destroy the darkness.

"Mother Durga! We are thy children, through thy grace, by thy influence may we become fit for the great work, for the great Ideal. Mother, destroy our smallness, our selfishness, our fear.

"Mother Durga! Thou art Kali... sword in hand, thou slayest the Asura. Goddess, do thou slay with thy pitiless cry the enemies who dwell within us, may none remain alive there, not one. May we become pure and spotless, this is our prayer, O Mother, make thyself manifest.

"Mother Durga! India lies low in selfishness and fearfulness and littleness. Make us great, make our efforts great, our hearts vast, make us true to our resolve. May we no longer desire the small, void of energy, given to laziness, stricken with fear.

"Mother Durga! Extend wide the power of Yoga. We are thy Aryan children, develop in us again the lost teaching, character, strength of intelligence, faith and devotion, force of austerity, power of chastity and true knowledge, bestow all that upon the world. To help mankind, appear, O Mother of the world, dispel all ills.

"Mother Durga! Slay the enemy within, then root out all obstacles abroad. May the noble heroic mighty Indian race, supreme in love and unity, truth and strength, arts and letters, force and knowledge, ever dwell in its holy woodlands, its fertile fields, under its sky-scraping hills, along the banks of its pure-streaming rivers. This is our prayer at the feet of the Mother. Make thyself manifest.

"Mother Durga! Enter our bodies in thy Yogic strength. We shall become thy instruments, thy sword slaying all evil, thy lamp dispelling all ignorance. Fulfil this yearning of thy young children, O Mother. Be the master and drive thy instrument, wield thy sword and slay the evil, hold up the lamp and spread the light of knowledge. Make thyself manifest."[1]

One would like to see in all countries the same veneration for the national soul, the same aspiration to become fit instruments for the manifestation of its highest ideal, the same ardour for progress and self-perfection enabling each people to identify itself with its national soul and thus find its true nature and role, which makes each one a living and immortal entity regardless of all the accidents of history.

Bulletin, August 1952

3

Advice to Newcomers

The International University Centre is being organised little by

---

[1] *Hymn to Durga*, translated by Sri Nolini Kanta Gupta from Sri Aurobindo's Bengali original.

little. Until it is possible to erect the new buildings where it will be permanently housed, and for which the plans are now ready, certain departments such as the library, the reading room and a limited number of classes have been accommodated in the old premises that are going to be pulled down. Already future teachers and future students are beginning to arrive, some from outside, new to the climate and customs of the country. They are arriving in the Ashram for the first time and know nothing of its life or its customs. Some of them come with a mental aspiration, either to serve or to learn; others come in the hope of doing yoga, of finding the Divine and uniting with Him; finally there are those who want to devote themselves entirely to the divine work upon earth. All of them come impelled by their psychic being, which wants to lead them towards self-realisation. They come with their psychic in front and ruling their consciousness; they have a psychic contact with people and things. Everything seems beautiful and good to them, their health improves, their consciousness grows more luminous; they feel happy, peaceful and safe; they think that they have reached their utmost possibility of consciousness. This peace and fullness and joy given by the psychic contact they naturally find everywhere, in everything and everybody. It gives an openness towards the true consciousness pervading here and working out everything. So long as the openness is there, the peace, the fullness and the joy remain with their immediate results of progress, health and fitness in the physical, quietness and goodwill in the vital, clear understanding and broadness in the mental and a general feeling of security and satisfaction. But it is difficult for a human being to keep up a constant contact with his psychic. As soon as he settles down and the freshness of the new experience fades away, the old person comes back to the surface with all its habits, preferences, small manias, shortcomings and misunderstandings; the peace is replaced by restlessness, the joy vanishes, the understanding is blinded and the feeling that the place is the same as everywhere else creeps in, because one has

45

become what one was everywhere else. Instead of seeing only what has been accomplished, he becomes aware more and more and almost exclusively of what has yet to be done; he becomes morose and discontented and blames people and things instead of blaming himself. He complains of the lack of comfort, of the unbearable climate, of the unsuitable food that makes his digestion painful. Taking support from Sri Aurobindo's teaching that the body is an indispensable basis for the yoga, that it should not be neglected and that, on the contrary, great care should be given to it, the physical consciousness concentrates almost exclusively on the body and tries to find ways of satisfying it. This is practically impossible, for, with a very few exceptions, the more it is given, the more it demands. Besides, the physical being is ignorant and blind; it is full of false notions, preconceived ideas, prejudices and preferences. Indeed, it cannot deal effectively with the body. Only the psychic consciousness has the knowledge and the insight needed to do the right thing in the right way.

You might well ask, what is the remedy for this state of affairs? For here we are going round in a vicious circle, since the whole trouble comes from drawing away from the psychic and only the psychic can find the solution to the problems. There is consequently only one remedy: be on your guard, hold fast to the psychic, do not allow anything in your consciousness to slip in between your psychic and yourself, close your ears and your understanding to all other suggestions and rely only on the psychic.

Usually, those who become conscious of their psychic being expect that it will liberate them from vital and physical attractions and activities; they seek to escape from the world in order to live in the joy of contemplation of the Divine, and in the immutable peace of constant contact with Him. The attitude of those who want to practise Sri Aurobindo's integral yoga is quite different. When they have found their psychic being and are united with it, they ask it to turn its gaze towards the physical being in order to act on it with the knowledge that comes from the contact with the Divine, and to transform the body so that it may be able to receive and manifest the divine consciousness and harmony.

This is the goal of our efforts here; this will be the culmination of your studies in the International University Centre.

So, to all those who come to join the University Centre, I shall say once more: never forget our programme and the deeper reason of your coming here. And if in spite of all your efforts the horizon sometimes darkens, if hope and joy fade away, if enthusiasm flags, remember that it is a sign that you have drawn away from your psychic being and lost contact with its ideal. In this way you will avoid making the mistake of throwing the blame on the people and things around you and thus quite needlessly increasing your sufferings and your difficulties.

Bulletin, November 1952

The Four Austerities
and the Four Liberations

TO PURSUE an integral education that leads to the supramental realisation, four austerities are necessary, and with them four liberations.

Austerity is usually confused with self-mortification, and when someone speaks of austerities, we think of the discipline of the ascetic who, in order to avoid the arduous task of spiritualising the physical, vital and mental life, declares it incapable of transformation and casts it away ruthlessly as a useless encumbrance, as a bondage and an impediment to all spiritual progress, in any case as something incorrigible, as a load that has to be borne more or less cheerfully until Nature, or divine Grace, delivers you from it by death. At best, life on earth is a field for progress and one should take advantage of it as best one can in order to reach as soon as possible the degree of perfection which will put an end to the ordeal by making it unnecessary.

For us the problem is quite different. Life on earth is not a passage or a means; by transformation it must become a goal and a realisation. Consequently, when we speak of austerities, it is not out of contempt for the body nor to detach ourselves from it, but because of the need for control and mastery. For there is an austerity which is far greater, far more complete and far more difficult than all the austerities of the ascetic: it is the austerity which is necessary for the integral transformation, the fourfold austerity which prepares the individual for the manifestation of the supramental truth. For example, one can say that few austerities are as strict as those which physical culture demands for the perfection of the body. But we shall return to this point in due time.

Before starting to describe the four kinds of austerity required, it is necessary to clarify one question which is a source of much misunderstanding and confusion in the minds of most people. It is the question of ascetic practices, which they mistake for spiritual disciplines. These practices, which consist of ill-treating the body in order, so they say, to liberate the spirit from it, are in fact a sensuous distortion of spiritual discipline; it is a kind of perverse need for suffering which drives the ascetic to self-mortification. The sadhu's recourse to the bed of nails or the Christian anchorite's resort to the whip and the hair-shirt are the result of a more or less veiled sadistic tendency, unavowed and unavowable; it is an unhealthy seeking or a subconscious need for violent sensations. In reality, these things are very far removed from all spiritual life, for they are ugly and base, dark and diseased; whereas spiritual life, on the contrary, is a life of light and balance, beauty and joy. They are invented and extolled by a sort of mental and vital cruelty towards the body. But cruelty, even with regard to one's own body, is nonetheless cruelty, and all cruelty is a sign of great unconsciousness. Unconscious natures need very strong sensations, for without them they can feel nothing; and cruelty, which is one form of sadism, brings very strong sensations. The avowed purpose of such practices is to abolish all sensation so that the body may no longer stand in the way of one's flight towards the spirit; but the effectiveness of this method is open to doubt. It is a recognised fact that in order to progress rapidly, one must not be afraid of difficulties; on the contrary, by choosing to do the difficult thing at every opportunity, one increases the will-power and strengthens the nerves. Now, it is much more difficult to lead a life of moderation and balance, in equanimity and serenity, than to try to contend with over-indulgence in pleasure and the obscuration it entails, by over-indulgence in asceticism and the disintegration it causes. It is much more difficult to achieve the harmonious and progressive development of one's physical being in calm and simplicity than to ill-treat it to the point of annihilation. It is much more difficult to live soberly and without desire than to deprive the body of its indispensable nourishment and cleanliness and boast proudly of one's abstinence. It is much more difficult to avoid or to surmount and conquer illness by an inner and outer harmony, purity and balance, than to disregard and ignore it and leave it free to do its work of destruction. And the most difficult thing of all is to maintain the consciousness constantly at the height of its capacity, never allowing the body to act under the influence of a lower impulse.

This is why we shall have recourse to the four austerities which will result in four liberations within us. The practice of these austerities will constitute a fourfold discipline or tapasya which can be defined as follows:

1) Tapasya of love
2) Tapasya of knowledge
3) Tapasya of power
4) Tapasya of beauty

These terms have been listed from top to bottom, so to say, but their order should not be taken to indicate anything superior or inferior, or more or less difficult, or the order in which these disciplines can and ought to be practised. The order, importance and difficulty vary with each individual and no absolute rule can be formulated. Each one must find and work out his own system according to his personal needs and capacities.

Accordingly, only an overall view will be given here, presenting an ideal procedure that is as complete as possible. Each one will then have to apply as much of it as he can in the best possible way.

The tapasya or discipline of beauty will lead us, through austerity in physical life, to freedom in action. Its basic programme will be to build a body that is beautiful in form, harmonious in posture, supple and agile in its movements, powerful in its activities and robust in its health and organic functioning.

To achieve these results, it will be good, as a general rule, to make use of habit as a help in organising one's material life, for the body functions more easily within the framework of a regular routine. But one must know how to avoid becoming a slave to one's habits, however good they may be; the greatest flexibility must be maintained so that one may change them each time it becomes necessary to do so.

One must build up nerves of steel in powerful and elastic muscles in order to be able to endure anything whenever it is indispensable. But at the same time great care must be taken not to demand more from the body than the effort which is strictly necessary, the expenditure of energy that fosters growth and progress, while categorically excluding everything that causes exhaustion and leads in the end to physical decline and disintegration.

A physical culture which aims at building a body capable of serving as a fit instrument for a higher consciousness demands very austere habits: a great regularity in sleep, food, exercise and every activity. By a scrupulous study of one's own bodily needs — for they vary with each individual — a general programme will be established; and once this has been done well, it must be followed rigorously, without any fantasy or slackness. There must be no little exceptions to the rule that are indulged in "just for once" but which are repeated very often — for as soon as one yields to temptation, even "just for once", one lessens the resistance of the will-power and opens the door to every failure. One must therefore forgo all weakness: no more nightly escapades from which one comes back exhausted, no more feasting and carousing which upset the normal functioning of the stomach, no more distractions, amusements and pleasures that only waste energy and leave one without the strength to do the daily practice. One must submit to the austerity of a sensible and regular life, concentrating all one's physical attention on building a body that comes as close to perfection as possible. To reach this ideal goal, one must strictly shun all excess and every vice, great or small; one must deny oneself the use of such slow poisons as tobacco, alcohol, etc., which men have a habit of

51

developing into indispensable needs that gradually destroy the will and the memory. The all-absorbing interest which nearly all human beings, even the most intellectual, have in food, its preparation and its consumption, should be replaced by an almost chemical knowledge of the needs of the body and a very scientific austerity in satisfying them. Another austerity must be added to that of food, the austerity of sleep. It does not consist in going without sleep but in knowing how to sleep. Sleep must not be a fall into unconsciousness which makes the body heavy instead of refreshing it. Eating with moderation and abstaining from all excess greatly reduces the need to spend many hours in sleep; however, the quality of sleep is much more important than its quantity. In order to have a truly effective rest and relaxation during sleep, it is good as a rule to drink something before going to bed, a cup of milk or soup or fruit-juice, for instance. Light food brings a quiet sleep. One should, however, abstain from all copious meals, for then the sleep becomes agitated and is disturbed by nightmares, or else is dense, heavy and dulling. But the most important thing of all is to make the mind clear, to quieten the emotions and calm the effervescence of desires and the preoccupations which accompany them. If before retiring to bed one has talked a lot or had a lively discussion, if one has read an exciting or intensely interesting book, one should rest a little without sleeping in order to quieten the mental activity, so that the brain does not engage in disorderly movements while the other parts of the body alone are asleep. Those who practise meditation will do well to concentrate for a few minutes on a lofty and restful idea, in an aspiration towards a higher and vaster consciousness. Their sleep will benefit greatly from this and they will largely be spared the risk of falling into unconsciousness while they sleep.

After the austerity of a night spent wholly in resting in a calm and peaceful sleep comes the austerity of a day which is sensibly organised; its activities will be divided between the progressive and skilfully graded exercises required for the culture of the body, and work of some kind or other. For both can and ought to form part of the physical tapasya. With regard to exercises, each one will choose the ones best suited to his body and, if possible, take guidance from an expert on the subject, who knows how to combine and grade the exercises to obtain a maximum effect. Neither the choice nor the execution of these exercises should be governed by fancy. One must not do this or that because it seems easier or more amusing; there should be no change of training until the instructor considers it necessary. The self-perfection or even simply the self-improvement of each individual body is a problem to be solved, and its solution demands much patience, perseverance and regularity. In spite of what many people think, the athlete's life is not a life of amusement or distraction; on the contrary, it is a life of methodical efforts and austere habits, which leave no room for useless fancies that go against the result one wants to achieve.

In work too there is an austerity. It consists in not having any preferences and in doing everything one does with interest. For one who wants to grow in self-perfection, there are no great or small tasks, none that are important or unimportant; all are equally useful for one who aspires for progress and self-mastery. It is said that one only does well what one is interested in doing. This is true, but it is truer still that one can learn to find interest in everything one does, even in what appear to be the most insignificant chores. The secret of this attainment lies in the urge towards self-perfection. Whatever occupation or task falls to your lot, you must do it with a will to progress; whatever one does, one must not only do it as best one can but strive to do it better and better in a constant effort for perfection. In this way everything without exception becomes interesting, from the most material chore to the most artistic and intellectual work. The scope for progress is infinite and can be applied to the smallest thing.

This leads us quite naturally to liberation in action. For, in one's action, one must be free from all social conventions, all moral prejudices. However, this does not mean that one should lead a life of licence and dissoluteness. On the contrary, one imposes on oneself a rule that is far stricter than all social rules, for it tolerates no hypocrisy and demands a perfect sincerity. One's entire physical activity should be organised to help the body to grow in balance and strength and beauty. For this purpose, one must abstain from all pleasure-seeking, including sexual pleasure. For every sexual act is a step towards death. That is why from the most ancient times, in the most sacred and secret schools, this act was prohibited to every aspirant towards immortality. The sexual act is always followed by a longer or shorter period of unconsciousness that opens the door to all kinds of influences and causes a fall in consciousness. But if one wants to prepare oneself for the supramental life, one must never allow one's consciousness to slip into laxity and inconscience under the pretext of pleasure or even of rest and relaxation. One should find relaxation in force and light, not in darkness and weakness. Continence is therefore the rule for all those who aspire for progress. But especially for those who want to prepare themselves for the supramental manifestation, this continence must be replaced by a total abstinence, achieved not by coercion and suppression but by a kind of inner alchemy, as a result of which the energies that are normally used in the act of procreation are transmuted into energies for progress and integral transformation. It is obvious that for the result to be total and truly beneficial, all sexual impulses and desires must be eliminated from the mental and vital consciousness as well as from the physical will. All radical and durable transformation proceeds from within outwards, so that the external transformation is the normal, almost inevitable result of this process.

A decisive choice has to be made between lending the body to Nature's ends in obedience to her demand to perpetuate the race as it is, and preparing this same body to become a step towards the creation of the new race. For it is not possible to do both at the same time; at every moment one has to decide whether one wants to remain part of the humanity of yesterday or to belong to the superhumanity of tomorrow.

One must renounce being adapted to life as it is and succeeding in it if one wants to prepare for life as it will be and to become an active and efficient part of it.

One must refuse pleasure if one wants to open to the delight of existence, in a total beauty and harmony.

This brings us quite naturally to vital austerity, the austerity of the sensations, the tapasya of power. For the vital being is the seat of power, of effective enthusiasm. It is in the vital that thought is transformed into will and becomes a dynamism for action. It is also true that the vital is the seat of desires and passions, of violent impulses and equally violent reactions, of revolt and depression. The normal remedy is to strangle and starve the vital by depriving it of all sensation; sensations are indeed its main sustenance and without them it falls asleep, grows sluggish and starves to death.

In fact, the vital has three sources of subsistence. The one most easily accessible to it comes from below, from the physical energies through the sensations.

The second is on its own plane, when it is sufficiently vast and receptive, by contact with the universal vital forces.

The third, to which it usually opens only in a great aspiration for progress, comes to it from above by the infusion and absorption of spiritual forces and inspiration.

To these sources men always strive more or less to add another, which is for them at the same time the source of most of their torments and misfortunes. It is the interchange of vital forces with their fellows, usually in groups of two, which they most often mistake for love, but which is only the attraction between two forces that take pleasure in mutual interchange.

Thus, if we do not wish to starve our vital, sensations must not be rejected or diminished in number and intensity. Neither should we avoid them; rather we must make use of them with wisdom and discernment. Sensations are an excellent instrument of knowledge and education, but to make them serve these ends, they must not be used egoistically for the sake of enjoyment, in a blind and ignorant search for pleasure and self-satisfaction.

The senses should be capable of enduring everything without disgust or displeasure, but at the same time they must acquire and develop more and more the power of discerning the quality, origin and effect of the various vital vibrations in order to know whether they are favourable to harmony, beauty and good health or whether they are harmful to the balance and progress of the physical being and the vital. Moreover, the senses should be used as instruments to approach and study the physical and vital worlds in all their complexity; in this way they will take their true place in the great endeavour towards transformation.

It is by enlightening, strengthening and purifying the vital, and not by weakening it, that one can contribute to the true progress of the being. To deprive oneself of sensations is therefore as harmful as depriving oneself of food. But just as the choice of food must be made wisely and solely for the growth and proper functioning of the body, so too the choice of sensations and their control should be made with a very scientific austerity and solely for the growth and perfection of the vital, of this highly dynamic instrument, which is as essential for progress as all the other parts of the being.

It is by educating the vital, by making it more refined, more sensitive, more subtle and, one should almost say, more elegant, in the best sense of the word, that one can overcome its violence and brutality, which are in fact a form of crudity and ignorance, of lack of taste.

In truth, a cultivated and illumined vital can be as noble and heroic and disinterested as it is now spontaneously vulgar, egoistic and perverted when it is left to itself without education. It is enough for each one to know how to transform in himself the search for pleasure into an aspiration for the supramental plenitude. If the education of the vital is carried far enough, with perseverance and sincerity, there comes a time when, convinced of the greatness and beauty of the goal, the vital gives up petty and illusory sensorial satisfactions in order to win the divine delight.

Bulletin, February 1953

2

The question of mental austerity immediately brings to mind long meditations leading to control of thought and culminating in inner silence. This aspect of yogic discipline is too well known to need dwelling upon. But there is another aspect of the subject which is usually given less attention, and that is control of speech. Apart from a very few exceptions, only absolute silence is set in opposition to loose talk. And yet it is a far greater and far more fruitful austerity to control one's speech than to abolish it altogether.

Man is the first animal on earth to be able to use articulate sounds. Indeed, he is very proud of this capacity and exercises it without moderation or discernment. The world is deafened with the sound of his words and sometimes one almost misses the harmonious silence of the plant kingdom.

Besides, it is a well-known fact that the weaker the mental power, the greater is the need to use speech. Thus there are primitive and uneducated people who cannot think at all unless they speak, and they can be heard muttering sounds more or less loudly to themselves, because this is the only way they can follow a train of thought, which would not be formulated in them but for the spoken word.

There are also a great many people, even among those who are educated but whose mental power is weak, who do not know what they want to say until they say it. This makes their speech interminable and tedious. For as they speak, their thought becomes clearer and more precise, and so they have to repeat the same thing several times in order to say it more and more exactly.

Some need to prepare beforehand what they have to say, and splutter when they are obliged to improvise, because they have not had time to elaborate step by step the exact terms of what they want to say.

Lastly, there are born orators who are masters of the spoken word; they spontaneously find all the words they need to say what they want to say and say it well.

None of this, however, from the point of view of mental austerity, goes beyond the category of idle talk. For by idle talk I mean every word that is spoken without being absolutely indispensable. One may ask, how can one judge? For this, one must first make a general classification of the various categories of spoken words.

First, in the physical domain, we have all the words that are spoken for material reasons. They are by far the most numerous and most probably also the most useful in ordinary life.

A constant babble of words seems to be the indispensable accompaniment to daily work. And yet as soon as one makes an effort to reduce the noise to a minimum, one realises that many things are done better and faster in silence and that this helps to maintain one's inner peace and concentration.

If you are not alone and live with others, cultivate the habit of not externalising yourself constantly by speaking aloud, and you will notice that little by little an inner understanding is established between yourself and others; you will then be able to communicate among yourselves with a minimum of words or even without any words at all. This outer silence is most favourable to inner peace, and with goodwill and a steadfast aspiration, you will be able to create a harmonious atmosphere which is very conducive to progress.

In social life, in addition to the words that concern material life and occupations, there will be those that express sensations, feelings and emotions. Here the habit of outer silence proves of valuable help. For when one is assailed by a wave of sensations or feelings, this habitual silence gives you time to reflect and, if necessary, to regain possession of yourself before projecting the sensation or feeling in words. How many quarrels can be avoided in this way; how many times one will be saved from one of those psychological catastrophes which are only too often the result of uncontrolled speech.

Without going to this extreme, one should always control the words one speaks and never allow one's tongue to be prompted by a movement of anger, violence or temper. It is not only the quarrel that is bad in its results, but the fact of allowing one's tongue to be used to project bad vibrations into the atmosphere; for nothing is more contagious than the vibrations of sound, and by giving these movements a chance to express themselves, one perpetuates them in oneself and in others.

Among the most undesirable kinds of idle talk must also be included everything that is said about others.

Unless you are responsible for certain people, as a guardian, a teacher or a departmental head, what others do or do not do is no concern of yours and you must refrain from talking about them, from giving your opinion about them and what they do, and from repeating what others may think or say about them.

It may happen that the very nature of your occupation makes it your duty to report what is taking place in a particular department, undertaking or communal work. But then the report should be confined to the work alone and not touch upon private matters. And as an absolute rule, it must be wholly objective. You should not allow any personal reaction, any preference, any like or dislike to creep in. And above all, never introduce your own petty personal grudges into the work that is assigned to you.

In all cases and as a general rule, the less one speaks of others, even to praise them, the better. It is already so difficult to know exactly what is happening in oneself — how can one know with certainty what is happening in others? So you must totally abstain from pronouncing upon anybody one of those final judgments which cannot but be foolish if not spiteful.

When a thought is expressed in speech, the vibration of the sound has a considerable power to bring the most material substance into contact with the thought, thus giving it a concrete and effective reality. That is why one must never speak ill of people or things or say things which go against the progress of the divine realisation in the world. This is an absolute general rule. And yet it has one exception. You should not criticise anything unless at the same time you have the conscious power and active will to dissolve or transform the movements or things you criticise. For this conscious power and active will have the capacity of infusing Matter with the possibility to react and refuse the bad vibration and ultimately to correct it so that it becomes impossible for it to go on expressing itself on the physical plane.

This can be done without risk or danger only by one who moves in the gnostic realms and possesses in his mental faculties the light of the spirit and the power of the truth. He, the divine worker, is free from all preference and all attachment; he has broken down the limits of his ego and is now only a perfectly pure and impersonal instrument of the supramental action upon earth.

There are also all the words that are uttered to express ideas, opinions, the results of reflection or study. Here we are in an intellectual domain and we might think that in this domain men are more reasonable, more self-controlled, and that the practice of rigorous austerity is less indispensable. It is nothing of the kind, however, for even here, into this abode of ideas and knowledge, man has brought the violence of his convictions, the intolerance of his sectarianism, the passion of his preferences. Thus, here too, one must resort to mental austerity and carefully avoid any exchange of ideas that leads to controversies which are all too often bitter and nearly always unnecessary, or any clash of opinion which ends in heated discussions and even quarrels, which are always the result of some mental narrowness that can easily be cured when one rises high enough in the mental domain.

For sectarianism becomes impossible when one knows that any formulated thought is only one way of saying something which eludes all expression. Every idea contains a little of the truth or one aspect of the truth. But no idea is absolutely true in itself.

This sense of the relativity of things is a powerful help in keeping one's balance and preserving a serene moderation in one's speech. I once heard an old occultist of some wisdom say, "Nothing is essentially bad; there are only things which are not in their place. Put each thing in its true place and you will have a harmonious world."

And yet, from the point of view of action, the value of an idea is in proportion to its pragmatic power. It is true that this power varies a great deal according to the individual on whom it acts. An idea that has great impelling force in one individual may have none whatsoever in another. But the power itself is contagious. Certain ideas are capable of transforming the world. They are the ones that ought to be expressed; they are the ruling stars in the firmament of the spirit that will guide the earth towards its supreme realisation.

Lastly, we have all the words that are spoken for the purpose of teaching. This category ranges from the kindergarten to the university course, not forgetting all the artistic and literary creations of mankind that seek to entertain or instruct. In this domain, everything depends on the worth of the creation, and the subject is too vast to be dealt with here. It is a fact that concern about education is very much in vogue at present and praiseworthy attempts are being made to make use of new scientific discoveries in the service of education. But even in this matter, austerity is demanded from the aspirant towards truth.

It is generally admitted that in the process of education a certain kind of lighter, more frivolous, more entertaining

61

productions are necessary to reduce the strain of effort and give some relaxation to the children and even to adults. From a certain point of view, this is true; but unfortunately this concession has served as an excuse to justify a whole category of things which are nothing but the efflorescence of all that is vulgar, crude and base in human nature. Its coarsest instincts, its most depraved taste find in this concession a good excuse to display and impose themselves as an inevitable necessity. They are nothing of the kind, however; one can relax without being dissolute, take rest without being vulgar, enjoy oneself without allowing the grosser elements in the nature to rise to the surface. But from the point of view of austerity, these needs themselves change their nature; relaxation is transformed into inner silence, rest into contemplation and enjoyment into bliss.

This generally recognised need for entertainment, slackening of effort and more or less long and total forgetfulness of the aim of life and the purpose of existence should not be considered as something altogether natural and indispensable, but as a weakness to which one yields because of lack of intensity in the aspiration, because of instability in the will, because of ignorance, unconsciousness and sloth. Do not justify these movements and you will soon realise that they are unnecessary; there will even come a time when they become repugnant and unacceptable to you. Then the greater part of human creation, which is ostensibly entertaining but in reality debasing, will lose its support and cease to be encouraged.

However, one should not think that the value of spoken words depends on the nature of the subject of conversation. One can talk idly on spiritual matters just as much as on any other, and this kind of idle talk may well be one of the most dangerous. For example, the neophyte is always very eager to share with others the little he has learnt. But as he advances on the path, he becomes more and more aware that he does not know very much and that before trying to instruct others, he must be very sure of the value of what he knows, until he finally becomes wise and realises that many hours of silent concentration are needed to be able to speak usefully for a few minutes. Moreover, where inner life and spiritual effort are concerned, the use of speech should be subjected to a still more stringent rule and nothing should be said unless it is absolutely indispensable.

It is a well-known fact that one must never speak of one's spiritual experiences if one does not want to see vanishing in a flash the energy accumulated in the experience, which was meant to hasten one's progress. The only exception which can be made to the rule is with regard to one's guru, when one wants to receive some explanation or teaching from him concerning the content and meaning of one's experience. Indeed, one can speak about these things without danger only to one's guru, for only the guru is able by his knowledge to use the elements of the experience for your own good, as steps towards new ascents.

It is true that the guru himself is subject to the same rule of silence with regard to what concerns him personally. In Nature everything is in movement; thus, whatever does not move forward is bound to fall back. The guru must progress even as his disciples do, although his progress may not be on the same plane. And for him too, to speak about his experiences is not favourable: the greater part of the dynamic force for progress contained in the experience evaporates if it is put into words. But on the other hand, by explaining his experiences to his disciples, he greatly helps their understanding and consequently their progress. It is for him in his wisdom to know to what extent he can and ought to sacrifice the one to the other. It goes without saying that no boasting or vainglory should enter into his account, for the slightest vanity would make him no longer a guru but an imposter.

As for the disciple, I would tell him: "In all cases, be faithful to your guru whoever he is; he will lead you as far as you can go. But if you have the good fortune to have the Divine as your guru, there will be no limit to your realisation."

Nevertheless, even the Divine, when incarnate on earth, is subject to the same law of progress. His instrument of manifestation, the physical being he has assumed, should be in a constant state of progress, and the law of his personal self-expression is in a way linked to the general law of earthly progress. Thus, even the embodied god cannot be perfect on earth until men are ready to understand and accept perfection. That day will come when everything that is now done out of a sense of duty towards the Divine will be done out of love for Him. Progress will be a joy instead of being an effort and often even a struggle. Or, more exactly, progress will be made in joy, with the full adherence of the whole being, instead of by coercing the resistance of the ego, which entails great effort and sometimes even great suffering.

In conclusion, I would say this: if you want your speech to express the truth and thus acquire the power of the Word, never think out beforehand what you want to say, do not decide what is a good or bad thing to say, do not calculate the effect of what you are going to say. Be silent in mind and remain unwavering in the true attitude of constant aspiration towards the All-Wisdom, the All-Knowledge, the All-Consciousness. Then, if your aspiration is sincere, if it is not a veil for your ambition to do well and to succeed, if it is pure, spontaneous and integral, you will then be able to speak very simply, to say the words that ought to be said, neither more nor less, and they will have a creative power.

Bulletin, April 1953

3

Of all austerities the most difficult is the austerity of feelings and emotions, the tapasya of love.

Indeed, in the domain of feelings, more perhaps than in any other, man has the sense of the inevitable, the irresistible, of a fatality that dominates him and which he cannot escape. Love (or at least what human beings call love) is particularly regarded as an imperious master whose caprice one cannot elude, who strikes you according to his fancy and forces you to obey him whether you will or not. In the name of love the worst crimes have been perpetrated, the greatest follies committed.

And yet men have invented all kinds of moral and social rules in the hope of controlling this force of love, of making it amenable and docile. But these rules seem to have been made only to be broken; and the restraint they impose on its free activity merely increases its explosive power. For it is not by rules that the movements of love can be disciplined. Only a greater, higher and truer power of love can subdue the uncontrollable impulses of love. Only love can rule over love by enlightening, transforming and exalting it. For here too, more than anywhere else, control does not consist of suppression and abolition but of transmutation — a sublime alchemy. This is because, of all the forces at work in the universe, love is the most powerful, the most irresistible. Without love the world would fall back into the chaos of inconscience.

Consciousness is indeed the creatrix of the universe, but love is its saviour. Conscious experience alone can give a glimpse of what love is, of its purpose and process. Any verbal transcription is necessarily a mental travesty of something which eludes all expression in every way. Philosophers, mystics, occultists, have all tried to define love, but in vain. I have no pretension of succeeding where they have failed. But I wish to state in the simplest possible terms what in their writings takes such an abstract and complicated form. My words will have no other aim than to lead towards the living experience, and I wish to be able to lead even a child to it.

Love is, in its essence, the joy of identity; it finds its ultimate expression in the bliss of union. Between the two lie all the phases of its universal manifestation.

At the beginning of this manifestation, in the purity of its origin, love is composed of two movements, two complementary poles of the urge towards complete oneness. On one hand there is the supreme power of attraction and on the other the irresistible need for absolute self-giving. No other movement could have better bridged the abyss that was created when in the individual being consciousness was separated from its origin and became unconsciousness.

What had been projected into space had to be brought back to itself without, however, annihilating the universe which had thus been created. That is why love burst forth, the irresistible power of union.

It brooded over the darkness and the inconscience; it was scattered and fragmented in the bosom of unfathomable night. And then began the awakening and the ascent, the slow formation of Matter and its endless progression. It is indeed love, in a corrupted and darkened form, that is associated with all the impulses of physical and vital Nature, as the urge behind all movement and all grouping, which becomes quite perceptible in the plant kingdom. In trees and plants, it is the need to grow in order to obtain more light, more air, more space; in flowers, it is the offering of their beauty and fragrance in a loving efflorescence. Then, in animals, it is love that lies behind hunger and thirst, the need for appropriation, expansion, procreation, in short, behind every desire, whether conscious or not. And among the higher species, it is in the self-sacrificing devotion of the female to her young. This brings us quite naturally to the human race in which, with the triumphant advent of mental activity, this association reaches its climax, for it has become conscious and deliberate. Indeed, as soon as terrestrial development made it possible, Nature took up this sublime force of love and put it at the service of her creative work by linking and mixing it with her movement of procreation. This association has even become so close, so intimate, that very few human beings are illumined enough in their consciousness to be able to dissociate these movements from each other and experience them separately. In this way, love has suffered every degradation; it has been debased to the level of the beast.

From then on, too, there clearly appears in Nature's works the will to rebuild, by steps and stages and through ever more numerous and complex groupings, the primordial oneness. Having made use of the power of love to bring two human beings together to form the biune group, the origin of the family, after having broken the narrow limits of personal egoism, changing it into a dual egoism, Nature, with the appearance of children, brought forth a more complex unit, the family. And in course of time, with multifarious associations between families, individual interchanges and mingling of blood, larger groupings were formed: clans, tribes, castes, classes, leading to the creation of nations. This work of group formation proceeded simultaneously in the various parts of the world, crystallising in the different races. And little by little, Nature will fuse these races too in her endeavour to build a real and material foundation for human unity.

In the consciousness of most men, all this is the outcome of chance; they are not aware of the existence of a global plan and take circumstances as they come, for better or for worse according to their temperament: some are satisfied, others discontented.

Among the contented, there is a certain category of people who are perfectly adapted to Nature's ways: these are the optimists. For them the days are brighter because of the nights, colours are vivid because of the shadows, joy is more intense because of suffering, pain gives a greater charm to pleasure, illness gives health all its value; I have even heard some of them say that they are glad to have enemies because it made them appreciate their friends all the more. In any case, for all these people, sexual activity is one of the most enjoyable of occupations, satisfaction of the palate is a delight of life that they cannot go without; and it is quite normal to die since one is born: death puts an end to a journey which would become tedious if it were to last too long.

In short, they find life quite all right as it is and do not care to know whether it has a purpose or a goal; they do not worry about the miseries of others and do not see any need for progress.

Never try to "convert" these people; it would be a serious mistake. If they were unfortunate enough to listen to you, they would lose the balance they have without being able to find a new one. They are not ready to have an inner life, but they are Nature's favourites; they have a very close alliance with her, and this realisation should not be needlessly disturbed.

To a lesser degree, and above all, in a less durable way, there are other contented people in the world whose contentment is due to the magic effect of love. Each time an individual breaks the narrow limitations in which he is imprisoned by his ego and emerges into the open air, through self-giving, whether for the sake of another human being or his family, his country or his faith, he finds in this self-forgetfulness a foretaste of the marvellous delight of love, and this gives him the impression that he has come into contact with the Divine. But most often it is only a fleeting contact, for in the human being love is immediately mixed with lower egoistic movements which debase it and rob it of its power of purity. But even if it remained pure, this contact with the divine existence could not last for ever, for love is only one aspect of the Divine, an aspect which here on earth has suffered the same distortions as the others.

Besides, all these experiences are very good and useful for the ordinary man who follows the normal way of Nature in her stumbling march towards the future unity. But they cannot satisfy those who want to hasten the movement, or rather, who aspire to belong to another line of more direct and rapid movement, to an exceptional movement that will liberate them from ordinary mankind and its interminable march, so that they may take part in the spiritual advance which will lead them along the swiftest paths towards the creation of the new race, the race that will express the supramental truth upon earth. These rare souls must reject all forms of love between human beings, for however beautiful and pure they may be, they cause a kind of short-circuit and cut off the direct connection with the Divine.

For one who has known love for the Divine, all other forms of love are obscure and too mixed with pettiness and egoism and darkness; they are like a perpetual haggling or a struggle for supremacy and domination, and even among the best they are full of misunderstanding and irritability, of friction and incomprehension.

Moreover, it is a well-known fact that one grows into the likeness of what one loves. Therefore if you want to be like the Divine, love Him alone. Only one who has known the ecstasy of the exchange of love with the Divine can know how insipid and dull and feeble any other exchange is in comparison. And even if the most austere discipline is required to arrive at this exchange, nothing is too hard, too long or too severe in order to achieve it, for it surpasses all expression.

This is the marvellous state we want to realise on earth; it is this which will have the power to transform the world and make it a habitation worthy of the Divine Presence. Then will pure and true love be able to incarnate in a body that will no longer be a disguise and a veil for it. Many a time, in order to make the discipline easier and to create a closer and more easily perceptible intimacy, the Divine has sought, in his highest form of love, to assume a physical body similar in appearance to the human body; but each time, imprisoned within the gross forms of Matter, he was able to express only a caricature of himself. And in order to manifest in the fullness of his perfection he waits only for human beings to have made some indispensable progress in their consciousness and in their bodies; for the vulgarity of man's vanity and the stupidity of his conceit mistake the sublime divine love, when it expresses itself in a human form, for a sign of weakness and dependence and need.

And yet man already knows, at first obscurely, but more and more clearly as he draws nearer to perfection, that love alone can put an end to the suffering of the world; only the ineffable joy of love in its essence can sweep away from the universe the burning pain of separation. For only in the ecstasy of the supreme union will creation discover its purpose and its fulfilment.

That is why no effort is too arduous, no austerity too rigorous if it can illumine, purify, perfect and transform the physical substance so that it may no longer conceal the Divine when he takes on an outer form in Matter. For then this marvellous tenderness will be able to express itself freely in the world, the divine love which has the power of changing life into a paradise of sweet joy.

This, you will say, is the culmination, the crown of the effort, the final victory; but what must be done in order to achieve it? What is the path to be followed and what are the first steps on the way?

Since we have decided to reserve love in all its splendour for our personal relationship with the Divine, we shall replace it in our relations with others by a total, unvarying, constant and egoless kindness and goodwill that will not expect any reward or gratitude or even any recognition. However others may treat you, you will never allow yourself to be carried away by any resentment; and in your unmixed love for the Divine, you will leave him sole judge as to how he is to protect you and defend you against the misunderstanding and bad will of others.

You will await your joys and pleasures from the Divine alone. In him alone will you seek and find help and support. He will comfort you in all your sorrows, guide you on the path, lift you up if you stumble, and if there are moments of failure and exhaustion, he will take you up in his strong arms of love and enfold you in his soothing sweetness.

To avoid any misunderstanding, I must point out here that because of the exigencies of the language in which I am expressing myself, I am obliged to use the masculine gender whenever I mention the Divine. But in fact the reality of love I speak of is above and beyond all gender, masculine or feminine; and when it incarnates in a human body, it does so indifferently in the body of a man or a woman according to the needs of the work to be done.

In summary, austerity in feelings consists then of giving up all emotional attachment, of whatever nature, whether for a person, for the family, for the country or anything else, in order to concentrate on an exclusive attachment for the Divine Reality. This concentration will culminate in an integral identification and will be instrumental to the supramental realisation upon earth.

This leads us quite naturally to the four liberations which will be the concrete forms of this achievement. The liberation of the feelings will be at the same time the liberation from suffering, in a total realisation of the supramental oneness.

The mental liberation or liberation from ignorance will establish in the being the mind of light or gnostic consciousness, whose expression will have the creative power of the Word.

The vital liberation or liberation from desire gives the individual will the power to identify itself perfectly and consciously with the divine will and brings constant peace and serenity as well as the power which results from them.

Finally, crowning all the others, comes the physical liberation or liberation from the law of material cause and effect. By a total self-mastery, one is no longer a slave of Nature's laws which make men act according to subconscious or semiconscious impulses and maintain them in the rut of ordinary life. With this liberation one can decide in full knowledge the path to be taken, choose the action to be accomplished and free oneself from all blind determinism, so that nothing is allowed to intervene in the course of one's life but the highest will, the truest knowledge, the supramental consciousness.

Bulletin, August 1953

To the Students, Young and Old

THERE are, in the history of the earth, moments of transition when things that have existed for thousands of years must give way to those that are about to manifest. A special concentration of the world consciousness, one might almost say, an intensification of its effort, occurs at such times, varying according to the kind of progress to be made, the quality of the transformation to be realised. We are at precisely such a turning-point in the world's history. Just as Nature has already created upon earth a mental being, man, so too there is now a concentrated activity in this mentality to bring forth a supramental consciousness and individuality.

Certain beings who, I might say, are in the secret of the gods, are aware of the importance of this moment in the life of the world, and they have taken birth on earth to play their part in whatever way they can. A great luminous consciousness broods over the earth, creating a kind of stir in its atmosphere. All who are open receive a ripple from this eddy, a ray of this light and seek to give form to it, each according to his capacity.

We have here the unique privilege of being at the very centre of this radiating light, at the fount of this force of transformation.

Sri Aurobindo, incarnating the supramental consciousness in a human body, has not only revealed to us the nature of the path to follow and the way to follow it in order to reach the goal, but has also by his own personal realisation given us the example; he has provided us, so to say, with the proof that the thing can be done and that the time has come to do it.

Consequently, we are not here to repeat what others have done, but to prepare ourselves for the blossoming of a new consciousness and a new life. That is why I address myself to you, the students, that is, to all who wish to learn, to learn always more and always better, so that one day you may be capable of opening yourselves to the new force and of giving it the possibility of manifesting on the physical plane. For that is our programme and we must not forget it. To understand the true reason why you are here, you must remember that we want to become instruments that are as perfect as possible, instruments that express the divine will in the world. And if the instruments are to be perfect, they must be cultivated, educated, trained. They must not be left like fallow land or a formless piece of stone. A diamond reveals all its beauty only when it is artistically cut. It is the same for you. If you want your physical being to be a perfect instrument for the manifestation of the supramental consciousness, you must cultivate it, sharpen it, refine it, give it what it lacks, perfect what it already possesses. That is why you go to school, my children, whether you are big or small, for one can learn at any age — and so you must go to your classes.

Sometimes, if you are not in a very good mood, you say, "How boring it is going to be!" Yes, perhaps the teacher who is taking your class does not know how to amuse you. He may be a very good teacher, but at the same time he may not know how to entertain you, for it is not always easy. There are days when one does not feel like being entertaining. There are days, for him as for you, when one would like to be elsewhere than in school. But still, you go to your class. You go because you must, for if you obey all your fancies you will never have any control over yourselves; your fancies will control you. So you go to your class, but instead of going there and thinking, "How bored I am going to be; I am sure it is not going to be interesting", you should tell yourselves, "There is not a single minute in life, not one circumstance that is not an opportunity for progress. So what progress am I going to make today? The class I am going to now is on a subject that does not interest me. But perhaps that is because something is lacking in me; perhaps, in my brain, a certain number of cells are deficient and that is why I cannot find any interest in the subject. If so, I shall try, I shall listen carefully, concentrate hard and above all drive out of my mind this aimlessness, this superficial shallowness which makes me feel bored when there is something I cannot grasp. I am bored because I do not make an effort to understand, because I do not have this will for progress." When one does not progress, one feels bored, everyone, young or old; for we are here on earth to progress. How tedious life would be without progress! Life is monotonous. Most often it is not fun. It is far from being beautiful. But if you take it as a field for progress, then everything changes, everything becomes interesting and there is no longer any room for boredom. Next time your teacher seems boring to you, instead of wasting your time doing nothing, try to understand why he bores you. Then if you have a capacity of observation and if you make an effort to understand, you will soon see that a kind of miracle has occurred and that you are no longer feeling bored at all.

This remedy is good in almost every case. Sometimes, in certain circumstances, everything seems dull, boring, stupid; this means that you are as boring as the circumstances and it clearly shows that you are not in a state of progress. It is simply a passing wave of boredom, and nothing is more contrary to the purpose of existence. At such a moment you might make an effort and ask yourself, "This boredom shows that I have something to learn, some progress to make in myself, some inertia to conquer, some weakness to overcome." Boredom is a dullness of the consciousness; and if you seek the cure within yourself, you will see that it immediately dissolves. Most people, when they feel bored, instead of making an effort to rise one step higher in their consciousness, come down one step lower; they come down even lower than they were before and do stupid things, they make themselves vulgar in the hope of amusing themselves. That is why men intoxicate themselves, spoil their health, deaden their brains. If they had risen instead of falling, they would have made use of this opportunity to progress.

In fact, the same thing holds true in all circumstances, when life gives you a severe blow, one of those blows which men call a misfortune. The first thing they try to do is to forget, as if they did not forget only too soon! And in order to forget, they do all kinds of things. When something is very painful, they try to distract themselves — what they call distracting themselves, that is, doing stupid things, lowering their consciousness instead of raising it. If something extremely painful happens to you, never try to deaden yourself; you must not forget, you must not sink into unconsciousness. Go right to the heart of the pain and there you will find the light, the truth, the strength and the joy which are hidden behind this pain. But for that you must be firm and refuse to let yourself slide.

In this way every event in life, great or small, can be an opportunity for progress. Even the most insignificant details can lead to revelations if you know how to profit from them. Whenever you are engaged in something which does not demand the whole of your attention, use it as an opportunity to develop your faculty of observation and you will see that you will make interesting discoveries. To help you to understand what I mean, I shall give you two examples. They are two brief moments in life which are insignificant in themselves, but still leave a deep and lasting impression.

The first example takes place in Paris. You have to go out into this immense city; here all is noise, apparent confusion, bewildering activity. Suddenly you see a woman walking in front of you; she is like most other women, her dress has nothing striking about it, but her gait is remarkable, supple, rhythmic, elegant, harmonious. It catches your attention and you are full of wonder. Then, this body moving along so gracefully reminds you of all the splendours of ancient Greece and the unparalleled lesson in beauty which its culture gave to the whole world, and you live an unforgettable moment — all that just because of a woman who knows how to walk!

The second example is from the other end of the world,

from Japan. You have just arrived in this beautiful country for a long stay and very soon you find out that unless you have at least a minimum knowledge of the language, it will be very difficult for you to get along. So you begin to study Japanese and in order to become familiar with the language you do not miss a single opportunity to hear people talking, you listen to them carefully, you try to understand what they are saying; and then, beside you, in a tram where you have just taken your seat, there is a small child of four or five years with his mother. The child begins to talk in a clear and pure voice and listening to him you have the remarkable experience that he knows spontaneously what you have to learn with so much effort, and that as far as Japanese is concerned he could be your teacher in spite of his youth.

In this way life becomes full of wonder and gives you a lesson at each step. Looked at from this angle, it is truly worth living.

Bulletin, November 1953

Foresight

TO FORESEE destiny! How many have attempted it, how many systems have been elaborated, how many sciences of divination have been created and developed only to perish under the charge of charlatanism or superstition. And why is destiny always so unforeseeable? Since it has been proved that everything is ineluctably determined, how is it that one cannot succeed in knowing this determinism with any certainty?

Here again the solution is to be found in Yoga. And by yogic discipline one can not only foresee destiny but modify it and change it almost totally. First of all, Yoga teaches us that we are not a single being, a simple entity which necessarily has a single destiny that is simple and logical. Rather we have to acknowledge that the destiny of most men is complex, often to the point of incoherence. Is it not this very complexity which gives us the impression of unexpectedness, of indeterminacy and consequently of unpredictability?

To solve the problem one must know that, to begin with, all living creatures, and more especially human beings, are made up of a combination of several entities that come together, interpenetrate, sometimes organising themselves and completing each other, sometimes opposing and contradicting one another. Each one of these beings or states of being belongs to a world of its own and carries within it its own destiny, its own determinism. And it is the combination of all these determinisms, which is sometimes very heterogeneous, that results in the destiny of the individual. But as the organisation and relationship of all these entities can be altered by personal discipline and effort of will, as these various determinisms act on each other in different ways according to the concentration of the consciousness, their combination is nearly always variable and therefore unforeseeable.

For example, the physical or material destiny of a being comes from his paternal and maternal forebears, from the physical conditions and circumstances in which he is born; one should be able to foresee the events of his physical life, his state of health and approximately how long his body will last. But then there comes into play the formation of his vital being (the being of desires and passions, but also of impulsive energy and active will) which brings with it its own destiny. This destiny affects the physical destiny and can alter it completely and often even change it for the worse. For example, if a man born with a very good physical balance, who ought to live in very good health, is driven by his vital to all kinds of excesses, bad habits and even vices, he can in this way partly destroy his good physical destiny and lose the harmony of health and strength which would have been his but for this unfortunate interference. This is only one example. But the problem is much more complex, for, to the physical and vital destinies, there must be added the mental destiny, the psychic destiny, and many others besides.

In fact, the higher a being stands on the human scale, the more complex is his being, the more numerous are his destinies and the more unforeseeable his fate seems to be as a consequence. This is however only an appearance. The knowledge of these various states of being and their corresponding inner worlds gives at the same time the capacity to discern the various destinies, their interpenetration and their combined or dominant action. Higher destinies are quite obviously the closest to the central truth of the universe, and if they are allowed to intervene, their action is necessarily beneficent. The art of living would then consist in maintaining oneself in one's highest state of consciousness and thus allowing one's highest destiny to dominate the others in life and action. So one can say without any fear of making a mistake: be always at the summit of your consciousness and the best will always happen to you. But that is a maximum which is not easy to reach. If this ideal condition turns out to be unrealisable, the individual can at least, when he is confronted by a danger or a critical situation, call upon his highest destiny by aspiration, prayer and trustful surrender to the divine will. Then, in proportion to the sincerity of his call, this higher destiny intervenes favourably in the normal destiny of the being and changes the course of events insofar as they concern him personally. It is events of this kind that appear to the outer consciousness as miracles, as divine interventions.

Bulletin, February 1950

Transformation

WE WANT an integral transformation, the transformation of the body and all its activities. But there is an absolutely indispensable first step that must be accomplished before anything else can be undertaken: the transformation of the consciousness. The starting-point is of course the aspiration for this transformation and the will to realise it; without that nothing can be done. But if in addition to the aspiration there is an inner opening, a kind of receptivity, then one can enter into this transformed consciousness at a single stroke and maintain oneself there. This change of consciousness is abrupt, so to say; when it occurs, it occurs all of a sudden, although the preparation for it may have been long and slow. I am not speaking here of a mere change in mental outlook, but of a change in the consciousness itself. It is a complete and absolute change, a revolution in the basic poise; the movement is like turning a ball inside out. To the transformed consciousness everything appears not only new and different, but almost the reverse of what it seemed to the ordinary consciousness. In the ordinary consciousness you advance slowly, by successive experiences, from ignorance to a very distant and often doubtful knowledge. In the transformed consciousness your starting-point is knowledge and you proceed from knowledge to knowledge. However, this is only a beginning; for the outer consciousness, the various planes and parts of the outer active being are transformed only slowly and gradually as a result of the inner transformation.

There is a partial change of consciousness which makes you lose all interest in things that you once found desirable; but it is only a change of consciousness and not what we call the transformation. For the transformation is fundamental and absolute; it is not merely a change, but a reversal of consciousness: the being turns inside out, as it were, and takes a completely different position. In this reversed consciousness the being stands above life and things and deals with them from there; it is at the centre of everything and directs its action outwards from there. Whereas in the ordinary consciousness the being stands outside and below: from outside it strives to reach the centre; from below, crushed by the weight of its own ignorance and blindness, it struggles desperately to rise above them. The ordinary consciousness is ignorant of what things are in reality; it sees only their shell. But the true consciousness is at the centre, at the heart of reality and has the direct vision of the origin of all movements. Seated within and above, it knows the source, the cause and effect of all things and forces.

I repeat, this reversal is sudden. Something opens within you and all at once you find yourself in a new world. The change may not be final and definitive to begin with; it sometimes requires time to settle permanently and become your normal nature. But once the change has taken place, it is there, in principle, once and for all; and then what is needed is to express it gradually in the details of practical life. The first manifestation of the transformed consciousness always seems to be abrupt. You do not feel that you are changing slowly and gradually from one state into another; you feel that you are suddenly awakened or newly born. No effort of the mind can lead you to this state, for with the mind you cannot imagine what it is and no mental description can be adequate.

Such is the starting-point of all integral transformation.

Bulletin, August 1950

The Fear of Death and
the Four Methods of Conquering It

GENERALLY speaking, perhaps the greatest obstacle in the way of man's progress is fear, a fear that is many-sided, multiform, self-contradictory, illogical, unreasoning and often unreasonable. Of all fears the most subtle and the most tenacious is the fear of death. It is deeply rooted in the subconscient and it is not easy to dislodge. It is obviously made up of several interwoven elements: the spirit of conservatism and the concern for self-preservation so as to ensure the continuity of consciousness, the recoil before the unknown, the uneasiness caused by the unexpected and the unforeseeable, and perhaps, behind all that, hidden in the depths of the cells, the instinct that death is not inevitable and that, if certain conditions are fulfilled, it can be conquered; although, as a matter of fact, fear in itself is one of the greatest obstacles to that conquest. For one cannot conquer what one fears, and one who fears death has already been conquered by it.

How can one overcome this fear? Several methods can be used for this purpose. But first of all, a few fundamental notions are needed to help us in our endeavour. The first and most important point is to know that life is one and immortal. Only the forms are countless, fleeting and brittle. This knowledge must be securely and permanently established in the mind and one must identify one's consciousness as far as possible with the eternal life that is independent of every form, but which manifests in all forms. This gives the indispensable psychological basis with which to confront the problem, for the problem remains. Even if the inner being is enlightened enough to be above all fear, the fear still remains hidden in the cells of the body, obscure, spontaneous, beyond the reach of reason, usually almost unconscious. It is in these obscure depths that one must find it out, seize hold of it and cast upon it the light of knowledge and certitude.

Thus life does not die, but the form is dissolved, and it is this dissolution that the physical consciousness dreads. And yet the form is constantly changing and in essence there is nothing to prevent this change from being progressive. Only this progressive change could make death no longer inevitable, but it is very difficult to achieve and demands conditions that very few people are able to fulfil. Thus the method to be followed in order to overcome the fear of death will differ according to the nature of the case and the state of the consciousness. These methods can be classified into four principal kinds, although each one includes a large number of varieties; in fact, each individual must develop his own system.

The first method appeals to the reason. One can say that in the present state of the world, death is inevitable; a body that has taken birth will necessarily die one day or another, and in almost every case death comes when it must: one can neither hasten nor delay its hour. Someone who craves for it may have to wait very long to obtain it and someone who dreads it may suddenly be struck down in spite of all the precautions he has taken. The hour of death seems therefore to be inexorably fixed, except for a very few individuals who possess powers that the human race in general does not command. Reason teaches us that it is absurd to fear something that one cannot avoid. The only thing to do is to accept the idea of death and quietly do the best one can from day to day, from hour to hour, without worrying about what is going to happen. This process is very effective when it is used by intellectuals who are accustomed to act according to the laws of reason; but it would be less successful for emotional people who live in their feelings and let themselves be ruled by them. No doubt, these people should have recourse to the second method, the method of inner seeking. Beyond all the emotions, in the silent and tranquil depths of our being, there is a light shining constantly, the light of the psychic consciousness. Go in search of this light, concentrate on it; it is within you. With a persevering will you are sure to find it and as soon as you enter into it, you awake to the sense of immortality. You have always lived, you will always live; you become wholly independent of your body; your conscious existence does not depend on it; and this body is only one of the transient forms through which you have manifested. Death is no longer an extinction, it is only a transition. All fear instantly vanishes and you walk through life with the calm certitude of a free man.

The third method is for those who have faith in a God, their God, and who have given themselves to him. They belong to him integrally; all the events of their lives are an expression of the divine will and they accept them not merely with calm submission but with gratitude, for they are convinced that whatever happens to them is always for their own good. They have a mystic trust in their God and in their personal relationship with him. They have made an absolute surrender of their will to his and feel his unvarying love and protection, wholly independent of the accidents of life and death. They have the constant experience of lying at the feet of their Beloved in an absolute self-surrender or of being cradled in his arms and enjoying a perfect security. There is no longer any room in their consciousness for fear, anxiety or torment; all that has been replaced by a calm and delightful bliss.

But not everyone has the good fortune of being a mystic.

Finally there are those who are born warriors. They cannot accept life as it is and they feel pulsating within them their right to immortality, an integral and earthly immortality. They possess a kind of intuitive knowledge that death is nothing but a bad habit; they seem to be born with the resolution to conquer it. But this conquest entails a desperate combat against an army of fierce and subtle assailants, a combat that has to be fought constantly, almost at every minute. Only one who has an indomitable spirit should attempt it. The battle has many fronts; it is waged on several planes that intermingle and complement each other.

The first battle to be fought is already formidable: it is the mental battle against a collective suggestion that is massive, overwhelming, compelling, a suggestion based on thousands of years of experience, on a law of Nature that does not yet seem to have had any exception. It translates itself into this stubborn assertion: it has always been so, it cannot be any different; death is inevitable and it is madness to hope that it can be anything else. The concert is unanimous and till now even the most advanced scientist has hardly dared to sound a discordant note, a hope for the future. As for the religions, most of them have based their power of action on the fact of death and they assert that God wanted man to die since he created him mortal. Many of them make death a deliverance, a liberation, sometimes even a reward. Their injunction is: submit to the will of the Highest, accept without revolt the idea of death and you shall have peace and happiness. In spite of all this, the mind must remain unshakable in its conviction and sustain an unbending will. But for one who has resolved to conquer death, all these suggestions have no effect and cannot affect his certitude which is based on a profound revelation.

The second battle is the battle of the feelings, the fight against attachment to everything one has created, everything one has loved. By assiduous labour, sometimes at the cost of great efforts, you have built up a home, a career, a social, lit- erary, artistic, scientific or political work, you have formed an environment with yourself at the centre and you depend on it at least as much as it depends on you. You are surrounded by a group of people, relatives, friends, helpers, and when you think of your life, they occupy almost as great a place as yourself in your thought, so much so that if they were to be suddenly taken away from you, you would feel lost, as if a very important part of your being had disappeared.

It is not a matter of giving up all these things, since they make up, at least to a great extent, the aim and purpose of your existence. But you must give up all attachment to these things, so that you may feel capable of living without them, or rather so that you may be ready, if they leave you, to rebuild a new life for yourself, in new circumstances, and to do this indefinitely, for such is the consequence of immortality. This state may be defined in this way: to be able to organise and carry out everything with utmost care and attention and yet remain free from all desire and attachment, for if you wish to escape death, you must not be bound by anything that will perish.

After the feelings come the sensations. Here the fight is piti-less and the adversaries formidable. They can sense the slightest weakness and strike where you are defenceless. The victories you win are only fleeting and the same battles are repeated indefi-nitely. The enemy whom you thought you had defeated rises up again and again to strike you. You must have a strongly tempered character, an untiring endurance to be able to withstand every defeat, every rebuff, every denial, every discouragement and the immense weariness of finding yourself always in contradiction with daily experience and earthly events.

We come now to the most terrible battle of all, the physical battle which is fought in the body; for it goes on without respite or truce. It begins at birth and can end only with the defeat of one of the two combatants: the force of transformation and the force of disintegration. I say at birth, for in fact the two movements are in conflict from the very moment one comes into the world, although the conflict becomes conscious and deliberate only much later. For every indisposition, every illness, every malformation, even accidents, are the result of the action of the force of disintegration, just as growth, harmonious devel-opment, resistance to attack, recovery from illness, every return to the normal functioning, every progressive improvement, are due to the action of the force of transformation. Later on, with the development of the consciousness, when the fight becomes deliberate, it changes into a frantic race between the two oppo-site and rival movements, a race to see which one will reach its goal first, transformation or death. This means a ceaseless effort, a constant concentration to call down the regenerating force and to increase the receptivity of the cells to this force, to fight step by step, from point to point against the devastating action of the forces of destruction and decline, to tear out of its grasp everything that is capable of responding to the ascending urge, to enlighten, purify and stabilise. It is an obscure and obstinate struggle, most often without any apparent result or any external sign of the partial victories that have been won and are ever uncertain — for the work that has been done always seems to need to be redone; each step forward is most often made at the cost of a setback elsewhere and what has been done one day can be undone the next. Indeed, the victory can be sure and lasting only when it is total. And all that takes time, much time, and the years pass by inexorably, increasing the strength of the adverse forces.

All this time the consciousness stands like a sentinel in a trench: you must hold on, hold on at all costs, without a quiver of fear or a slackening of vigilance, keeping an unshakable faith in the mission to be accomplished and in the help from above which inspires and sustains you. For the victory will go to the most enduring.

There is yet another way to conquer the fear of death, but it is within the reach of so few that it is mentioned here only as a matter of information. It is to enter into the domain of death deliberately and consciously while one is still alive, and then to return from this region and re-enter the physical body, resuming the course of material existence with full knowledge. But for that one must be an initiate.

Bulletin, February 1954

REPLY TO QUESTIONS
*Raised by the last paragraph of "The Fear of Death
and the Four Methods of Conquering It"*

All these questions can be reduced to a single one: what is this
knowledge or discipline which gives the capacity to face death
without fear?

Until now, nothing has been said here about this method of
knowledge, which is also a method of action, because the study
and practice of this science cannot be put into the hands of one
and all. To talk about occult things is of little value; one must
gain experience of them. And this experimentation demands
not only special capacities that very few men possess but also
a psychological development that very few people can achieve.
In the modern world, this knowledge is hardly recognised as
scientific, and yet it is so, for it fulfils the conditions usually
required for a science. It is a system of knowledge organised
according to certain principles; it follows precise processes, and
by reproducing exactly the same conditions, one obtains the
same results. It is also a progressive knowledge; one can devote
oneself to studying it and develop it in a regular and logical way,
just like any other recognised science of today. But this study
deals with realities which do not belong to the most material
world. In order to take it up, one must possess special senses, for
the domain in which it moves lies beyond our ordinary senses.
These special senses are latent in men. Just as we have a physical
body, so too we have other more subtle bodies with their own
senses; these senses are much more refined and precise, much
more powerful than our physical senses. But of course, as education does not usually deal with this domain, these senses are
not normally developed and the worlds in which they function
elude our ordinary knowledge. And yet children spontaneously
live a great deal in this domain. They see all kinds of things
that are as real for them as physical objects. When they speak
about them, most often they are told that they are stupid or

88

liars, because they mention phenomena of which others have no experience, but which for them are as true, as tangible, as real as what everyone can see. The dreams that children so often have either in sleep or while they are awake are extremely vivid and have a great importance in their lives. Only with intensive mental development do these capacities fade away in children and even sometimes disappear in the end. Yet there are people who have the good fortune to be born with spontaneously developed inner senses and nothing can prevent these senses from remaining awake and even developing. If these people, before it is too late, meet someone who has the knowledge and can help them in the methodical education of the subtle senses, they will become very interesting instruments of research and discovery in the occult worlds.

In all ages, there have been isolated individuals or small groups on earth who were the guardians of a very ancient tradition, corroborated by their own experiences, and who practised this type of science. They sought out especially gifted individuals and gave them the necessary training. Usually these groups lived more or less in secret or in hiding, because ordinary men are very intolerant of this kind of capacity and activity, which is beyond them and frightens them. But there have been great periods in human history when recognised schools of initiation were established and were highly esteemed and respected, as in ancient Egypt, ancient Chaldea, ancient India, and even to some extent in Greece and Rome. Even in Europe, in the Middle Ages, there were institutions that taught occult science, but they had to conceal themselves very carefully, for they were pursued and persecuted by the official Christian religion. And if by chance it was discovered that a man or a woman practised this occult science, they were burnt alive at the stake as sorcerers. Now this knowledge is almost lost; very few people possess it. But with the knowledge, the intolerance has gone too. In our times, it is true, most educated people prefer to deny the existence of this science or to dub it imagination or even fraud in order to hide from themselves their own ignorance and the uneasiness they would feel if they had to recognise the reality of a power over which they have no control. And even among those who do not deny it, most of them are not very fond of these things; they are disturbed and troubled by them. However, they are obliged to admit that it is not a crime. And people who practise occultism are no longer burnt at the stake or thrown into prison. Only, since it is no longer necessary to hide, many people claim to have the knowledge, but very few of them really know anything. Some unscrupulous and ambitious people take advantage of the mystery which formerly used to shroud occult science and use it as a means of mystification and deceit. But it is not by these people that we should judge the knowledge which they wrongly claim to possess. In every domain of human activity, there are charlatans and imposters, but we should not allow their tricks to throw discredit upon a true science which they falsely claim to possess. That is why, during the great periods when this science was flourishing, when there were recognised schools where it could be practised, before anyone was allowed to undertake this study, he had to undergo for a very long time, sometimes for many years, a very strict twofold discipline of self-development and self-mastery. On one hand, the sincerity and disinterestedness of the aspirant's intentions, the purity of his motives, of his capacity for self-forgetfulness and self-abnegation, his sense of sacrifice and unselfishness were ascertained, as far as possible. In this way the loftiness and nobility of the candidate's aspiration were proved, while on the other hand he was subjected to a series of ordeals intended to show that his capacities were adequate and that he could without danger practise the science to which he wished to devote himself. These ordeals laid a special emphasis on the mastery of passions and desires, on the establishment of an unshakable calm, and above all on the absence of all fear, for in this endeavour an unflinching fearlessness is an essential condition of safety.

In one of its aspects, occult science is like a kind of chemistry applied to the play of forces and the structure of the worlds and individual forms of the inner dimensions. Just as in the chemistry of Matter the manipulation of certain substances is not without danger, so too in the occult worlds the wielding of certain forces and contact with them involve risks which only a great self-control and an unshakable calm can render innocuous.

In another of its aspects, occult science is, for the individual seeker, like the discovery and exploration of unknown countries whose laws and customs one often learns at one's own cost. Some of these realms are even rather terrifying for the beginner, who finds himself surrounded by new and unexpected perils. However, most of these dangers are more imaginary than real, and if one faces them without fear they lose the greater part of their reality.

In any case, at all times it has been recommended that one should take up these studies only under a very reliable guide who can point out the paths to follow, put you on guard against dangers, whether illusory or not, and give protection when needed.

Thus it is difficult to give more details here about the science itself, except to say that the indispensable basis of occult studies is a recognition of the concrete and objective reality of the many states of being and the inner worlds, which is a psychological application of the theory of four-dimensional or multi-dimensional space.

Occult science could thus be defined as a concrete objectification, in the world of forms, of what spiritual disciplines teach from the purely psychological point of view. The two should complement each other for the perfection of self-development and integral action. Occult knowledge without spiritual discipline is a dangerous instrument, for the one who uses it as for others, if it falls into impure hands. Spiritual knowledge without occult science lacks precision and certainty in its objective results; it is all-powerful only in the subjective world. The two, when combined in inner or outer action, are irresistible and are fit instruments for the manifestation of the supramental power.

Bulletin, April 1954

A Dream

THERE should be somewhere on earth a place which no nation could claim as its own, where all human beings of goodwill who have a sincere aspiration could live freely as citizens of the world and obey one single authority, that of the supreme truth; a place of peace, concord and harmony where all the fighting instincts of man would be used exclusively to conquer the causes of his sufferings and miseries, to surmount his weaknesses and ignorance, to triumph over his limitations and incapacities; a place where the needs of the spirit and the concern for progress would take precedence over the satisfaction of desires and passions, the search for pleasure and material enjoyment. In this place, children would be able to grow and develop integrally without losing contact with their souls; education would be given not for passing examinations or obtaining certificates and posts but to enrich existing faculties and bring forth new ones. In this place, titles and positions would be replaced by opportunities to serve and organise; the bodily needs of each one would be equally provided for, and intellectual, moral and spiritual superiority would be expressed in the general organisation not by an increase in the pleasures and powers of life but by increased duties and responsibilities. Beauty in all its artistic forms, painting, sculpture, music, literature, would be equally accessible to all; the ability to share in the joy it brings would be limited only by the capacities of each one and not by social or financial position. For in this ideal place money would no longer be the sovereign lord; individual worth would have a far greater importance than that of material wealth and social standing. There, work would not be a way to earn one's living but a way to express oneself and to develop one's capacities and possibilities while being of service to the community as a whole, which, for its own part, would provide for each individual's subsistence and sphere of action. In short, it would be a place where human relationships, which are normally based almost exclusively on competition and strife, would be replaced by relationships of emulation in doing well, of collaboration and real brotherhood.

The earth is certainly not ready to realise such an ideal, for mankind does not yet possess sufficient knowledge to understand and adopt it nor the conscious force that is indispensable in order to execute it; that is why I call it a dream.

And yet this dream is in the course of becoming a reality; that is what we are striving for in Sri Aurobindo's Ashram, on a very small scale, in proportion to our limited means. The realisation is certainly far from perfect, but it is progressive; little by little we are advancing towards our goal which we hope we may one day be able to present to the world as a practical and effective way to emerge from the present chaos, to be born into a new life that is more harmonious and true.

Bulletin, August 1954

Helping Humanity

F OR THOSE who practise the integral Yoga, the welfare of humanity can be only a consequence and a result, it cannot be the aim. And if all the efforts to improve human conditions have miserably failed in the end in spite of all the ardour and enthusiasm and self-consecration they have inspired at first, it is precisely because the transformation of the conditions of human life can only be achieved by another preliminary transformation, the transformation of the human consciousness or at least of a few exceptional individuals capable of laying the foundations for a more widespread transformation.

But we shall return to this subject later on; it will form our conclusion. First of all, I want to tell you about two striking examples chosen from among the adepts of true philanthropy.

Two outstanding beings at the two extremes of thought and action, two of the finest human souls expressing themselves in sensitive and compassionate hearts, received the same psychic shock when they came into contact with the misery of men. Both devoted their whole lives to finding the remedy for the suffering of their fellow-men, and both believed they had found it. But because their solutions, which may be described as contraries, were each in its own domain incomplete and partial, both of them failed to relieve the suffering of humanity.

One in the East, Prince Siddhartha, later known as the Buddha, and the other in the West, Monsieur Vincent, who came to be called Saint Vincent de Paul after his death, stood, so to say, at the two poles of human consciousness, and their methods of assistance were diametrically opposite. Yet both believed in salvation through the spirit, through the Absolute, unknowable to thought, which one called God and the other Nirvana.

Vincent de Paul had an ardent faith and preached to his flock that one must save one's soul. But on coming into contact with human misery, he soon discovered that in order to find one's soul one must have time to look for it. And when do those who labour from morning till night and often from night till morning to eke out a living really have time to think of their souls? So in the simplicity of his charitable heart he concluded that if the poor were at least assured of the barest necessities by those who possess more than they need, these unfortunate people would have enough leisure to lead a better life. He believed in the virtue and efficacy of social work, of active and material charity. He believed that misery could be cured by the multiplication of individual cures, by bringing relief to a greater number, to a very large number of individuals. But this is only a palliative, not a cure. The fullness of consecration, self-abnegation and courage with which he carried on his work has made of him one of the most beautiful and touching figures in human history. And yet his endeavour seems to have rather multiplied than diminished the number of the destitute and the helpless. Certainly the most positive result of his apostleship was to create an appreciable sense of charity in the mentality of a certain section of the well-to-do. And because of this, the work was truly more useful to those who were giving charity than to those who were the object of this charity.

At the other extreme of consciousness stands the Buddha with his pure and sublime compassion. For him the suffering arising out of life could only be abolished by the abolition of life; for life and the world are the outcome of the desire to be, the fruit of ignorance. Abolish desire, eliminate ignorance, and the world will disappear and with it all suffering and misery. In a great effort of spiritual aspiration and silent concentration he elaborated his discipline, one of the most uplifting and the most effective disciplines ever given to those who are eager for liberation.

Millions have believed in his doctrine, although the number of individuals capable of putting it into practice has been very small. But the condition of the earth has remained practically the same and there has been no appreciable diminution in the mass of human suffering.

However, men have canonised the first and deified the second in their attempt to express their gratitude and admiration. But very few have sincerely tried to put into practice the lesson and example that were given to them, although that is truly the only effective way of showing one's gratitude. And yet, even if that had been done, the conditions of human life would not have been perceptibly improved. For to help is not the same as to cure, nor is escaping the same as conquering. Indeed, to alleviate physical hardships, the solution proposed by Vincent de Paul can in no way be enough to cure humanity of its misery and suffering, for not all human sufferings come from physical destitution and can be cured by material means — far from it. Bodily well-being does not inevitably bring peace and joy; and poverty is not necessarily a cause of misery, as is shown by the voluntary poverty of the ascetics of all countries and all ages, who found in their destitution the source and condition of a perfect peace and happiness. Whereas on the contrary, the enjoyment of worldly possessions, of all that material wealth can provide in the way of comfort and pleasure and external satisfaction is powerless to prevent one who possesses these things from suffering pain and sorrow.

Neither can the other solution, escape, the solution of the Buddha, present a practical remedy to the problem. For even if we suppose that a very large number of individuals are capable of practising the discipline and achieving the final liberation, this can in no way abolish suffering from earth and cure others of it, all the others who are still incapable of following the path that leads to Nirvana.

Indeed, true happiness is the happiness one can feel in any circumstances whatsoever, because it comes from regions which cannot be affected by any external circumstances. But this happiness is accessible only to a very few individuals, and most of the human race is still subject to terrestrial conditions. So we can say on one hand that a change in the human consciousness is absolutely indispensable and, on the other, that without an integral transformation of the terrestrial atmosphere, the conditions of human life cannot be effectively changed. In either case, the remedy is the same: a new consciousness must manifest on earth and in man. Only the appearance of a new force and light and power accompanying the descent of the supramental consciousness into this world can raise man out of the anguish and pain and misery in which he is submerged. For only the supramental consciousness bringing down upon earth a higher poise and a purer and truer light can achieve the great miracle of transformation.

Nature is striving towards this new manifestation. But her ways are tortuous and her march is uncertain, full of halts and regressions, so much so that it is difficult to perceive her true plan. However, it is becoming more and more clear that she wants to bring forth a new species out of the human species, a supramental race that will be to man what man is to the animal. But the advent of this transformation, this creation of a new race which Nature would take centuries of groping attempts to bring about, can be effected by the intelligent will of man, not only in a much shorter time but also with much less waste and loss.

Here the integral Yoga has its rightful place and utility. For Yoga is meant to overcome, by the intensity of its concentration and effort, the delay that time imposes on all radical transformation, on all new creation.

The integral Yoga is not an escape from the physical world which leaves it irrevocably to its fate, nor is it an acceptance of material life as it is without any hope of decisive change, or of the world as the final expression of the Divine Will.

The integral Yoga aims at scaling all the degrees of consciousness from the ordinary mental consciousness to a supramental and divine consciousness, and when the ascent is completed, to return to the material world and infuse it with the supramental force and consciousness that have been won, so that this earth may be gradually transformed into a supramental and divine world.

The integral Yoga is especially intended for those who have realised in themselves all that man can realise and yet are not satisfied, for they demand from life what it cannot give. Those who yearn for the unknown and aspire for perfection, who ask themselves agonising questions and have not found any definitive answers to them, they are the ones who are ready for the integral Yoga.

For there is a series of fundamental questions which those who are concerned about the fate of mankind and are not satisfied with current formulas inevitably ask themselves. They can be formulated approximately as follows:

Why is one born if only to die?

Why does one live if only to suffer?

Why does one love if only to be separated?

Why does one think if only to err?

Why does one act if only to make mistakes?

The sole acceptable answer is that things are not what they ought to be and that these contradictions are not only not inevitable but they are rectifiable and will one day disappear. For the world is not irremediably what it is. The earth is in a period of transition that certainly seems long to the brief human consciousness, but which is infinitesimal for the eternal consciousness. And this period will come to an end with the appearance of the supramental consciousness. The contradictions will then be replaced by harmonies and the oppositions by syntheses.

This new creation, the appearance of a superhuman race, has already been the object of much speculation and controversy. It pleases man's imagination to draw more or less flattering portraits of what the superman will be like. But only like can know like, and it is only by becoming conscious of the divine nature in its essence that one will be able to have a conception of what the divine nature will be in the manifestation. Yet those who have realised this consciousness in themselves are usually more anxious to become the superman than to give a description of him.

However, it may be useful to say what the superman will certainly not be, so as to clear away certain misunderstandings. For example, I have read somewhere that the superhuman race would be fundamentally cruel and insensitive; since it is above suffering, it will attach no importance to the suffering of others and will take it as a sign of their imperfection and inferiority. No doubt, those who think in this way are judging the relations between superman and man from the manner in which man behaves towards his lesser brethren, the animals. But such behaviour, far from being a proof of superiority, is a sure sign of unconsciousness and stupidity. This is shown by the fact that as soon as man rises to a little higher level, he begins to feel compassion towards animals and seeks to improve their lot. Yet there is an element of truth in the conception of the unfeeling superman: it is this, that the higher race will not feel the kind of egoistic, weak and sentimental pity which men call charity. This pity, which does more harm than good, will be replaced by a strong and enlightened compassion whose only purpose will be to provide a true remedy to suffering, not to perpetuate it.

On the other hand, this conception describes fairly well what the reign of a race of vital beings upon earth would be like. They are immortal in their nature and much more powerful than man in their capacities, but they are also incurably anti-divine in their will, and their mission in the universe seems to be to delay the divine realisation until the instruments of this realisation, that is to say, men, become pure and strong and perfect enough to overcome all obstacles. It might not perhaps be useless to put the poor afflicted earth on guard against the possibility of such an evil domination.

Until the superman can come in person to show man what his true nature is, it might be wise for every human being of goodwill to become conscious of what he can conceive as the most beautiful, the most noble, the truest and purest, the most luminous and best, and to aspire that this conception may be realised in himself for the greatest good of the world and men.

Bulletin, November 1954

The Problem of Woman

I WISH to speak to you about the problem of woman, a problem as old as mankind in appearance, but infinitely older in origin. For if we want to find the law that governs and solves it, we must go back to the origin of the universe, even beyond the creation.

Some of the most ancient traditions, perhaps even the most ancient, ascribed the cause of the creation of the universe to the will of a Supreme Absolute to manifest by his own self-objectification; and the first act of this objectification was said to be the emanation of the creative Consciousness. Now, these ancient traditions usually speak of the Absolute in the masculine gender and of the Consciousness in the feminine, thus making this primordial gesture the origin of the differentiation between man and woman and at the same time giving a kind of priority to the masculine over the feminine. In fact, although they are one, identical and coexistent before the manifestation, the masculine took the original decision and emanated the feminine to carry it out, which amounts to saying that while there is no creation without the feminine, neither is there any feminine manifestation without the previous decision of the masculine.

We could certainly ask whether this explanation is not a little too human. But, to tell the truth, all the explanations that men can give must always necessarily be human, at least in their formulation. For, in their spiritual ascent towards the Unknowable and Unthinkable, certain exceptional individuals have been able to transcend human nature and identify themselves with the object of their seeking in a sublime and, in a way, unformulable experience. But as soon as they sought to share the benefit of their discovery with others, they had to formulate it, and in order to be comprehensible their formula had, of necessity, to be human and symbolic.

We could also ask whether these experiences and their disclosure are responsible for the sense of superiority which man nearly always feels towards woman, or whether, on the contrary, it is this widespread sense of superiority that is responsible for the form given to the experiences....

In any case, the indisputable fact remains: man feels superior and wants to dominate, woman feels oppressed and revolts, openly or secretly; and the eternal quarrel between the sexes is perpetuated from age to age, identical in essence, innumerable in its forms and hues.

Of course man throws the whole blame on woman, just as woman throws the entire blame on man. In truth the blame should be equally distributed between the two and neither can boast of being superior to the other. Moreover, until this notion of superiority and inferiority is eliminated, nothing and no one can put an end to the misunderstanding that divides the human species into two opposite camps, and the problem will not be solved.

So many things have been said and written on this problem, it has been approached from so many angles, that a whole volume would not be enough to expound all its aspects. Generally speaking, the theories are excellent, or, in any case, all have their own virtues; but the practice has proved less successful and I do not know whether from the point of view of realisation we have made any headway since the Stone Age. For in their mutual relationships, man and woman are at once rather despotic masters and somewhat pitiable slaves to each other.

Yes, slaves; for so long as one has desires, preferences and attachments, one is a slave of these things and of the people on whom one is dependent for their satisfaction.

Thus woman is enslaved to man because of the attraction she feels for the male and his strength, because of the desire for a home and the security it brings, and lastly because of the attachment to motherhood. Man too on his side is enslaved to woman, because of his possessiveness, his thirst for power and domination, because of his desire for sexual relations and because of his attachment to the little comforts and conveniences of married life.

That is why no law can liberate women unless they liberate themselves; likewise, men too, in spite of all their habits of domination, will cease to be slaves only when they have freed themselves from all inner enslavement.

And this state of veiled struggle, often unavowed but always present in the subconscient even in the best cases, seems unavoidable, unless human beings rise above their ordinary consciousness to identify themselves with the perfect consciousness and unite with the Supreme Reality. For as soon as one attains this higher consciousness one realises that the difference between man and woman reduces itself to a purely physical difference.

As a matter of fact, there may have been on earth in the beginning a pure masculine type and a pure feminine type, each with its own special and clearly differentiated characteristics; but in course of time, the inevitable mixture, heredity, all the sons that looked like their mothers, all the daughters that looked like their fathers, social progress, similar occupations — all this has made it impossible today to discover one of these pure types: all men are feminine in many respects and all women are masculine in many traits, especially in modern societies. But unfortunately, because of the physical appearance, the habit of quarrelling is perpetuated, perhaps even aggravated by a spirit of rivalry.

In their best moments, both man and woman can forget their difference of sex, but it reappears at the slightest provocation; the woman feels she is a woman, the man knows he is a man and the quarrel is revived indefinitely in one form or another, open or veiled, and perhaps all the more bitter the less it is admitted. And one wonders whether it will not be so until there are no longer any men or women, but living souls expressing their identical origin in sexless bodies.

For one dreams of a world in which all these oppositions will at last disappear and where a being will be able to live and prosper who will be the harmonious synthesis of all that is best in the human race, uniting conception and execution, vision and creation in one single consciousness and action.

Until such a happy and radical solution is reached, India remains, on this point as on many others, the land of violent and conflicting contrasts, which can nevertheless be resolved by a very wide and comprehensive synthesis.

Indeed, is it not in India that we find the most intense adoration, the most complete veneration of the Supreme Mother, creatrix of the universe, conqueror of all enemies, mother of all the gods and all the worlds, dispenser of all boons?

And is it not in India too that we find the most radical condemnation, the uttermost contempt for the feminine principle, Prakriti, Maya, corrupting illusion, cause of every fall and every misery, Nature that deceives and defiles and lures away from the Divine?

The whole life of India is shot through with this contradiction; she suffers from it in both mind and heart. Everywhere feminine deities are erected on her altars; the children of India await salvation and liberation from their Mother Durga. And yet is it not one of her children who said that the Avatar would never incarnate in the body of a woman, because no right-minded Hindu would recognise him! Fortunately, the Divine is not affected by such a narrow sectarian spirit or moved by such petty considerations. And when it pleases him to manifest in a terrestrial body, he cares very little whether or not he is recognised by men. Besides, in all his incarnations, he seems always to have preferred children and simple hearts to the learned.

In any case, until the manifestation of a new conception and consciousness compels Nature to create a new species which would no longer have to yield to the necessity of animal procreation and thus be under the obligation of dividing into two complementary sexes, the best that can be done for the progress of the present human race is to treat both sexes on a footing of perfect equality, to give them the same education and training and to teach them to find, through a constant contact with a Divine Reality that is above all sexual differentiation, the source of all possibilities and harmonies.

And it may be that India, the land of contrasts, will also be the land of new realisations, even as she was the cradle of their conception.

Bulletin, April 1955

Part Two

Messages, Letters and Conversations

I

Sri Aurobindo International
Centre of Education

During the 1920s and 1930s, the Mother's educational guidance was limited to instructing a few individuals in French and offering general counsel in other courses of study. At that time, children were not permitted, as a rule, to live in the Ashram. In the early 1940s, a number of families were admitted to the Ashram and instruction was initiated for the children. On 2 December 1943, the Mother formally opened a school for about twenty children. She herself was one of the teachers. The number of pupils gradually increased during the next seven years.

On 24 April 1951, the Mother presided over a convention where it was resolved to establish an "international university centre". On 6 January 1952, she inaugurated the Sri Aurobindo International University Centre. The name was changed in 1959 to the Sri Aurobindo International Centre of Education.

At present, the Centre of Education has about 150 full or part-time teachers and 500 students, ranging from nursery to advanced levels. The curriculum includes the humanities, languages, fine arts, sciences, engineering, technology and vocational training. Facilities include libraries, laboratories, workshops, and a theatre and studios for drama, dance, music, painting, etc.

The Centre of Education seeks to develop every aspect of the individual, rather than to concentrate exclusively on mental training. It employs what is called the "Free Progress System", which is, in the Mother's words, "a progress guided by the soul and not subject to habits, conventions or preconceived ideas."

The student is encouraged to learn by himself, choose his subjects of study, progress at his own pace and ultimately to take charge of his own development. The teacher is more an advisor and source of information than an instructor. In practice, the system is adapted to the temperament of teacher and student, and some still prefer the traditional methods of education, utilising prescribed courses of study with direct instruction by the teacher.

Sciences and mathematics are studied in French, other subjects in English. Each student is encouraged to learn his mother-tongue, and some study additional languages, both Indian and European.

The Centre of Education does not award degrees or diplomas, since it seeks to awaken in its students a joy of learning and an aspiration for progress that are independent of outer motives.

Messages

*The effective manifestation
of Ishwara and Ishwari
in union.*

SIGNIFICANCE OF THE SYMBOL OF THE
SRI AUROBINDO INTERNATIONAL CENTRE OF EDUCATION

*

One of the most recent forms under which Sri Aurobindo conceived of the development of his work was to establish at Pondicherry an International University Centre open to students from all over the world.

It is considered that the most fitting memorial to his name would be to found this University now so as to give concrete expression to the fact that his work continues with unabated vigour.

1951

*

INAUGURAL MESSAGE FOR THE
SRI AUROBINDO MEMORIAL CONVENTION

Sri Aurobindo is present in our midst, and with all the power of his creative genius he presides over the formation of the University Centre which for years he considered as one of the best means of preparing the future humanity to receive the supramental light that will transform the élite of today into a new race manifesting upon earth the new light and force and life.

In his name I open today this convention meeting here with the purpose of realising one of his most cherished ideals.

24 April 1951

*

STUDENTS' PRAYER[1]

Make of us the hero warriors we aspire to become. May we fight successfully the great battle of the future that is to be born, against the past that seeks to endure; so that the new things may manifest and we may be ready to receive them.

6 January 1952

*

I am perfectly sure, I am quite confident, there is not the slightest doubt in my mind, that this University, which is being established here, will be the greatest seat of knowledge upon earth.

It may take fifty years, it may take a hundred years, and you may doubt about my being there; I may be there or not, but these children of mine will be there to carry out my work.

And those who collaborate in this divine work today will have the joy and pride of having participated in such an exceptional achievement.

28 May 1953

*

[1] Given at the inauguration of the Sri Aurobindo International University Centre.

We are not here to do (only a little better) what the others do.

We are here to do what the others *cannot do* because they do not have the idea that it can be done.

We are here to open the way of the Future to children who belong to the Future.

Anything else is not worth the trouble and not worthy of Sri Aurobindo's help.

6 September 1961

*

MESSAGES FOR THE ANNUAL RE-OPENING OF CLASSES

Another year has passed, leaving behind it its burden of lessons, some hard, some even painful.

Now, a new year begins, bringing possibilities of progress and of realisation. But to take full advantage of these possibilities, we must understand the previous lessons.

It is more important to know that all accidents are the effect of unconsciousness. However, externally, one of their chief causes is a spirit of indiscipline, a kind of contempt for discipline.

It is left to us to prove, by a sustained and disciplined effort, that we are sincere in our aspiration for a life more conscious and more true.

16 December 1966

*

Let the Truth be your master and your guide.

We aspire for the Truth and its triumph in our being and our activities.

Let the aspiration for the Truth be the dynamism of our efforts.

O Truth! We want to be guided by Thee. May Thy reign come upon earth.

16 December 1967

*

113

When one lives in the truth, one is above all contradictions.

16 December 1968

*

You must have lived what you want to teach.

To speak of the new consciousness, let it penetrate you and reveal to you its secrets. For only then can you speak with any competence.

To rise into the new consciousness, the first condition is to have enough modesty of mind to be convinced that all that you think you know is nothing in comparison to what yet remains to be learnt.

All that you have learnt outwardly must be just a step allowing you to rise towards a higher knowledge.

16 December 1969

*

It is only in the calm that one can know and do. All that is done in agitation and violence is an aberration and a folly. The first sign of the divine presence in the being is peace.

We are here to do better than elsewhere and to prepare ourselves for a supramental future. This should never be forgotten. I appeal to the sincere goodwill of all so that our ideal may be realised.

16 December 1971

*

MESSAGES TO
THE MOTHER'S INTERNATIONAL SCHOOL, DELHI

A new Light has appeared upon earth. Let this new School opened today be guided by it.

Blessings.

23 April 1956

*

Teach us to be really sincere in our effort towards the Truth.

23 April 1957

*

Let yesterday's realisation be a springboard for tomorrow's achievement.

23 April 1958

*

Let us prepare ourselves for the new life that is manifesting upon earth.

23 April 1959

*

The best students are those who want to know, not those who want to show.

23 April 1966

*

The Mother's School. Sincerity.

23 April 1967

*

The measure of the sincerity is the measure of the success.

23 April 1968

*

The Future is full of promise. Prepare yourself for it.
Blessings.

23 April 1969

*

MESSAGE FOR THE INAUGURATION OF
SRI MIRAMBIKA HIGH SCHOOL, AHMEDABAD

Faith and Sincerity are the twin agents of success.
Blessings.

14 June 1966

115

Aims

Why are we here in the Sri Aurobindo Ashram?

There is an ascending evolution in nature which goes from the
stone to the plant, from the plant to the animal, from the animal
to man. Because man is, for the moment, the last rung at the
summit of the ascending evolution, he considers himself as the
final stage in this ascension and believes there can be nothing on
earth superior to him. In that he is mistaken. In his physical nature he is yet almost wholly an animal, a thinking and speaking
animal, but still an animal in his material habits and instincts.
Undoubtedly, nature cannot be satisfied with such an imperfect
result; she endeavours to bring out a being who will be to man
what man is to the animal, a being who will remain a man in its
external form, and yet whose consciousness will rise far above
the mental and its slavery to ignorance.

Sri Aurobindo came upon earth to teach this truth to men.
He told them that man is only a transitional being living in a
mental consciousness, but with the possibility of acquiring a new
consciousness, the Truth-consciousness, and capable of living a
life perfectly harmonious, good and beautiful, happy and fully
conscious. During the whole of his life upon earth, Sri Aurobindo gave all his time to establish in himself this consciousness
he called supramental, and to help those gathered around him
to realise it.

You have the immense privilege of having come quite young
to the Ashram, that is to say, still plastic and capable of being
moulded according to this new ideal and thus become the rep-
resentatives of the new race. Here, in the Ashram, you are in the
most favourable conditions with regard to the environment, the
influence, the teaching and the example, to awaken in you this
supramental consciousness and to grow according to its law.

116

Now, all depends on your will and your sincerity. If you have the will no more to belong to ordinary humanity, no more to be merely evolved animals; if your will is to become men of the new race realising Sri Aurobindo's supramental ideal, living a new and higher life upon a new earth, you will find here all the necessary help to achieve your purpose; you will profit fully by your stay in the Ashram and eventually become living examples for the world.

24 July 1951

*

What is the real purpose, the aim of our Education Centre? Is it to teach Sri Aurobindo's works? And these only? And all or some of these? Or is it to prepare students to read Sri Aurobindo's works and Mother's? Is it to prepare them for the Ashram life or also for other 'outside' occupation? There are so many opinions floating around, and even those older people whom we expect to know make so many different statements, that one does not know what to believe and act by. Then on what basis can we work without any real sure knowledge? I pray, Mother, give us your guidance.

It is not a question of preparing to read these works or other works. It is a question of pulling all those who are capable to do so, out of the general human routine of thought, feeling and action; it is to give all opportunities to those who are here to cast off from them the slavery to the human way of thinking and doing; it is to teach all those who want to listen that there is another and truer way of living, that Sri Aurobindo has taught us how to live and become a *true being* — and that the aim of the education here is to prepare the children and make them fit for *that life*.

For all the rest, the human ways of thinking and living, the world is vast and there is place out there for everybody.

It is not a number that we want — it is a selection; it is not brilliant students that we want, it is living souls.

*

It should be known and we should not hesitate to say openly that the purpose of our school is to discover and encourage those in whom the need for progress has become conscious enough to orient their life.

*

From the worldly standpoint, from the point of view of result achieved certainly things can be done better. But I am speaking of the effort put in, effort in the deepest sense of the word. Work is prayer done with the body. With that effort in your work the Divine is satisfied; the eye of the Consciousness that has viewed it is indeed pleased. Not that from the human standpoint one cannot do better. For us, however, this particular endeavour is one among many; it is only one movement in our Sadhana. We are engaged in many other things. To bring one particular item of work to something like perfection requires time and means and resources which are not at our disposal. But we do not seek perfection in one thing, our aim is an integral achievement.

An outside view may find many things to criticise and criticise much, but from the inner view what has been done has been done well. In an outside view, you come with all kinds of mental, intellectual formations and find there is nothing uncommon in what is done here. But thereby you miss what is behind: the Sadhana. A deeper consciousness would see the march towards a realisation that surpasses all. The outside view does not see the spiritual life; it judges by its own smallness.

There are people who write wanting to join our University and they ask what kind of diploma or degree we prepare for, the career we open out. To them I say: go elsewhere, please, if you want that; there are many other places, very much better than ours, even in India, in that respect. We do not have their equipment or magnificence. You will get there the kind of success you look for. We do not compete with them. We move in a different sphere, on a different level.

But this does not mean that I ask you to feel superior to others. The true consciousness is incapable of feeling superior. It is only the small consciousness that seeks to show its superiority. Even a child is superior to such a being: for it is spontaneous in its movements. Rise above all that. Do not be interested in anything other than your relation with the Divine, what you wish to do for Him. That is the only thing interesting.§[1]

30 November 1955

*

We are not here to lead an easy and comfortable life. We are here to find the Divine, to become divine, to manifest the Divine.

What happens to us is the Divine's affair, not ours.

---

[1] Whenever the symbol § appears, it indicates a spoken comment of the Mother which was noted from memory by a sadhak and approved by the Mother for publication.

The Divine knows better than we do what is good for the world's progress and for our own.

23 August 1967

*

To develop the spirit of service is part of the training here and it completes the other studies.

13 June 1971

*

You must not confuse a religious teaching with a spiritual one.

Religious teaching belongs to the past and halts progress.

Spiritual teaching is the teaching of the future — it illumines the consciousness and prepares it for the future realisation.

Spiritual teaching is above religions and strives towards a global Truth.

It teaches us to enter into direct relations with the Divine.

12 February 1972

*

The aim of education is not to prepare a man to succeed in life and society, but to increase his perfectibility to its utmost.

*

Do not aim at success. Our aim is perfection. Remember you are on the threshold of *a new world*, participating in its birth and instrumental in its creation. There is nothing more important than the transformation. There is no interest more worthwhile.

*

In a general way, education, culture, refinement of the senses are the means of curing movements of crude instinct and desire and passion. To obliterate them is not curing them; instead they should be cultivated, intellectualised, refined. That is the surest way of curing them. To give them their maximum growth in view of the progress and development of consciousness, so that one may attain to a sense of harmony and exactitude of perception is a part of culture and education for the human being.

Students

You who are young, are the hope of the country. Prepare yourselves to be worthy of this expectation.

Blessings.

*

Of one thing you can be sure — *your future is in your hands.* You will become the man you *want to be* and the higher your ideal and your aspiration, the higher will be your realisation, but you must keep a firm resolution and never forget your true aim in life.

2 April 1963

*

To be young is to live in the future.

To be young is to be always ready to give up what we are in order to become what we must be.

To be young is never to accept the irreparable.

28 March 1967

*

Only those years that are passed uselessly make you grow old.

A year spent uselessly is a year during which no progress has been accomplished, no growth in consciousness has been achieved, no further step has been taken towards perfection.

Consecrate your life to the realisation of something higher and broader than yourself and you will never feel the weight of the passing years.

21 February 1958

*

It is not the number of years you have lived that makes you grow old. You become old when you stop progressing.

As soon as you feel you have done what you had to do, as soon as you think you know what you ought to know, as soon as you want to sit and enjoy the results of your effort, with the feeling you have worked enough in life, then at once you become old and begin to decline.

When, on the contrary, you are convinced that what you know is nothing compared to all which remains to be known, when you feel that what you have done is just the starting-point of what remains to be done, when you see the future like an attractive sun shining with the innumerable possibilities yet to be achieved, then you are young, however many are the years you have passed upon earth, young and rich with all the realisations of tomorrow.

And if you do not want your body to fail you, avoid wasting your energies in useless agitation. Whatever you do, do it in a quiet and composed poise. In peace and silence is the greatest strength.

21 February 1968

*

For a happy and effective life, the essentials are sincerity, humility, perseverance and an insatiable thirst for progress. Above all, one must be convinced of a limitless possibility of progress. Progress is youth; at a hundred years of age one can be young.

14 January 1972

*

If the growth of consciousness were considered as the principal goal of life, many difficulties would find their solution.

The best way of not becoming old is to make progress the goal of our life.

18 January 1972

*

To know how to be reborn into a new life at every moment is the secret of eternal youth.

*

One must learn always not only intellectually but also psychologically, one must progress in regard to character, one must cultivate the qualities and correct the defects; everything should be made an occasion to cure ourselves of ignorance and incapacity; life becomes then tremendously interesting and worth the trouble of living it.

27 January 1972

*

The child does not worry about his growth, he simply grows.

*

There is a great power in the simple confidence of a child.

17 November 1954

*

When a child lives in normal conditions, it has a spontaneous confidence that all it needs will be given to it.

This confidence should persist, unshaken, throughout life; but the limited idea, ignorant and superficial, of its needs which a child has, must be replaced progressively by a wider, deeper and truer conception which culminates in the perfect conception of needs in accordance with the supreme wisdom, until we realise that the Divine alone knows what our true needs are and rely upon Him for everything.

19 November 1954

*

The most important condition is trust, a child-like trust, the candid feeling that knows that needed things will come, that there is no question about it. When the child has need of anything he is certain that it is coming. This kind of simple trust or reliance is the most important condition.

*

Why do children have fear? Because they are weak.

Physically they are weaker than the grown-ups around them and, generally, they are also weaker vitally and mentally.

Fear stems from a sense of inferiority.

However, there is a way to be free from it: it is to have faith in the Divine Grace and to rely on It to protect you in all circumstances.

The more you grow up, the more will you get over your fear if you let the contact with your soul develop in you — that is to say, with the truth of your being — and if you always strive that all you think, all you speak, all you do should be more and more the expression of this deep truth.

When you will consciously live in it, you will fear nothing any longer, in any domain of your being, because you will be united with the universal Truth which governs the world.

8 August 1964

*

Sweet Mother,
How can a child know without the help of his parents or teachers, what he is?

You must find it out yourself, but not with your mind.

It is only the psychic that can tell you.

*

125

Divine Mother,
When we are children, we are told what is good and
what is bad. That's why we repeat the same all our life,
"This is good! That is bad!". How should one know, in
fact, what is good and what is bad?

You can know the truth only when you are conscious of the
Divine.

*

How can I abstain from error?

By knowing what is true.

*

Lord, we pray to Thee:
May we understand better why we are here,
May we do better what we have to do here,
May we be what we ought to become here,
So that Thy will may be fulfilled harmoniously.

15 January 1962

*

Let our effort of every day and all time be to know You better
and to serve You better.

1 January 1973

*

Permit, Sweet Mother, that we be,
Now and for ever more,
Thy simple children, loving thee
More and still more.

*

I have a sweet little mother sitting close in my heart.
We are so happy together; never will we part.

*

Sweet Mother,
    Can you hear me whenever I call you?

My dear child,
    Be sure that I hear you each time you call and my help and force go straight to you.
    With my blessings.

1 June 1960

*

Bonne Fête.
    I embrace you with all my heart and give you my blessings for the fulfilment of your highest aspiration.
    With my love.

30 August 1963

*

Bonne Fête.
    With a whole bunch of roses (surrender) so that your aspiration may be fulfilled and you become my ideal child aware of your soul and the true goal of your life.
    With my blessings and my love.

30 August 1964

*

MESSAGES TO STUDENT BOARDING HOUSES

Prayer Given to the Children of Dortoir Boarding

We all want to be the true children of our Divine Mother. But for that, sweet Mother, give us patience and courage, obedience, goodwill, generosity and unselfishness, and all the necessary virtues.

127

This is our prayer and aspiration.

15 January 1947

*

To Big Boys' Boarding

May this day be for you the beginning of a new life in which you will strive to understand better and better why you are here and what is expected of you.

Live always in the aspiration of realising your most complete and most true perfection.

And for a beginning take care to be honest, sincere, straightforward, noble and pure in a rigorous discipline that you will impose on yourselves.

I shall always be present to help you and to guide you.

My blessings.

1963

*

To Dortoir Boarding Annex

Today, we who are united in a common remembrance aspire that this intensity may be the symbol of a true oneness based on a common effort towards ever truer and more perfect realisations.

15 January 1968

*

Young Man's Boarding

Be always faithful to your Ideal and sincere in your action.

*

STUDY

My dear child,

The true wisdom is to be ready to learn from whatever source the knowledge can come.

We can learn things from a flower, an animal, a child, if we are eager to know always more, because there is only One Teacher in the world — the Supreme Lord, and He manifests through everything.

With all my love.

9 March 1967

*

To do good work one must have good taste.

Taste can be educated by study and the help of those who have good taste.

To learn, it is necessary to feel first that one does not know.

15 December 1965

*

When you feel that you know nothing then you are ready to learn.[1]

December 1965

*

The whole question is to know whether the students go to school to increase their knowledge and to learn what is needed to know how to live well — or whether they go to school to *pretend* and to have good marks which they can boast about.

Before the Eternal Consciousness, one drop of sincerity has more value than an ocean of pretence and hypocrisy.

*

[1] Message for the inauguration of a course in technology.

You see, my child, the unfortunate thing is that you are too busy with yourself. At your age I was exclusively occupied with my studies — informing myself, learning, understanding, knowing. That was my interest, even my passion. My mother, who loved us — my brother and myself — very much, never allowed us to be bad-tempered or dissatisfied or lazy. If we went and complained to her about something or other and told her that we were not satisfied, she would laugh at us and scold us and say to us, "What is this foolishness? Don't be ridiculous, off you go and work, and don't take any notice of your good or bad moods! That is not interesting at all."

My mother was perfectly right and I have always been very grateful to her for having taught me discipline and the necessity of self-forgetfulness in concentration on what one is doing.

I have told you this because the anxiety you speak of comes from the fact that you are far too busy with yourself. It would be far better for you to attend more to what you are doing (painting or music), to develop your mind which is still very uncultivated and to learn the elements of knowledge which are indispensable to a man if he does not want to be ignorant and uncultured.

If you worked regularly eight to nine hours a day, you would be hungry and you would eat well and sleep peacefully, and you would have no time to wonder whether you are in a good or a bad mood.

I am telling you these things with all my affection, and I hope that you will understand them.

Your mother who loves you.

15 May 1934

*

O Mother, I want to act according to Your will and nothing else.

Then quickly leave the path you have taken — don't waste your time wandering about and talking to girls. Start working in earnest again, study, educate yourself, occupy your mind with interesting and useful things and not with futile chatter, and do not give false excuses for your vital attractions. If your wish is truly sincere you can be sure that you will have my force to help you conquer.

27 September 1934

*

On the days when I do not study I feel worse. But when I begin to study, happiness comes. I do not understand this process.

What do you mean by process? It is not a process; the disappearance of the bad feeling is the very natural result of concentrating the mind on study, which on the one hand provides it with a healthy activity, and on the other draws its attention away from this morbid contemplation of the little physical ego.

3 December 1934

*

Mother, is it good to go to D's house to read the poems he has written in Gujarati?

It all depends on the effect it has on you. If you come away feeling more peaceful and content, it is all right. If, on the contrary, it makes you feel melancholy and dissatisfied it would be better not to go there. You can simply observe and see how it affects you and decide accordingly.

13 December 1934

*

In the dream I saw You had written, "My dear child, why have you stopped studying?" You had written much more, and I would like You to write it here, if possible.

Yes, in fact last night I asked you why you had not studied, and I told you that to yield like that to the impulses of the

131

vital was certainly not the way to control it. You must create a discipline for yourself and impose it on yourself at all costs if you want to put an end to vital bad will and mental depressions. Without discipline one cannot do anything in life and all yoga is impossible.

*

For physical work it is not difficult, but for study it becomes difficult to follow the discipline when I feel bad. All the same, I have decided that on the days when I do not study, I will not eat my lunch.

What a funny idea you have! To punish your body for a fault the vital has committed! It is not fair.

22 December 1934

*

Just this morning there is a very big depression and so it is becoming impossible to study.

This will not do.

*

O Mother, what shall I do?

Force yourself to study and your depression will go away. Can you imagine a student in school coming and telling his teacher, "Sir, I did not do my homework today because I felt depressed"? The teacher would certainly punish him very severely.

16 January 1935

*

*I think there is one thing You do not like very much —
that I do not apply myself to my studies.*

Studies strengthen the mind and turn its concentration away
from the impulses and desires of the vital. Concentrating on
study is one of the most powerful ways of controlling the mind
and the vital; that is why it is so important to study.

28 January 1935

*

*My mind does not become peaceful, I think, because
I do not study hard. Studying does not give me much
pleasure.*

One does not study for the sake of pleasure — one studies to
learn and to develop one's brain.

1 February 1935

*

*It is quite impossible for me to study, because inertia
came.*

If you do not study the inertia will go on increasing.

4 March 1935

*

*I do not know how to spend my time, understanding
nothing.*

Study, that is the best way to understand.

*

133

You tell me to study, but I do not like studying.

You do not give enough time to study, that is why it does not interest you. Everything one does with care necessarily becomes interesting.

10 April 1935

*

Which path must I take then? What is the right and true way of making the effort?

Do what I explained to you yesterday — make your brain work by studying regularly and systematically; then during the hours when you are not studying, your brain, having worked enough, will be able to rest and it will be possible for you to concentrate in the depths of your heart and find there the psychic source; with it you will become conscious of both gratitude and true happiness.

22 May 1935

*

My studies are suffering because of constant depression.

I have told you that it is *by study* that you can overcome the depression.

27 July 1935

*

I would like to know whether as a general rule it is good for little children to play all the time.

For children there should be a time for work and study and a time for play.

16 November 1936

*

134

Do You think my mind is developing?

Regular study certainly cannot fail to develop it.

7 December 1936

*

I am turning more and more towards study and giving less attention to my sadhana. I do not know whether this is desirable.

It is all right; study can become part of the sadhana.

8 December 1936

*

If someone is teaching me, is it necessary for him to identify himself with me, to concentrate on me?

Without concentration one cannot achieve anything.

18 May 1937

*

Do You think that the tiredness comes from too much mental work?

No, it comes from *mental tamas.*

21 January 1941

*

(A teacher wrote that his students did not work very hard.)

Continue to be patient — it is some kind of mental tamas; one day they will wake up.

*

135

The students cannot learn their lessons, even when they have their books.

One must have a lot of patience with young children, and repeat the same thing to them several times, explaining it to them in various ways. It is only gradually that it enters their mind.

*

Intelligence and capacity of understanding are surely more important than regularity in work. Steadiness may be acquired later on.

*

Mother, how can one get rid of laziness?

Laziness comes from weakness, or from lack of interest. For curing the first — one must become strong.
For curing the second — one must do something interesting.

*

Sweet Mother,
You have told me that one must become strong to cure weakness. Mother, would you tell me how one can become strong?

First you must want it integrally and then you must do what is needed.

*

How to get rid of mental inertia?

The cure is not in trying to wake up the mind but in turning it, immobile and silent, upward towards the region of intuitive light, in a steady and quiet aspiration, and to wait in silence, for the light to come down and flood your brain which will, little by little, wake up to this influence and become capable of receiving and expressing the intuition.

Love and blessings.

26 September 1967

*

Sweet Mother,

We do not know what is the matter this year. We are unable to make any progress, either in our studies or at the Playground. Our minds are always restless and troubled. We have lost our concentration. We are wasting our time gossiping and thinking about bad things. We are not able to overcome our failings. Sweet Mother, we beg you to deliver us from this painful situation. We want to progress. We want to be your true children. Please show us the way.

Crying does not help at all.

You must have the will and make the necessary effort.

*

What is to be done to make the will stronger?

To educate it, to exercise it as one exercises the muscles by using them.

23 March 1934

*

Concentration and will can be developed as well as muscles; they grow by regular training and exercise.

*

Mother, how can one strengthen one's will-power?

By exercise.

*

137

It takes more than a few months to learn something. One must work assiduously to make progress.

12 November 1954

*

It is a passing impulse which pushes me so much to study.

So long as you need to form yourself, to build your brain, you will feel this strong urge to study; but when the brain is well formed, the taste for studies will gradually die away.

*

What is the utility of reason in our life?

Without reason, human life would be incoherent and unregulated; we would be like impulsive animals or unbalanced madmen.

6 April 1961

*

Mother, what are knowledge and intelligence? Have they important roles to play in our life?

Knowledge and intelligence are precisely the qualities of the higher mind in man which differentiate him from the animal.

Without knowledge and intelligence, one is not a man but an animal in human form.

Blessings.

30 December 1969

*

In Your Conversations *You have said that the intellect is like a mediator between the true knowledge and its realisation down here. Does it not follow that intellectual*

*culture is indispensable for rising above the mind to find
there the true knowledge?*

Intellectual culture is indispensable for preparing a good mental
instrument, large, supple and rich, but its action stops there.

In rising above the mind, it is more often a hindrance than
a help, for, in general, a refined and educated mind finds its
satisfaction in itself and rarely seeks to silence itself so as to be
surpassed.

*

All that you know, however fine it may be, is nothing in comparison with what you can know, if you are able to use other
methods.

*

The best way to understand is always to rise high enough in
the consciousness to be able to unite all contradictory ideas in a
harmonious synthesis.

And for the correct attitude, to know how to pass flexibly
from one position to another without ever losing sight even for
a moment of the one goal of self-consecration to the Divine and
identification with Him.

29 April 1964

*

The important point is to know that the mind is incapable of
understanding the One Supreme — that is why all that is said
and thought about it is a travesty and an approximation and is
necessarily full of irreconcilable contradictions.

That is also why it has always been taught that mental
silence is indispensable in order to have true knowledge.

31 August 1965

*

A very, very quiet head is indispensable for a clear understanding and vision and a right action.

*

Please help me to distinguish between the bubbling of ideas and an inner vision of necessities.

The mind must be quiet and silent before you can receive an inspiration from above.

*

The mind must remain quiet to let the Force flow through it for an integral manifestation.

*

How does one teach a student to think correctly?

Mental capacity is developed in silent meditation.

23 March 1966

*

I shall try to work with the help of intuition. Help me in my efforts.

Calm the vital.
Silence the mind.
Keep the brain silent and still like an even surface turned upwards and attentive.
And wait....

29 September 1967

*

It is not by mental activity that you can quiet your mind, it is from a higher or deeper level that you can receive the help you need. And both can be reached in silence only.

18 December 1971

*

How to stop discussions in the mind?

The first condition is to talk as little as possible.

The second is to think just of what you are doing at the moment and not of what you have to do or of what you have done before.

Never regret what is past or imagine what will be.

Check pessimism in your thoughts as much as you can and become a voluntary optimist.

*

Mother, a free, quiet, silent mind is such a nice thing; I would like to have more of that. I want to be free from the constant whirlwinds of thoughts and emotions within me, tossing me like a toy.

It comes progressively.

Do not strain.

Be calm and confident.

12 March 1973

*

Now, what the intellect has understood let the whole being realise. Mental knowledge must be replaced by the flaming power of progress.

*

READING

Sweet Mother, You have said that I do not think well. How can one develop one's thought?

You must read with great attention and concentration, not novels or dramas, but books that make you think. You must meditate on what you have read, reflect on a thought until you have

141

understood it. Talk little, remain quiet and concentrated and speak only when it is indispensable.

*

*I am reading a book on motor-cars, but I read it hastily;
I skip the descriptions of complicated mechanisms.*

If you don't want to learn a thing thoroughly, conscientiously and in all its details, it is better not to take it up at all. It is a great mistake to think that a little superficial and incomplete knowledge of things can be of any use whatsoever; it is good for nothing except making people conceited, for they imagine they know and in fact know nothing.

*

Read carefully whatever you read, and read it again a second time if you have not understood it properly.

*

Y has just written to me about the great number of novels that you read. I do not think that this kind of reading is good for you — and if it is to study style, as you told me, an attentive study of one good book by a good author, done with care, teaches much more than this hasty and superficial reading.

*I had two reasons for reading novels, to learn words and
style.*

In order to learn you must read very carefully and choose with care what you read.

*

Do You think I should stop reading Gujarati literature?

It all depends on the effect this literature has on your imagination. If it fills your head with undesirable ideas and your vital with desires, it is certainly better to stop reading this kind of book.

2 November 1934

*

Is there any harm in my reading novels in French?

Reading novels is never beneficial.

24 April 1937

*

When one reads dirty books, an obscene novel, does not
the vital enjoy through the mind?

In the mind also there are perversions. It is a very poor and unrefined vital which can take pleasure in such things!

*

In unformed minds what they read sinks in without any regard to its value and imprints itself as truth. It is advisable therefore to be careful about what one gives them to read and to see that only what is true and useful for their formation gets a place.

3 June 1939

*

I do not approve of these literature classes in which, ostensibly for the sake of knowledge, they flounder in the mud of a state of mind which is out of place here and which cannot in any way help to build up the consciousness of tomorrow. I repeated this to X yesterday in connection with your letter, and I explained briefly to him how I saw the transition period between what was and what will be.

143

If we could discover, either here or there, the expression of a sincere and luminous aspiration, it could be made into an opportunity for study and become an interesting development.

Examine the matter together and let me know what you decide.

In any case: no more "literature classes".§

18 July 1959

*

What is the value of literature?

It depends on what you want to be or do. If you want to be a littérateur, you must read a lot of literature. Then you will know what has been written and you won't repeat old things. You have to keep an alert mind and know how to say things in a striking manner.

But if you want real knowledge, you can't find it in literature. To me, literature as such is on a pretty low level — it is mostly a work of the creative vital, and the highest it reaches is up to the throat centre, the external expressive mind. This mind puts one in relation with outside things. And, in its activity, literature is all a game of fitting ideas to ideas and words to ideas and words to one another. It can develop a certain skill in the mind, some capacity for discussion, description, amusement and wit.

I haven't read much of English literature — I have gone through only a few hundred books. But I know French literature very well — I have read a whole library of it. And I can say that it has no great value in terms of Truth. Real knowledge comes from above the mind. What literature gives is the play of a lot of common or petty ideas. Only on a rare occasion does some ray from above come in. If you look into thousands and thousands of books, you will find just one small intuition here and there. The rest is nothing.

I can't say that the reading of literature equips one better to understand Sri Aurobindo. On the contrary, it can be a hindrance. For, the same words are used and the purpose for which they are used is so different from the purpose for which Sri Aurobindo has made use of them, the manner in which they have been put together to express things is so different from Sri Aurobindo's that these words tend to put one off from the light which Sri Aurobindo wants to convey to us through them. To get to Sri Aurobindo's light we must empty our minds of all that literature has said and done. We must go inward and stay in a receptive silence and turn it upward. Then alone we get something in the right way. At the worst, I have seen that the study of literature makes one silly and perverse enough to sit in judgment on Sri Aurobindo's English and find fault with his grammar!

But, of course, I am not discouraging the teaching of literature altogether. Many of our children are in a crude state and literature can help to give their minds some shape, some suppleness. They need a good deal of carving in many places. They have to be enlarged, made active and agile. Literature can serve as a sort of gymnastics and stir up and awaken the young intelligence.

I may add that the whole controversy that has gone on among the teachers recently on the value of literature is a storm in a tea-cup. It is really part of a problem which concerns the whole basis of education. All that has been going on in every department of our School is to me one single problem at bottom. When I look at the education everywhere, I feel like the Yogi who was told to sit and meditate in front of a wall. I find myself facing a wall. It is a greyish wall, with some streaks of blue running across it — these are the efforts of the teachers to do something worthwhile — but everything goes on superficially and behind it all is like this wall here on which I am striking my hand now. It is hard and impenetrable, it shuts out the true light. There is no door — one can't enter through it and pass into that light.

When the young students come to me and tell me about their work, each time I want to say something useful I find the same solid wall blocking me.

I have the intention of taking in hand the problem of education. I am preparing myself for it. It may take two years. But I have warned Pavitra that when I intervene and remould things, it may seem like a cyclone. People may feel that they can no longer stand on their legs! So many matters will get upset. There will be all-round bewilderment at first. But, as a result of the cyclone, the wall will break down and the true light burst in.

I thought it fair to say beforehand that there would be a radical change. This way the teachers can be prepared for it.

I do not wish to doubt or ignore the goodwill among the teachers of literature. And there are some old teachers who are sincerely doing their best. I appreciate all this. And in my decision on the alternatives set before me by the School I have taken everything into consideration. But the whole discussion, I repeat, has been a lot of unnecessary excitement — what could be called a quarrel among ants or, as one says in French, "Il n'y a pas de quoi fouetter un chat."[2]§

*

There is a subtle world where you can see all possible subjects for paintings, novels, plays of all kinds, even the cinema.

It is from there that most authors receive their inspiration.

*

(*A teacher suggested that books dealing with subjects like crime, violence and licentiousness should not be available to young people.*)

It is not so much a question of subject-matter but of vulgarity of mind and narrowness and selfish common-sense in the conception of life, expressed in a form devoid of art, greatness or refinement, which must be carefully removed from the

---

[2] "There is nothing to beat a cat about."

reading-matter of children both big and small. All that lowers and degrades the consciousness must be excluded.

1 November 1959

*

The selection [of books] has to be carefully done. Some of the books contain ideas which are sure to lower the consciousness of our children. Only such books are to be recommended as have some bearing on our Ideal or contain historic tales, adventures or explorations.

One is never too careful with books which have the most pernicious effect.

Blessings.

17 April 1967

*

I have been laying great stress on the stories of the Ramayana and Mahabharata and on the songs of Kabir, Mira, etc. Is it against your way to continue these old things?

Not at all — it is the attitude that is important. The past must be a spring-board towards the future, not a chain preventing from advancing. As I said, all depends on the attitude towards the past.

*

Some of the best poets and saints have written about the love of Radha and Krishna as if it were carnal love.

I always considered it as an incapacity of finding the true words and the correct language.

*

147

Stop reading all this nonsense. The occultism that can be found in books is vital and most dangerous.

*

If you want to know what is really happening in the world, you should not read newspapers of any sort, for they are full of lies.

To read a newspaper is to take part in the great collective falsehoods.

2 February 1970

*

Mother,

How can one know what is happening in other countries and even in our own, if we do not read papers? At least we get some idea from them, don't we? Or would it be better not to read them at all?

I did not say that you must not read papers. I said that you must not blindly believe in all that you read, you must know that truth is quite another thing.

Blessings.

4 February 1970

*

I want to see what will happen to me if I stop reading completely.

It is difficult to keep one's mind always fixed on the same thing, and if it is not given enough work to occupy it, it begins to become restless. So I think it is better to choose one's books carefully rather than stop reading altogether.

*

(*Written on a slip placed in a copy of* Prières et Méditations de la Mère)

Do not read this book unless you have the intention of putting
it into practice.

*

A library should be an intellectual sanctuary where one comes
to find light and progress.

*

CONDUCT

WHAT A CHILD SHOULD ALWAYS REMEMBER

The necessity of an absolute sincerity.
The certitude of Truth's final victory.
The possibility of constant progress with the will to achieve.

*

AN IDEAL CHILD

IS GOOD-TEMPERED

He does not become angry when things seem to go against him
or decisions are not in his favour.

IS GAME

Whatever he does he does it to the best of his capacity and keeps
on doing in the face of almost certain failure. He always thinks
straight and acts straight.

149

IS TRUTHFUL

He never fears to say the truth whatever may be the consequences.

IS PATIENT

He does not get disheartened if he has to wait a long time to see the results of his efforts.

IS ENDURING

He faces the inevitable difficulties and sufferings without grumbling.

IS PERSEVERING

He never slackens his effort however long it has to last.

IS POISED

He keeps equanimity in success as well as in failure.

IS COURAGEOUS

He always goes on fighting for the final victory though he may meet with many defeats.

IS CHEERFUL

He knows how to smile and keep a happy heart in all circumstances.

IS MODEST

He does not become conceited over his success, neither does he feel himself superior to his comrades.

IS GENEROUS

He appreciates the merits of others and is always ready to help another to succeed.

IS FAIR AND OBEDIENT

He observes the discipline and is always honest.

Bulletin, August 1950

*

The ideal child is intelligent. He understands everything he is told, he knows his lesson before he has learnt it and answers every question he is asked.

*

He has faith in the future which is rich with all the realisations that are to come, full of beauty and light.

Childhood is the symbol of the future and the Hope of all the victories to come.

*

THE IDEAL CHILD

... likes to study when he is at school,
... he likes to play when he is in the playground,
... he likes to eat at meal-time,
... he likes to sleep at bed-time,
... and always he is full of love for all those around him,
... full of confidence in the divine Grace,
... full of deep respect for the Divine.

*

The things to be taught to a child

1) The necessity of absolute sincerity.
2) The certitude of the final victory of Truth.
3) The possibility and the will to progress.
Good temper, fair-play, truthfulness.
Patience, endurance, perseverance.
Equanimity, courage, cheerfulness.

*

What should be the main concern in education for children aged eleven to thirteen?

The most important thing to teach them is the absolute necessity of being sincere.

All untruth, however slight, should be refused.

They should also be taught to progress constantly, for as soon as one stops making any progress, one falls back and that is the beginning of decay.

*

According to what I see and know, as a general rule, children over 14 should be allowed their independence and should be given advice only if and when they ask for it.

They should know that they are responsible for managing their own existence.

*

I am very pleased to hear the ideas and sentiments you have expressed just now and I give you my blessings. Only I wish that your ideas did not remain as mere ideals, but became realities. That should be your vow, to materialise the ideal in your life and character. I take this occasion, however, to tell you something that I have wanted to tell you for a long time. It is with regard to your studies. Naturally there are exceptions, but it is the exceptions that give force to the rule. For instance, you asked for leave today. I did not think you required more relaxation. Your life here is organised on a routine of almost constant relaxation. However, I agreed to your request. But the way in which you received the "good news" pained me. Some of you even seemed to consider it a victory. But I ask, victory of what, against what? The victory of inconscience against the joy of learning and knowing more and more? The victory of unruliness against order and rule? The victory of the ignorant and superficial will over the endeavour towards progress and self-conquest?

This is, you must know, the very ordinary movement of those who live in the ordinary condition of life and education. But as for you, if you wish to realise the great ideal that is our goal, you must not remain content with the ordinary and futile reactions of ordinary people who live in the blind and ignorant conditions of ordinary life.

It looks as if I were very conservative when I say so, still I must tell you that you should be very careful about outside influences and ordinary habits. You must not allow them to shape your feelings and ways of life. Whatever comes from an outside and foreign atmosphere should not be permitted to jump into you — all that is mediocre and ignorant. If you wish to belong to the family of the new man, do not imitate pitifully the children of today and yesterday. Be firm and strong and full of faith; fight in order to win, as you say, the great victory. I have trust in you and I count upon you.

Until now I have not published what I told you on the anniversary day of the University. I hoped you would profit by the lesson and mend your ways, but to my great regret I am compelled to note that the situation has not improved: it seems some students have chosen the time when they are in the class to bring out the worst they have in them, they behave like street urchins; they not only take no advantage of the teacher given

153

to them, but seem to take a mischievous pleasure in preventing others from benefiting by the lessons.

We want to show to the world what must be the new man of tomorrow. Is this the example that we will set before them?§

Published in April 1953

*

(An extract from the minutes of teachers' meeting:) The meeting felt concern over lack of discipline, good manners and right behaviour among some students.

I insist on the necessity of having good manners. I do not see anything grand in the manners of a gutter-snipe.

4 March 1960

*

True strength and protection come from the Divine Presence in the heart.

If you want to keep this Presence constantly in you, avoid carefully all vulgarity in speech, behaviour and acts.

Do not mistake liberty for license and freedom for bad manners: the thoughts must be pure and the aspiration ardent.

26 February 1965

*

Isn't this immense freedom we are given dangerous for those who are not yet awake, who are still unconscious? How can we account for this good fortune we have been given?

Danger and risk form part of all forward movement. Without them, nothing would ever move; besides, they are indispensable in forming the character of those who want to progress.

13 April 1966

*

Two things need to be done. Children must be taught:

    a) not to tell a lie, whatever the consequences;

    b) to control violence, rage, anger.

If these two things can be done, they can be led towards superhumanity.

There is an idea that if one breaks conventions, restrictions, one is free from the limitations of ordinary humanity. But this is wrong.

Those two things must be achieved to be able to be what may be called "superman": not to tell lies and to control oneself.

A complete devotion to the Divine is the last condition, but these are the first two things to be achieved.§

18 July 1971

*

Discipline is indispensable to be a man. Without discipline one is nothing but an animal. I give you two weeks to show that you really want to change and become disciplined. If you become disciplined and obedient I am willing to give you another chance. But do not try to be deceitful... At the least sign of insincerity, I shall have to send you away.

One begins to be a man only when one aspires to a higher and truer life and accepts a discipline of transformation.

For this one must begin by mastering one's lower nature and one's desires.

8 March 1972

*

To the students

To be noisy in class is an act of selfish stupidity.

If you don't intend to attend the class silently and attentively, it is better not to come.

*

155

It is forbidden to fight at school, to fight in class, to fight in the playground, to fight in the street, to fight at home (whether at your parents' house or in a boarding).

Always and everywhere children are forbidden to fight among themselves, for each time that one gives a blow to another, one gives it to one's own soul.

15 January 1963

*

I suggest the same remedy as the one I was using in my childhood when disagreeing with my young playmates. I was at that time, as you are, very sensitive and I felt hurt when abused by them, especially by those whom I had shown only sympathy and kindness. I used to tell myself: "Why be sorry and feel miserable? If they are right in what they say, I have only to be glad for the lesson and correct myself; if they are wrong, why should I worry about it — it is for them to be sorry for their mistake. In both cases the best and the most dignified thing I can do is to remain strong, quiet and unmoved."

This lesson which I was giving myself and trying to follow when I was eight years old, still holds good in all similar cases.

17 April 1932

*

Some words to the children.

1. Never make fun of anyone if you do not want others to make fun of you.

2. Always act in a respectable way if you want others to respect you.

3. Love everybody if you want everybody to love you.

*

As girls and boys are educated together here we have always insisted on the relations between them to be those of simple comradeship without any mixture of sex feeling and sensuality; and to avoid all temptation they are forbidden to go in one another's room and to meet anywhere privately. This has been made clear to everybody. And if these rules are strictly followed, nothing unpleasant can happen.

16 August 1960

*

Astrologers say that those who are born in November will be mad about sex.

Why do you believe in what the astrologers say? It is the belief that brings the trouble.

Sri Aurobindo says that a man becomes what he thinks he is.

Try this method of thinking that you are a good boy and will become sex-free.

Try this method for *five* years persistently and obstinately without admitting any doubt or discouragement, and after five years you will tell me the result.

Be very careful never to have a doubt about the result.

1965

You are attaching too much importance to this sex affair.

Do not think of it at all — be interested in *more interesting* activities, try to grow in knowledge and consciousness and kick away the sex thought and the sex impulse when it comes — then you can hope of becoming one of my soldiers.

1965

*

I have already asked of you all not to think that you are girls or boys, but *human beings* equally endeavouring to find, become and manifest the Divine.

16 February 1966

*

157

A complete lack of knowledge about sex can produce serious trouble. I want to give some information to children whom I know.

A simple notion of medical knowledge may be useful in taking away this silly old harmful feeling of shame which brings perversion.

*

Students say we are looking forward towards a sexless society, so why should we bother about genders in the language?

This is just a joke... or a twist of the mind and a clever way of refusing to understand what is meant by the advice.

*

Some good students give so much importance to money that it gives a shock. Can we discuss the matter?

Yes, try — it is very much needed. Money seems to have become the Supreme Lord these days — truth is receding in the background, as for Love, it is quite out of sight!

I mean Divine Love because what human beings call love is a very good friend of money.

*

When a child wants to impress you by telling you stories of the wealth of his family, you must not keep quiet. You must explain to him that worldly wealth does not count here, only the wealth that has been offered to the Divine has some value; that you do not become big by living in big houses, travelling by first-class and spending money lavishly. You can increase in stature only by being truthful, sincere, obedient and grateful.§

*

158

I have said, and I insist on this decision, that children below 15 should not go to bed later than 9 o'clock — those who do are being disobedient and this is regrettable.

*

Mother, why are the hours before midnight better for sleep than the later hours?

Because, symbolically, during the hours till midnight, the sun is setting, while from the very first hour after midnight the sun begins to rise.

Blessings.

22 August 1969

*

Mother, how is it better to go to bed early and to get up early?

When the sun sets, a kind of peace descends upon the earth and this peace is helpful for sleep.

When the sun rises, a vigorous energy descends upon the earth and this energy is helpful for work.

When you go to bed late and get up late, you contradict the forces of Nature and that is not very wise.

Blessings.

21 December 1969

*

Mother, what should be our attitude towards the captains and teachers here?

An obedient, docile and affectionate attitude. They are your elder brothers and sisters who take a lot of trouble for the sake of helping you.

Blessings.

1 February 1970

*

159

HOLIDAYS

There are two rumours in the Ashram concerning holidays.

The first is that You said that this time You are allowing us to go out during the holidays, but that You will not allow it next year. The second is that You do not want us to go out.

I would like to know which rumour is true, because many students have already received Your permission to go out during the holidays.

Neither one nor the other is true.

Neither one nor the other is false.

Both of them, and many others, are the more or less distorted expression of my synthesising and harmonising will.

To each one individually my reply, if he is sincere, is the expression of his need.

17 October 1964

*

Mother, why and how does one lose one's spiritual gain by going outside? One can make a conscious effort and your protection is always there, is it not?

To go to one's parents is to return to an influence generally stronger than any other: and few are the cases where parents help you in your spiritual progress, because they are generally more interested in a worldly realisation.

Parents who are chiefly interested in spiritual realisation do not usually ask their children to go back to visit them.

Blessings.

8 November 1969

*

The students who are not present for the beginning of the school-year on 16th December will not be allowed to attend classes for the entire school-year.

November 1969

*

Holidays

Shall we say *holy days*? There are two kinds of them: traditionally, the Lord for six days (or aeons) worked to create his world and the seventh He stopped for rest, concentration and contemplation. This can be called the day of God.

The second one is: the men, the creatures, during six days work for their personal interests and egoistic motives, and the seventh they stop working to take rest and have time to look inwardly or upwardly, in contemplation of the source and origin of their existence and consciousness, in order to take a dip in It and renew their energies.

It is scarcely necessary to mention the modern manner of understanding the word or the thing, that is to say, all the possible ways of wasting time in a futile attempt at amusing oneself.

*

For those in Auroville who want to be true servitors, is Sunday a holiday?

In the beginning the organisation of the week was conceived in this way: six days of work for the collectivity to which the individual belonged; the seventh day of the week was reserved for the inner quest for the Divine and the offering of one's being to the divine will. This is the only meaning and the only true reason for the so-called Sunday rest.

161

Needless to say, sincerity is the essential condition for realisation; all insincerity is a degradation.

25 October 1971

*

STUDIES ELSEWHERE

I intended to let you go for your studies to England without telling you anything about it, because each one must be free to follow the path he has chosen. But after what you have written I feel compelled to write to you.

No doubt from the exterior point of view, you will find in England all that you want for learning what human beings generally call knowledge, but from the point of view of Truth and Consciousness, you can find nowhere the atmosphere in which you are living here. Elsewhere you can meet with a religious or a philosophic spirit, but true spirituality, direct contact with the Divine, constant aspiration to realise Him in life, mind and action are in the world realised only by very rare and scattered individuals and not as a living fact behind any university teaching however advanced it may be.

Practically, as far as you are concerned, there will be a great risk of drifting away from the experience you have realised and then you cannot know what will happen to you.

That is all I wanted to say — now it is left to you to choose and decide.

22 October 1952

*

We see many people leaving the Ashram, either to seek a career or to study; they are those who have been here since childhood. There is a kind of uncertainty in our young people when they see others leave here and they say cautiously: "Who knows whether it will not be my

162

*turn one day!" I feel there is a force behind all that.
What is it?*

This uncertainty and these departures are caused by the lower
nature which resists the influence of the yogic power and tries to
slow down the divine action, not through ill-will, but in order
to be sure that nothing is forgotten or neglected in the haste
to reach the goal. Few are those ready for a total consecration.
Many children who have studied here need to come to grips with
life before they can be ready for the divine work and that is why
they leave in order to go through the test of the ordinary life.

11 November 1964

*

*(A student received an invitation to follow a course of
practical studies in Calcutta.)*

Those who *sincerely wish* to learn, have here all the possibilities
to do so. The only thing that one has outside, but does not have
here, is the moral constraint of an external discipline.

Here one is free and the only constraint is the one that one
sets *oneself*, when one is SINCERE.

Now it is for you to decide.

3 August 1966

*

*What answer should we give or what attitude should
we take with regard to some of the boys and girls who
say that they have come here only for studies, not for
sadhana and that therefore they can do what they like?*

They can be told that they should not be here. We are not im-
posing any Yoga on them; but they should lead a hygienic and
decent life, and if they do not want it, they should go elsewhere.

163

Mother, can they be sent away from here?

You can bring me one of them who is really very poor in studies. I shall not speak, but I'll try something. If it succeeds, then you can bring me the others.§

*

(*A teacher wrote that some students were not satisfied with the Centre of Education.*)

You can tell them that if they do not believe they can learn here something that is not taught elsewhere, they can very well change schools. We shall not miss them.

It is better to have a selected few than a commonplace mass.

*

(*A student had nearly completed his course of studies. Uncertain whether to attend college in the United States or to remain at the Ashram to live and work, he asked the Mother to make the decision.*)

I can tell you immediately that all depends on what you expect from life. If it is to live an ordinary or even successful life according to the usual old type, go to America and try your best.

If, on the contrary, you aspire at getting ready for the future and the new creation it prepares, remain here and prepare yourself for what is to come.

17 January 1969

*

We want here only those children who want to prepare themselves for a new life and who put progress before success in life. We do not want those who want to prepare themselves to earn a living and to achieve worldly success. They can go elsewhere.

The children — to understand what we expect of them, they should be over ten years of age — who are ready for a new

164

adventure, who want a new life, who are ready for a higher realisation, who want that the world should change and no longer be what it has been for so long, *these* are welcome.

We shall help them.§

January 1972

*

Au revoir, my child, never forget what your experience was, and do not let any external darkness penetrate and veil your consciousness.

I am with you.

*

Au revoir, my children, I wish that life may prove happy for you, and that one day you may be born into the Light and Truth.

Teachers

To love to learn is the most precious gift that one can make to a child, to learn always and everywhere.

*

It is an invaluable possession for every living being to have learnt to know himself and to master himself. To know oneself means to know the motives of one's actions and reactions, the why and the how of all that happens in oneself. To master oneself means to do what one has decided to do, to do nothing but that, not to listen to or follow impulses, desires or fancies.

To give a moral law to a child is evidently not an ideal thing; but it is very difficult to do without it. The child can be taught, as he grows up, the relativity of all moral and social laws so that he may find in himself a higher and truer law. But here one must proceed with circumspection and insist on the difficulty of discovering that true law. The majority of those who reject human laws and proclaim their liberty and their decision to "live their own life" do so only in obedience to the most ordinary vital movements which they disguise and try to justify, if not to their own eyes, at least to the eyes of others. They give a kick to morality, simply because it is a hindrance to the satisfaction of their instincts.

No one has a right to sit in judgment over moral and social laws, unless he has taken his seat above them; one cannot abandon them, unless one replaces them by something superior, which is not so easy.

In any case, the finest present one can give to a child would be to teach him to know himself and to master himself.

July 1930

*

Personality Traits of a Successful Teacher[1]

1. Complete self-control not only to the extent of not showing any anger, but remaining absolutely quiet and undisturbed under all circumstances.

2. In the matter of self-confidence, must also have a sense of the relativity of his importance.

Above all, must have the knowledge that the teacher himself must always progress if he wants his students to progress, must not remain satisfied either with what he is or with what he knows.

3. Must not have any sense of essential superiority over his students nor preference or attachment whatsoever for one or another.

4. Must know that all are equal spiritually and instead of mere tolerance must have a global comprehension or understanding.

5. "The business of both parent and teacher is to enable and to help the child to educate himself, to develop his own intellectual, moral, aesthetic and practical capacities and to grow freely as an organic being, not to be kneaded and pressured into form like an inert plastic material." (Sri Aurobindo, *The Human Cycle*)

Published in June 1954

*

Never forget that to be a good teacher one has to abolish in oneself all egoism.[2]

10 December 1959

*

[1] These comments were written by the Mother after she was shown a questionnaire on the subject which had been submitted to the Centre of Education by a training college for teachers.
[2] Message for the Annual Meeting of Teachers.

And to be worthy of teaching according to the supramental truth given us by Sri Aurobindo there should no longer be any ego.[3]

December 1960

*

All studies, or in any case the greater part of studies consists in learning about the past, in the hope that it will give you a better understanding of the present. But if you want to avoid the danger that the students may cling to the past and refuse to look to the future, you must take great care to explain to them that the purpose of everything that happened in the past was to prepare what is taking place now, and that everything that is taking place now is nothing but a preparation for the road towards the future, which is truly the most important thing for which we must prepare.

It is by cultivating intuition that one prepares to live for the future.

18 September 1967

*

Think rather of the future than of the past.[3]

15 December 1972

*

TEACHING

The school should be an opportunity for progress for the teacher as well as for the student. Each one should have the freedom to develop freely.

A method is never so well applied as when one has discovered it oneself. Otherwise it is as boring for the teacher as for the student.

*

[3] Message for the Annual Meeting of Teachers.

There is one thing that I must emphasise. Don't try to follow what is done in the universities outside. Don't try to pump into the students mere data and information. Don't give them so much work that they may not get time for anything else. You are not in a great hurry to catch a train. Let the students understand what they learn. Let them assimilate it. Finishing the course should not be your goal. You should make the programme in such a way that the students may get time to attend the subjects they want to learn. They should have sufficient time for their physical exercises. I don't want them to be very good students, yet pale, thin, anaemic. Perhaps you will say that in this way they will not have sufficient time for their studies, but that can be made up by expanding the course over a longer period. Instead of finishing a course in four years, you can take six years. Rather it would be better for them; they will be able to assimilate more of the atmosphere here and their progress will not be just in one direction at the cost of everything else. It will be an all-round progress in all directions.§

10 September 1953

*

To avoid giving too much work to the students of the Higher Course, but without lowering the general standard, the ones who feel that they have too much to do could be invited to give up a few courses. They would then be able to concentrate their time and energy on those they wish to keep. This would be better than lightening the courses, which would as a result lose their value for the other students. It is only natural that besides gifted students who have no difficulty in following, we should have less gifted students who cannot follow at the same pace. The latter could set aside certain subjects and take them up later by doing an extra year. Is this a good solution?

169

That depends. It cannot be made the general rule; for many of them it would not be much use. They have not reached a stage where they would be able to concentrate more on certain subjects if they had fewer subjects to study. The only result would be to encourage them to slacken — the very opposite of concentration! — and it would lead to a waste of time.

The solution does not lie there. What you should do is to teach the children to take interest in what they are doing — that is not the same thing as interesting the students! You must arouse in them the desire for knowledge, for progress. One can take an interest in anything — in sweeping a room, for example — if one does it with concentration, in order to gain an experience, to make a progress, to become more conscious. I often say this to the students who complain of having a bad teacher. Even if they don't like the teacher, even if he tells them useless things or if he is not up to the mark, they can always derive some benefit from their period of class, learn something of great interest and progress in consciousness.

Most teachers want to have *good students*: students who are studious and attentive, who understand and know many things, who can answer well — good students. This spoils everything. The students begin to consult books, to study, to learn. Then they rely only on books, on what others say or write, and they lose contact with the superconscient part which receives knowledge by intuition. This contact often exists in a small child but it is lost in the course of his education.

For the students to be able to progress in the right direction, it is obvious that the teachers should have understood this and changed their old way of seeing and teaching. Without that, my work is at a standstill.§

16 December 1959

*

(*There was disagreement among the teachers about whether the study of English literature should be made*

170

compulsory or optional for literature students of the Higher Course. When the matter was referred to the Mother for decision, she replied:)

To the teachers:

It is not so much the details of organisation as the *attitude* that must change.

It seems that unless the teachers themselves get above the usual intellectual level, it will be difficult for them to fulfil their duty and accomplish their task.

10 August 1960

*

It is not through uniformity that you obtain unity.

It is not through uniformity of programmes and methods that you will obtain the unity of education.

Unity is obtained through a constant reference, silent or expressed, as the case demands, to the central ideal, the central force or light, the purpose and the goal of our education.

The true, the supreme Unity expresses itself in diversity. It is mental logic that demands sameness. In practice, each one must find and apply his own method, that which he understands and feels. It is only in this way that education can be effective.

13 October 1960

*

Mother, would you please define in a few words what you mean essentially by "free progress"?

A progress guided by the soul and not subjected to habits, conventions or preconceived ideas.

*

(Several teachers submitted a report which expressed concern about the irregular study and class attendance of

171

the students. In the opinion of the teachers, only a few students were doing satisfactory work. As a solution, they suggested a more strict organisation of classes. The Mother commented:)

First for the teachers:

I am satisfied with the figures indicated in the report. In spite of what one might think, the proportion of very good students is satisfactory. If out of 150 students, there are 7 individuals of genuine value, it is very good.

Now for the organisation:

The classes as a whole may be reorganised so as to fulfil the needs of the majority, that is to say, of those who, in the absence of any outside pressure or imposed discipline, work badly and make no progress.

But it is essential that the present system of education in the new classes should be maintained, in order to allow outstanding individuals to show themselves and develop freely. That is our true aim. It should be known — we should not hesitate to proclaim it — that the whole purpose of our school is to discover and encourage those in whom the need for progress has become conscious enough to direct their lives. It ought to be a privilege to be admitted to these Free Progress classes.

At regular intervals (every month, for example) a selection should be made and those who cannot take advantage of this special education should be sent back into the normal stream.

The criticisms made in the report apply to the teachers as much as to the students. For students of high capacity, one teacher well versed in his subject is enough — even a good textbook, together with encyclopedias and dictionaries would be enough. But as one goes down the scale and the capacity of the student becomes lower, the teacher must have higher and higher capacities: discipline, self-control, consecration, psychological understanding, infectious enthusiasm, to awaken in the student the part which is asleep the will to know, the need for progress, self-control, etc.

Just as we organise the school in such a way as to be able to discover and help outstanding students, in the same way, the responsibility for classes should be given to outstanding teachers.

So I ask each teacher to consider his work in the school as the best and quickest way of doing his Yoga. Moreover, every difficulty and every difficult student should be an opportunity for him to find a divine solution to the problem.

5 August 1963

*

Mother, my students tell me that Z has told them that latent faculties could be developed by methodical exercises and that You had indicated these exercises to him. He added that we should experiment with this here in our Centre of Education.

On Z's insistence, I had indicated a first exercise — but the results were rather unfortunate, and I had to stop.

When the time has come, these things come naturally, spontaneously, so to say, and it is better not to make any arbitrary resolutions.

*

The education we are given here at present differs little from the education that is given elsewhere. This is precisely why we should try here to educate the latent and spiritual faculties of the student. But how can we do this in school?

This cannot be done by any external method. It depends almost entirely on the teacher's attitude and consciousness. If he does not have the vision and the inner knowledge himself, how can he transmit them to his students?

173

To tell the truth, we rely mainly on the all-surrounding atmosphere charged with spiritual force, which has an effect even if it is not perceived or felt.

20 April 1966

*

To the teachers and students:

The "Vers la Perfection" classes[4] are in accord with the teaching of Sri Aurobindo.

They lead towards the realisation of the Truth.

Those who do not understand that are turning their backs on the future.

September 1966

*

(*A teacher complained that trivial and useless things were being taught — that, for example, in the language classes students were asked to read foolish stories and given insignificant details about the life and customs of the people.*)

Your difficulty comes from the fact that you have still the old belief that in life some things are high and others low. It is not exact. It is not the things or the activities that are high or low, it is the consciousness of the doer which is true or false.

If you unite your consciousness with the Supreme Consciousness and manifest It, all you think, feel or do becomes luminous and true. It is not the subject of the teaching which is to be changed, it is the consciousness with which you teach that must be enlightened.

31 July 1967

*

---

[4] The name given by the Mother to a group of classes based on the Free Progress System.

*I don't even know whether I have a soul, but as a teacher
I am expected to help the students and "insist on the
growth of the soul" — some light please.*

The contradiction comes from the fact that you want to *"mentalise"* and this is impossible. It is an attitude, an inside attitude mostly but which governs the outside action as much as *possible*. It is something to be *lived* much more than to be taught.

*

*If we are to have a new system, what exactly will this
system be?*

It will be put into practice in the best way possible, according to the capacity of each teacher.

25 July 1967

*

*(A teacher suggested reorganising the curriculum of the
students of a certain age-group. He advised reducing
the number of scheduled classes; teachers would give
individual assistance to their students in the mornings
and meet them as a class only in the afternoons. His
letter ended:)*
    *Many teachers feel that the division between X's
classes and what is called the "Old System" is not desirable. With the reorganisation we suggest, the differences
between the two will be greatly diminished. Do you
think that this division should continue? Must we go
on waiting for it to disappear?*

It would be infinitely preferable that the division should disappear immediately. The effectiveness of what you suggest will become apparent only in practice. Therefore it seems to me that the best thing is to try, either for a full year if the results are slow to show themselves, or for three months if the results are clearly apparent by then.

With sincerity and flexibility you should be able to solve the problem.

6 November 1967

∗

A meeting of the teachers of the Higher Course was held on the 9th of November 1967 in order to discuss suggestions for possible changes in the Higher Course.

A proposal was made that the Higher Course may be reorganised as follows:[5]

1. The choice of a subject for study should be freely made by each student, and it should reflect a real and serious quest of the student;

2. Each topic thus selected would constitute a short or a long project, according to the nature of the topic;

3. In exploring each project, students would take the help of the teacher or teachers that they might choose from among the teachers competent to deal with it;

4. There will be no fixed oral classes; but teachers may by agreement with their students arrange for oral classes as and when necessary, preferably in the afternoons;

5. The exact quantum of work to be covered by each student for his selected course cannot be determined, but in order to have completed his Course, he should have shown regularity of sustained effort, development of capacities, understanding of his subjects and the power of answering relevant questions orally and in writing with sufficient clarity and precision. The quality of the work will be more important than the quantity of the

---

[5] Here are listed only five of the fourteen proposals upon which the Mother's reply is based.

work, although the latter too should not be meagre, but commensurate with our high standards.

The above proposal was met with a general approval with some exceptions and it was decided to refer it to the Mother to seek Her guidance with regard to it.

It is all right. Now the important point is to apply it with sincerity and thoroughness.

Blessings.

November 1967

*

X said that we should ask Mother if the project method, under which each student will be asked to select one or a few topics for intensive study and exploration, should not be accompanied by a more comprehensive study intended to impart to the students a wider understanding of the important branches of knowledge.

School is just a preparation to make the students capable of thinking, studying, progressing and becoming intelligent if they can — all that must be done during the *entire life* and not only in school.

November 1967

*

Up to the secondary level, it is understood that the children are too young to know about Yoga and to decide whether they want to take up Yoga or not. So the education to them is education and nothing else.

But for the Higher Course, I think, it must be made clear that only those who are here for Yoga can be admitted as members of this Course — then the education becomes Yoga.

If Mother gives Her directive on this point, it will make things very clear to many of us.

177

School is just
a preparation
to make the
students capable
of thinking,
studying, progressing
and becoming
intelligent if
they care —
all that must
be done during
the entire life
and not only in school.

It is not quite like that. In all the sections, Primary, Secondary and Higher Course, the children will follow yogic methods in their education and prepare and try to bring down new knowledge. So all the students can be said to be doing Yoga.

A distinction must be made, however, between those doing Yoga and the disciples. To be a disciple one has to surrender and the decision to do so must be full and spontaneous. Such decisions have to be taken individually — when the call comes — and it cannot be imposed or even suggested.§

Blessings.[6]

16 November 1967

*

(Concerning a choice of textbooks for a mathematics class)

The French book is the only one that seems possible to me — the others are forbidding and make you disinclined to work.

But I would not advise giving this French book to the students. They do not really need books. The teacher or teachers should use the book to prepare lessons that are adapted to the knowledge, the capacity and the needs of the students. That is to say that the teachers should learn what is in the book and transcribe it and explain it to the students, bit by bit, a little at a time, with plenty of explanations, comments and practical examples so as to make the subject accessible and attractive, that is, a living application instead of dead, dry theory.

3 December 1967

*

Sweet Mother,
It is about a week that we started our new experiment in the Higher Course. And already a few questions

---

[6] After reading this report of her comment, the Mother wrote "Blessings" and her signature.

179

have arisen with regard to which I seek Thy Light and Guidance.

The organisation and the programme of the teachers and students have been so framed as to give preeminent importance to the free growth and progress of the individual.

1. Some teachers have said that this is all right for the élite, but not for the common or average students.

But, Mother, should we not so endeavour as to gradually turn the average students into the élite? And, if so, would it not be good to so organise that the stress is laid on the training of the élite, and to allow now and then, for shorter or slightly longer periods, some concessions for the average students — but aiming always to eliminate ultimately such concessions?

We want here only children that can be considered as an élite. The organisation must be made for them. Those who cannot fit in, they have only to go after a one year trial.

2. Some teachers have said that there is a conflict between the needs of the individual's progress and those of the progress of the group of which the individual in question is a member. How to reconcile and resolve this conflict?

It has been contended that if the individual remains more or less with his group, he gets the advantage of sharing the group's experience, of group discussions and of a collective study.

All that is useless — if the individual can progress at his maximum the group will necessarily benefit by it. If the individual is submitted to the possibility and capacity of the group, he loses his chance of total progress.

22 December 1967

180

*

X asked me some time ago whether I would like to work in the Free Progress classes. At present I am teaching in classes where what is called the "old way" is used.

Mother, tell me whether I should remain where I am now or whether I should work in the Free Progress classes?

The old method of teaching is obviously outdated and will be gradually abandoned throughout the whole world.

But to tell the truth, each teacher, drawing his inspiration from modern ideas, should discover the method which he finds best and most suited to his nature. Only if he does not know what to do may he join his class to those of X.

*

Ordinary classes belong to the past and will gradually disappear. As for the choice between working alone or joining the "Vers la Perfection" classes, that depends on you. Because to teach and to conduct a class one must move away from theory and intellectual speculations to a very concrete application which has to be worked out in all its details.

Learning to teach while taking a class is certainly very good for the would-be teacher, but certainly less useful for the students.

To join "Vers la Perfection" is a kind of training which may be very useful for a beginner, who can easily learn the practical side of teaching there.

The choice is yours.

*

I have observed two contradictory kinds of ideas in myself: one kind in favour of individual work, another in favour of group work.

Isn't it possible to divide the class time into two parts (equal or unequal according to the need) and to try out both systems? This would give diversity to the teaching and provide a wider field for observation of the students and their capacities.

*

(Below is a summary of questions concerning two groups of classes for children of fourteen to eighteen. Though both groups were based on the Free Progress System, the programme of "En Avant" was more structured than that of "Vers la Perfection".)

1. There are some differences of opinion among the teachers about the direction that should be taken by our school. How to do away with these differences?

2. Should there be fixed classes and a fixed programme for children below fourteen or can they also be given the freedom to choose their line of work and to work at their own pace?

3. Is it or is it not our essential task to realise the conditions in which the inner soul of the child will find it possible to come forward and guide his development?

4. Should we envisage a fusion of the two groups "Vers la Perfection" and "En Avant"?

All of them are both right and wrong at the same time.

First of all it seems that after the age of seven, those who have a living soul are so awake that they are ready to find it, if they are helped. Below seven this is exceptional.

There are great differences among our children. First there are those who have a living soul. For them there is no question. We must help them to find it.

But there are others, the ones who are like little animals. If they are children from the outside, whose parents expect them to be taught — for them the "En Avant" classes are suitable. It is of no importance.

The problem is not whether to have classes and programmes or not. The problem is to choose the children.

Up to the age of seven, children should enjoy themselves. School should all be a game, and they learn as they play. As they play they develop a taste for learning, knowing and understanding life. The system is not very important. It is the attitude of the teacher that matters. The teacher should not be something that one endures under constraint. He should always be the friend whom you love because he helps and amuses you.

Above the age of seven, the new system can be applied to those who are ready, provided that there is a class where the others can work in the ordinary way. And for that class the teacher should be convinced that what he is doing is the right method. He should not feel that he is relegated to an inferior task.

When people do not agree, it is their pettiness, their narrowness which prevents them from doing so. They may be right in their idea... but they may not be doing the right thing, if they don't have the necessary opening.

These things should be above considerations of personality. It is a weakness to mix the two. There should be no considerations of personality.

There are some things that we cannot do. For example, if we wanted to bring up all the children by the new method, we would have to take them all on trial for one or two months, find out those who can follow, and send the others back to their families. It is impossible.

We must therefore produce the solution *within*. There are children who don't like the new method — responsibility worries them. I have received intimations of this in letters from children. We can only leave them as they are.

Everyone, without exception, *without exception*, should

know that he is not someone who knows and applies what he knows. Everyone is learning to be what he should be and to do what he should do.§

16 November 1968

*

I have read with satisfaction what you say about your work and I approve of it for *your own work*.

But you must understand that other teachers can conceive their own work differently and be equally right.

I am surprised at your criticism of Y, for it does not correspond to what I know of him and his attitude.

I take this opportunity to assure you that spiritual progress and the service of Truth are based on harmony and not on division and criticism.

25 November 1968

*

Progress lies in widening, not in restriction.

There must be a bringing together of all points of view by putting each one in its true place, not an insistence on some to the exclusion of others.

True progress lies in the widening of the spirit and the abolition of all limits.

22 October 1971

*

The teachers have to grow into the needed consciousness, emphasis should be on the actual experiences of work and there should be no difference in the child's mind between work and play — all should be a joy of interest. It is the teacher's job to create that interest.

If the interest is there, the right work will follow.

1 November 1971

*

R was absent today and I found, after the class, that he has Your permission to stop coming to my class and take woodwork instead.

He told me he liked much better to do manual work instead of studies. I thought he was right in his instinct and his choice was the best for his nature. So I gave him the permission required.

26 March 1946

*

You must be very careful to see that there is no overlapping in the lessons that you teach. Your subjects are related to each other. If two teachers begin to speak on the same point, naturally there will be some difference in their points of view. The same thing seen from different angles looks different. This will bring confusion in the young minds of the students and they will start comparison amongst the teachers, which is not very desirable. So each one should try to take up his own subject without wandering about in other subjects.§

10 September 1953

*

Regarding the questions that will be put to the students, I would ask the teachers to think with *ideas* instead of with *words*.

And, a little later, when it becomes normal for them to think with ideas, I shall ask of them a greater progress, which will be the decisive progress, that is, instead of thinking with ideas, to think with *experiences*. When one can do that, one really begins to understand.

*

You have asked the teachers "to think with ideas *instead of with* words*". You have also said that later on you*

185

*will ask them to think with experiences. Will you throw
some light on these three ways of thinking?*

Our house has a very high tower; at the very top of that tower
there is a bright and bare room, the last one before we emerge
into the open air, into the full light.

Sometimes, when we are at leisure to do so, we climb up
to this bright room, and there, if we remain very quiet, one or
more visitors call on us; some are tall, others small, some single,
others in groups; all are bright and graceful.

Usually, in our joy at their arrival and in our haste to receive
them well, we lose our tranquillity and come galloping down to
rush into the large hall which forms the base of the tower and
which is the store-room of words. Here, more or less excited,
we select, reject, assemble, combine, disarrange, rearrange all
the words within our reach in an attempt to transcribe this or
that visitor who has come to us. But most often the picture we
succeed in making of her is more like a caricature than a portrait.

And yet if we were wiser, we would remain up there at
the summit of the tower, quite still, in joyful contemplation.
Then, after a certain length of time, we would see the visitors
themselves descending slowly, gracefully, calmly, without losing
anything of their elegance or their beauty and, as they cross the
store-room of words, clothing themselves effortlessly, automatically, with the words needed to make them perceptible even in
the material house.

This is what I call thinking with ideas.

When this process is no longer mysterious to you, I shall
explain what is meant by thinking with experiences.

31 May 1960

*

When you think with words, you can express what you think
with those words only. To think with ideas is to be able to put
the same idea in many kinds of words. The words can also

be of different languages, if you happen to know more than one language. This is the first, the most elementary thing about thinking with ideas.

When you think with experience, you go much deeper and you can express the same experience with many kinds of ideas. Then thought can take this form or that form in any language and through all of them the essential realisation will remain unchanged.

*

To be convincing when you speak, think not in ideas but in experiences.

*

Did you attend the teachers' meeting with X? They were meeting because in addition to their studies they wanted to give everyone a special project. They wanted to help them to discover what the scientists are discovering at the moment — "What is water?", "Why does sugar dissolve in water?" — and all these things that are leading scientists to the conclusion that they know nothing.

So I asked them the question: "What is death?"

It is very important. For hundreds of years men have been asking this question. They don't know.

The students will say that they don't know what death is, but they will find out by investigation. To understand this, you must know that (*Mother makes a gesture indicating several directions*), and in the end the knowledge is much wider than if one follows a straight line.

In silence, one comes into contact with the Truth. Later, the idea descends, passes through the "library" of words and picks out the most suitable ones. At first it comes hazily. You must continue until it becomes precise. You can note it down, but you should remain quiet and continue. Then you get the exact word. The word that comes then is used in its essential sense, but not in its conventional sense.

It is not quite the reality; they are the words which come closest to the reality. The teachers should do that. It would be very useful instead of (*gesture of going round and round in the head*).

(*Silence*)

I don't know whether you have tried to get mental silence. You can spend your whole life on that and achieve almost nothing, whereas this is extremely interesting.

At first nothing happens. You must stay like that: not actively — be in an aspiration towards the Divine. There must be no movement in the mind; it is not even surrender, it is a movement of perfect... something between self-giving and self-abdication. And if the mind makes an offering of its way of being, one day the answer comes spontaneously. It falls like a light.

The calmer you are, the more confidence you have, the more attentive you are, the more clearly it comes. A time comes when one has only to do that (*gesture of opening*).... The student asks a question. You remain (*same gesture*)....

And above all, do not think actively: "I want to know... What should I say to him?" No!

Then you will always get the answer for the student. Perhaps not the answer to the question he has asked, but the answer he needs. And it will always be interesting....

Up there, one knows. When you come to believe that the mind is powerless, that it knows nothing, you fall silent. You are more and more convinced that up there, there is a consciousness that not only knows but has the power, perceives the smallest detail and consequently the student's need, and replies to that. When you are convinced of that, you give up your personal intervention and say: "Take my place."§

31 July 1967

*

I let these three boys "drug" themselves with their games, hoping that they would grow out of it more quickly.

And in fact that is what happened at the beginning of the third week: the three children are putting their names down for individual games and forgetting their noisy games.

May I continue to do this: to let this "out of school" abscess form and then burst, not caring about the time that goes by and that seems to be wasted from the academic point of view?

Certainly, it is the best thing to do.

Within the framework of the school, should we allow "out of school" games of a certain type, such as hide-and-seek, ball-games (cricket), building a house.... Seeing the children clamouring for them, it gave us the idea that our children may have been cut off from a certain kind of activity: being able sometimes to play in complete freedom in a big park! Is this a real need in the children?

Undoubtedly.

23 September 1960

*

It is very difficult to choose games which are useful and profitable for a child. It asks for much consideration and reflection, and all that one does unthinkingly can have unhappy consequences.

*

If the children, even very small, are taught to put things in order, classify objects by kind, etc. etc., they like it very much and learn very well. There is a wonderful opportunity to give them good lessons of arrangement and tidiness, *practical, effective lessons,* not theory.

Try and I am sure the children will help you to arrange things.

Love and blessings.

14 December 1963

*

It has been noticed that quite a good number of students do not have the correct posture while sitting and writing. When they write they do not keep the notebook in front of them. It is kept at an angle of 45 to 90 degrees.

Perhaps it would be good for the teachers themselves to learn first the proper posture while writing?

With my blessings.

*

Sri Aurobindo, in one of his letters, has written about the young people and their readiness for sadhana. I enclose a copy of this letter for you to see. I should like to know from you if the warning given by Sri Aurobindo in this letter against enthusiastically communicating to the young people the ideas and feelings about spiritual life should be kept in mind while speaking to our students in the class? Is there a danger of "lighting an imitative and unreal fire" in them as Sri Aurobindo says here?

Sri Aurobindo's letter: "It may be said generally that to be over-anxious to pull people, especially very young people, into the sadhana is not wise. The sadhak who comes to this yoga must have a real call, and even with the real call the way is often difficult enough. But when one pulls people in in a spirit of enthusiastic propagandism, the danger is of lighting an imitative and unreal fire, not the true Agni, or else a short-lived fire which cannot last and is submerged by the uprush of the vital waves. This is especially so with young people who are plastic and easily caught hold of by ideas and communicated feelings not their own — afterwards the vital rises with its unsatisfied demands and they are swung between two contrary forces or rapidly yield to the strong pull of the ordinary life and action and satisfaction of desire which is the natural bent of adolescence. Or else the unfit adhar tends to suffer under the stress of a call for which it was not ready, or at least not yet ready. When one has the real thing in oneself, one goes through and finally takes the full way of sadhana, but it is only a minority that does so. It is better to receive only people who come of themselves and of these only those in whom the call is genuinely their own and persistent."[7]

This quotation is splendid and very, very useful.

Certainly the warning given by Sri Aurobindo must be strictly kept in mind when speaking to the young people who are bound to change their mind easily.

In class you must remain very objective.

Blessings.   *2 June 1967*

*

I should like to know what exactly you mean by "objective" in the above answer. Do you mean that no personal feeling must be allowed to enter in thought and speech while explaining Sri Aurobindo's and your views concerning sadhana to the students?

Yes, that.

Do not speak of yourself or your own experience.

5 June 1967

*

---

[7] *Letters on Yoga*, Cent. Vol. 24, pp. 1615-16.

191

Teachers must not be absent on the days and at the times of their classes. If a person is obliged to have external activities during school-hours, he cannot be a teacher.

11 March 1970

*

DISCIPLINE

Constraint is not the best or most effective principle of education. The true education should open out and reveal what is already there in these developing beings. Just as flowers open out in the sun, children open out in joy. Obviously joy does not mean weakness, disorder and confusion, — but a luminous kindliness that encourages what is good and does not severely emphasise what is bad. Grace is always closer to the truth than justice.

1961

*

Mother, what should be done in a class when a child refuses to conform to a discipline? Should he be left to do as he likes?

Generally speaking, above the age of twelve all children need discipline.

*

Some teachers believe that you are opposed to discipline.

For them, discipline is an arbitrary rule that they impose on the little ones, without conforming to it themselves. I am opposed to that kind of discipline.

*

So discipline is a rule which the child should impose on himself. How can he be led to recognise the need for it? How can he be helped to follow it?

Example is the most powerful instructor. Never demand from a child an effort of discipline that you do not make yourself. Calm, equanimity, order, method, absence of useless words, ought to be constantly practised by the teacher if he wants to instil them into his pupils.

The teacher should always be punctual and come to the class a few minutes before it begins, always properly dressed. And above all, so that his students should never lie, he must never lie himself; so that his students should never lose their tempers, he should never lose his temper with them; and to have the right to say to them, "Rough play often ends in tears", he should never raise his hand against any of them.

These are elementary and preliminary things which ought to be practised in all schools without exception.§

*

One can be in psychological control of the children only when one is in control of one's own nature.

16 July 1963

*

First, know thoroughly what you have to teach. Try to get a good understanding of your students and their particular needs.

Be very calm and very patient, never get angry; one must be master of oneself in order to be a master of others.

7 December 1964

*

If you have to exercise authority, have authority over yourself first. If you cannot keep discipline amongst the children, don't beat or shout or get agitated — that is not permissible. Bring

193

down calm and peace from above and under their pressure things will improve.§

*

And what should we do for the little children, Mother?

Oh, little children are wonderful! I see a lot of little children. People have got into the habit of bringing them to me. And the consciousness that is already there in those who are less than two years old, is magnificent. They are conscious. They don't have the means to express themselves, the words are not there, but they are very conscious. And so to scold a child, that seems...!

The other day, the day before yesterday, one was brought to me, and he was grumbling. And of course his mother... So I gave him a rose: "See! It's for you!" Of course, he didn't understand the words, but he turned the rose this way and that, and he calmed down. Little children are wonderful. It is quite enough to surround them with things and to let them be. Never interfere unless it is absolutely necessary. And let them be. And never scold them.§

31 July 1967

*

You are a good teacher but it is your way of dealing with the children that is objectionable.

The children must be educated in an atmosphere of love and gentleness.

No violence, never.

No scolding, never.

Always a gentle kindness and the teacher must be the *living example* of the virtues the child must acquire.

The children must be *happy* to go to school, *happy* to learn, and the teacher must be their best friend who gives them the example of the qualities they must acquire.

And all that depends exclusively on the teacher. What he does and how he behaves.

*

The students talk so much in the class that I have to scold them often.

It is not with severity but with *self-mastery* that children are controlled.

*

I must tell you that if a teacher wants to be respected, he must be *respectable*. X is not the only one to say that you use violence to make yourself obeyed; nothing is less respectable. You must first control yourself and never use brute force to impose your will.

*

I have always thought that something in the teacher's character was responsible for the indiscipline of his students.

I hope you will give me precise instructions which will help me to keep order in my classes.

The most important is to master yourself and never lose your temper. If you don't have control over yourself, how can you expect to control others, above all, children, who feel it immediately when someone is not master of himself?

*

195

To the teachers of all the infant classes

One rule which must be rigorously applied:

It is *absolutely forbidden* to hit the children — all blows are forbidden, even the slightest little slap or the so-called friendly punch. To give a blow to a child because he does not obey or does not understand or because he is disturbing the others indicates a lack of self-control, and it is harmful for both teacher and student.

Disciplinary measures may be taken if necessary, but in complete calm and not because of a personal reaction.

*

What can I do to achieve a silent atmosphere in the classroom?

Be completely silent yourself.

Bring a piece of cardboard with you, about one metre long, on which you write in very big letters, black on white,

SILENCE

(much bigger than that) and as soon as the students start talking, put the cardboard in front of you.

Blessings.

*

Never tell a child something it has to forget in order to truly know. Never do something in front of a child that it must not do when it is grown up.

*

Never forget that a little child under six knows much more than he can express.

*

196

HOMEWORK

All the students complain that their teachers think only of their own classes and want to give them homework, each one thinking that he is giving very little and not understanding that all these little bits together make up a considerable amount.

I cannot say they are wrong.

All the teachers who give lessons to a certain group of students should agree among themselves to allot the work so that the students are not overworked and can enjoy a rest and a relaxation that are *indispensable.*

This collective preparation must be ready before I can give any useful advice.

As for the subjects, it is indispensable to choose those which coincide with their *personal* experience so as to encourage introspection, observation and analysis of personal impressions.

December 1959

*

(A teacher of mathematics asked whether he should strictly adhere to the policy at that time, that children below the age of ten should not be given homework; a few of his students had asked for problems to do at home. The Mother wrote:)

This homework is a very thorny matter. Let those who want to do homework write to me directly about it.

1960

*

197

In our arithmetic class we would like to be given some homework to do.

If only you could write French a little more correctly!

You may do some homework if you really want to — but it is better to do a little well than to do much without care or concentration.

If you want to be able to do anything at all, you must learn to discipline yourselves and to concentrate.

28 June 1960

*

I do not agree that children should work at home. At home, they must be free to do what they wish.

The solution to the problem can be found in the silence room.[8]

14 September 1967

*

This has come up after receiving many letters from both parents and children complaining that because of homework, the children go to bed late and are very tired as they do not sleep enough.

I know that all these complaints are exaggerated, but they are also the indication that some progress must be made in the routine.

This project has to be worked out in its details with plasticity and suppleness.

I am not for treating all the children in the same way; it makes a kind of uniform level, advantageous for those that are backward but detrimental for those who can rise above the common height.

---

[8] A room where students sit or study in silence.

Those who want to work and learn must be encouraged. But the energy of those who dislike studies must be turned to another outlet.

Things are to be arranged and organised. The details of execution will be fixed later on.

Blessings.

26 September 1967

*

TESTS

Sometime I would like to know, Mother, Your intentions with regard to regrouping these classes in the new year, whether with an examination or without.

I consider an examination as quite necessary. In any case there will be one in French.

My love and blessings.

29 October 1946

*

It is not by conventional examinations that students can be selected for a class. It is only by developing in oneself the true psychological sense.

Select children who want to learn, not those who want to push themselves forward.

29 October 1965

*

(Concerning cheating in tests)
What should I do? Must we do what is done outside — put three teachers in a room to invigilate? The teachers do not like doing things in this way here in the Ashram.

199

Or should we abolish tests? I find this proposal doubtful, since the same thing happens with homework and essays.

In any case the problem exists, and in order to find the real solution we should understand why the children behave like this.

Please tell me the cause of this misbehaviour and the solution to this problem.

It is very simple. It is because most of the children study because they are compelled to do so by their families, by custom and prevalent ideas, and not because they want to *learn and know*. As long as their motive for studying is not rectified, as long as they do not work because they *want to know*, they will find all kinds of tricks to make their work easier and to obtain results with a minimum of effort.

June 1967

*

(The Mother indicated that repetition of the statement below, a hundred or a thousand times each day, until it becomes a living vibration, would help the student to instil in himself the right will and motive for studying.)

To be repeated each day by all the students:

It is not for our family, it is not to secure a good position, it is not to earn money, it is not to obtain a diploma, that we study.

We study to learn, to know, to understand the world, and for the sake of the joy that it gives us.

June 1967

*

The only solution is to annul this test and all that are to come. Keep all the papers with you in a closed bundle — as something that has not been — and continue quietly your classes.

At the end of the year you will give notes to the students, not based on written test-papers, but on their behaviour, their concentration, their regularity, their promptness to understand and their openness of intelligence.

For yourself you will take it as a discipline to rely more on inner contact, keen observation, and impartial outlook.

For the students it will be the necessity of understanding truly what they learn and not to repeat as a parrot what they have not fully understood.

And thus a true progress will have been made in the teaching.

With blessings.

21 July 1967

*

I find tests an obsolete and ineffective way of knowing if the students are intelligent, willing and attentive.

A silly, mechanical mind can very well answer a test if the memory is good and these are certainly not the qualities required for a man of the future.

It is by tolerance for the old habits that I consented that those who want tests can have them. But I hope that in future this concession will not be necessary.

To know if a student is good needs, if the tests are abolished, a little more inner contact and psychological knowledge for the teacher. But our teachers are expected to do Yoga, so this ought not to be difficult for them.

22 July 1967

*

Naturally the teacher has to test the student to know if he or she has learnt something and has made a progress. But this test must be individual and adapted to each student, not the same mechanical test for all of them. It must be a spontaneous and unexpected test leaving no room for pretence and insincerity. Naturally also, this is much more difficult for the teacher but so much more living and interesting also.

I enjoyed your remarks about your students. They prove that you have an individual relation with them — and that is essential for good teaching.

Those who are insincere do not truly want to learn but to get good marks or compliments from the teacher — they are not interesting.

25 July 1967

*

What should be the criteria for giving prizes in our "Free Progress Classes"?

The prizes certainly should not be based on competitive grades.

A prize of appreciation, of equivalent value, could be given to those who have exceeded a certain level of (1) capacity, plus (2) goodwill and regularity of effort.

Both should be there to warrant the prize.

Curriculum

STUDY OF WORKS OF SRI AUROBINDO
AND THE MOTHER

Sweet Mother, how should one read your books and the books of Sri Aurobindo so that they might enter into our consciousness instead of being understood only by the mind?

To read my books is not difficult because they are written in the simplest language, almost the spoken language. To draw profit from them, it is enough to read with attention and concentration and an attitude of inner goodwill with the desire to receive and to live what is taught.

To read what Sri Aurobindo writes is more difficult because the expression is highly intellectual and the language is much more literary and philosophic. The brain needs a preparation to be able truly to understand and generally a preparation takes time, unless one is specially gifted with an innate intuitive faculty.

In any case, I advise always to read *a little* at a time, keeping the mind as tranquil as one can, without making an effort to understand, but keeping the head as silent as possible, and letting the *force contained in what one reads enter deep within.* This force received in the calm and the silence will do its work of light and, if needed, will create in the brain the necessary cells for the understanding. Thus, when one re-reads the same thing some months later, one perceives that the thought expressed has become much more clear and close, and even sometimes altogether familiar.

It is preferable to read regularly, a little every day, and at a fixed hour if possible; this facilitates the brain-receptivity.

2 November 1959

*

Sweet Mother, with what attitude should I read Sri Auro-
bindo's books when they are difficult and when I do not
understand? Savitri, The Life Divine, *for example.*

Read a little at a time, read again and again until you have
understood.

23 May 1960

*

What is the true method for studying Sri Aurobindo's
works?

The true method is to read a little at a time, with concentration,
keeping the mind as silent as possible, without actively trying to
understand, but turned upwards, in silence, and aspiring for the
light. Understanding will come little by little.

And later, in one or two years, you will read the same thing
again and then you will know that the first contact had been
vague and incomplete, and that true understanding comes later,
after having tried to put it into practice.

14 October 1967

*

You came to earth to learn to know yourself.

Read Sri Aurobindo's books and look carefully within yourself as deeply as you can.

4 July 1969

*

This year, Sri Aurobindo's centenary year, tell us how
we, the teachers and students of the school, can serve Sri
Aurobindo.

First of all read what Sri Aurobindo has written on education.
Then you will have to find a way to put it into practice.

1972

*

Sri Aurobindo came upon the earth to announce the manifestation of the supramental world and not merely did he announce this manifestation but embodied also in part the supramental force and showed by example what one must do to prepare oneself for manifesting it. The best thing we can do is to study all that he has told us and endeavour to follow his example and prepare ourselves for the new manifestation.

This gives life its real sense and will help us to overcome all obstacles.

Let us live for the new creation and we shall grow stronger and stronger by remaining young and progressive.

30 January 1972

*

For Sri Aurobindo's centenary, what is the best offering that I can personally make to Sri Aurobindo?

Offer him your mind in all sincerity.

13 November 1970

*

To be able to offer my mind to Sri Aurobindo in all sincerity, is it not very necessary to develop a great power of concentration? Will you tell me by what method I could cultivate this precious faculty?

Fix a time when you can be quiet every day.

Take one of Sri Aurobindo's books. Read a sentence or two. Then remain silent and concentrated to understand the deeper meaning. Try to concentrate deeply enough to obtain mental silence and begin again daily until you obtain a result.

Naturally you should not fall asleep.

3 February 1972

*

If one reads Sri Aurobindo carefully one finds the answers to all that one wants to know.

25 October 1972

*

By studying carefully what Sri Aurobindo has said on *all subjects* one can easily reach a complete knowledge of the things of this world.

*

Mother, how can one become wise?

Read Sri Aurobindo.

*

It is not by books that Sri Aurobindo ought to be studied but by subjects — what he has said on the Divine, on Unity, on religion, on evolution, on education, on self-perfection, on supermind, etc., etc.

*

Is the [English] Board right in taking it for granted that in the school course of English studies Sri Aurobindo's and Mother's works should be included?

Yes.

*

Is it preferable to choose entire books or selections from different works?

For the *school*, selections are better.

*

Should any extract be chosen from works on Yoga?

Very simple things as in "Elements of Yoga".

*

In what way should these books or extracts be used for the study of English? Should they be explained or only read through? Specially, if Mother approves of works on Yoga, how should these be studied?

Not from the Yoga point of view.

*

Should these extracts be prepared by each individual teacher[1] *according to the needs of the class, subject to the approval of the Board (in consultation with the University Board)?*

Or should the Board undertake to draw up (in consultation with the University Board) a graded selection from the extracts recommended by the individual teachers?

No, because it would not be plastic enough.

*

There are five periods a week allotted to English in each class. Should a period or periods out of these be given entirely to Sri Aurobindo's and Mother's works?

Yes.

*

---

[1] Mother underlined these words and commented "Yes" in the margin.

Should an additional period or periods be given for this purpose?

No.

*

Is there any limit of language level below which these works should not be given in class? If so, which of the English groups need not be included?

It depends entirely on the capacities of the students.

*

Note to the Professors of the Higher Course

The Mother has suggested the following procedure for the study of Sri Aurobindo's works in the Higher Course.

(1) The teacher first presents a subject and gives the necessary elements of information to the students.

(2) Next, he gives to the students, without comments, the most significant passage (or passages) from Sri Aurobindo, relevant to the subject, and asks them to read and ponder over the same.

(3) The students are then requested to express orally at the next class or in a short essay what they have understood and the conclusions they have reached.

25 October 1959

Regarding (1) above: Is it the Mother's intention that while presenting the subject, the teacher should do so without reading anything from Sri Aurobindo's book?

Surely the teacher can read to the students passages from Sri Aurobindo whenever he finds it useful.

Regarding (2): Should the teacher, after presenting the subject, only point out the relevant passages from the book to the students, but not himself read any of them in the class? Could he ask the students to read these passages in the class itself, if there is time? Or should they be asked to read at home only?

He may read them himself, ask the students to read them aloud or silently, in the class or at home; it depends on the time and circumstances. The important thing is that Sri Aurobindo's writings should not be chewed and presented to the students as a semi-digested food. The teacher may give all the elements of appreciation but the students should have the direct contact, the joy of illumination. The teacher should be careful not to interpose himself as a screen between the mind of the student and the great consciousness of Sri Aurobindo.

Regarding (3): Is it the Mother's wish that the students should be asked to express orally or in writing what they have understood in a class at every next class? If a topic or a chapter takes more than one class to complete, could they be asked to express themselves when the topic or chapter is completed?

This is naturally left to the teacher.

There are certain subjects which have been prescribed for study as introduction to the chief task of studying Sri Aurobindo's works. Instead of teaching these subjects separately before taking up Sri Aurobindo's book, can the teachers teach them simultaneously, explaining the relevant ideas from them while presenting the given subject in Sri Aurobindo's book?

You may do as you prefer, but as told above, care must always be taken that Sri Aurobindo comes to the students after they have received the necessary information and preparation, but with all his freshness and power.

While teaching a particular book of Sri Aurobindo, can the teacher include some selections from other works of Sri Aurobindo containing his views on the subjects under study? Similarly, can the teacher include selections from the Mother's writings as well?

Why hesitate and limit yourself? You may surely quote other books of Sri Aurobindo or the Mother.§

10 November 1959

*

(*The outline of a study project "On the Spiritual History of India" was read to the Mother. She commented:*)

No! It won't do. It is not to be done that way. You should begin with a big BANG!

You were trying to show the continuity of history, with Sri Aurobindo as the outcome, the culmination. It is false entirely.

Sri Aurobindo does not belong to history; he is outside and beyond history.

Till the birth of Sri Aurobindo, religions and spiritualities were always centred on past figures, and they were showing as "the goal" the negation of life upon earth. So, you had a choice between two alternatives: either

— a life *in* this world with its round of petty pleasures and pains, joys and sufferings, threatened by hell if you were not behaving properly, or

— an escape *into* another world, heaven, nirvana, moksha....

Between these two there is nothing much to choose, they are equally bad.

210

Sri Aurobindo has told us that this was a fundamental mistake which accounts for the weakness and degradation of India. Buddhism, Jainism, Illusionism were sufficient to sap all energy out of the country.

True, India is the only place in the world which is still aware that something else than Matter exists. The other countries have quite forgotten it: Europe, America and elsewhere.... That is why she still has a message to preserve and deliver to the world. But at present she is splashing and floundering in the muddle.

Sri Aurobindo has shown that the truth does not lie in running away from earthly life but in remaining *in* it, to *transform it, divinise it*, so that the Divine can manifest HERE, in this PHYSICAL WORLD.

You should say all this at the first sitting. You should be square and frank... like that! (*With her hands Mother makes a big square sign on the table.*)

Then, when this is told, strongly, squarely, and there is no doubt about it — and then only — you can go on and amuse them with the history of religions and religious or spiritual leaders.

Then — and then only — you will be able to show the seed of weakness and falsehood that they have harboured and proclaimed.

Then — and then only — you will be able to discern, from time to time, from place to place, an "intuition" that something else is possible; in the Vedas, for instance (the injunction to descend deep into the cave of the Panis); in the Tantras also... a little light is burning.§

31 March 1967

*

Sri Aurobindo does not belong to the past nor to history.

Sri Aurobindo is the Future advancing towards its realisation.

Thus we must shelter the eternal youth required for a speedy advance, in order not to become laggards on the way.

2 April 1967

*

About the proposal of not making any subject com-pulsory,[2] X said that we should ask Mother if this could apply to the study of Sri Aurobindo's teaching also.

Yes.

He said that when the Higher Course was instituted some years back, it was Mother's chief intention that all the students should have a sufficient understanding of Sri Aurobindo's teachings and it was She who had made the Common Course compulsory for that purpose. Our Education Centre is primarily intended to impart and imbibe Sri Aurobindo's teachings, so how can their study be kept optional? In fact, it would be very strange to suppose that any student of our Centre would not be interested in studying Sri Aurobindo's works. And if he is not, how can he be expected to be a student of our Centre?

Yes, to those who want to learn in school but not for those who wish to study alone.

November 1967

*

It has been suggested that it is desirable that the Mother's talks and other important articles in the Bulletin *which are primarily meant for the children of the Education*

---

[2] "The choice of a subject for study should be freely made by each student, and it should reflect a real and serious quest of the student." (Proposal 1: see page 176)

Centre may be read out and explained to them in the class. For that purpose it is suggested that one or two periods in a month may be allotted to this subject. As to the language in which these classes should be taken we pray to the Mother to decide.

If you want to use my articles or conversations, you should do it *in French*.

27 July 1959

*

Sri Aurobindo should be read in English, and I should be read in French.

4 March 1966

*

You have said that it would take one or two years to understand Sri Aurobindo. So are the teachers justified in asking us questions (on the texts of Sri Aurobindo studied in class)?

I said it would take years to understand properly. But if you are intelligent you can understand something *immediately*; and the teacher wants to assess your degree of intelligence.

7 October 1967

*

The nature of my work is such that I have constantly to go on reading and writing and thinking — with the result that I live mostly in my mind. This constant preoccupation in mental activity stands in the way of the opening of the psychic centre. It has also made my life very dry and top-heavy. You have said in the Bulletin *that this sort of constant mental activity is not good for receiving the New Consciousness that is now manifesting. But, then, if the work that I have to do demands it, how can I help it?*

You seem to forget that Sri Aurobindo wrote for so many years the whole of the *Arya*[3] in perfect mental silence leaving the inspiration from above to go through and manifest through his hands on the typewriter.

7 March 1969

*

It is indeed a very good idea to study the *Arya*. The little you can understand by yourself is better and more effective than an ocean of explanation from another.

*

You may profitably teach biology. And at the same time continue your study of Sri Aurobindo.

It is better to do what you do thoroughly and most seriously, than to multiply your occupations.

To be a good teacher is not easy; but it is very interesting and a good opportunity to develop oneself.

As for reading the works of Sri Aurobindo, it opens the door of the future to us.

16 November 1972

*

All that we read, study or learn seems to be a heap of falsehood compared to Sri Aurobindo's writings. Then why waste time on them?

I suppose it is only as a gymnastic for the mind!

*

---

[3] A monthly review (1914-1921) in which Sri Aurobindo's major prose works first appeared.

214

*My beloved Mother, I want to follow a systematic course
of metaphysics and ethics. I am also thinking of reading*
The Life Divine.

If you read metaphysics and ethics, you must do it just as *mental
gymnastics* to give a little exercise to your brain, but never lose
sight of the fact that *this is not a source of knowledge* and that
it is not in this way that one can get knowledge. Naturally, this
does not hold good for *The Life Divine....*

*

It seems to me that apart from the work at the Building Service,
if you feel like studying, it would be more worthwhile to read
Sri Aurobindo's books seriously and carefully without rushing.
That will help you more than anything else for your sadhana.

9 March 1941

*

Which of Sri Aurobindo's books should I start with?

The Life Divine.
   My blessings.

11 March 1941

*

*(The Mother wrote out the following programme for a
study group.)*

1. Prayer (Sri Aurobindo, Mother — grant us your help in our
endeavour to understand your teaching.)
2. *Reading of Sri Aurobindo's book.*
3. A moment of silence.
4. One question can be put by whoever wants to put a question
on *what has been read.*
5. Answer to the question.
6. *No general discussion.*

215

This is *not* the meeting of a *group* but simply a class for studying Sri Aurobindo's books.

31 October 1942

*

LANGUAGES

To unite East and West, to give the best of one to the other and make a true synthesis, a university will be established for all kinds of studies. Our school will form a nucleus of that university.

In our school I have put French as the medium of instruction. One of the reasons is that French is the cultural language of the world. The children can learn the Indian languages at a later stage. If more stress is laid upon Indian languages at present, then the natural tendency of the Indian mind will be to fall back upon the ancient literature, culture and religion. You know very well that we realise the value of ancient Indian things, but we are here to create something new, to bring down something that will be quite fresh for the earth. In this endeavour, if your mind is tied down to the ancient things, then it will refuse to go forward. The study of the past has its place, but it must not hamper the work for the future.§

*

Should French be considered as a special language, to bring the children into contact first with you and then with a certain vibration of beauty?

Something like that.

All I can say is that we are considered to be one of the best — perhaps the very best — school in India for teaching French and I think it would be a good thing to deserve this appreciation.

In my relations with the children here, I always speak to them in French.

*

Why should science be taught in French?

There are many reasons of which the deeper ones you ought to know in your heart without needing to be told.

Among the exterior ones I can say that French, being a very precise language, is better for Science than English which is far superior for poetry.

There are also a few practical reasons among which is the fact, for all those who will have to earn their living when they are grown up, that all those who know French thoroughly well have most easily found employment.

Blessings.

9 February 1969

*

French is indeed the most precise and clearest language. But from the spiritual point of view it is not true that French is the best language to use; for English has a suppleness, a fluidity which French does not have, and this suppleness is indispensable for not deforming what is vaster and more comprehensive in the experience than what mental expression can formulate.

January 1950

*

(*Concerning translation*)

Bonté = Kindness and goodwill; *Bienveillance* is to see the good side of everything. It is not mere optimism which closes its eyes from bad. It is rather a psychic vision which sees the Good everywhere.

217

There are many words which cannot be translated. Sri Aurobindo's humour and irony cannot be translated into French. English humour when translated into French sounds stupid and flat; French humour when translated into English becomes cruel and meaningless. These two languages seem to be so similar and yet their genius is quite apart.

4 July 1956

*

I shall send you the book [*Prières et Méditations*] tomorrow; but you must study grammar well if you want to understand what you read.

20 June 1932

*

Where should I learn good French style?

It is taught in advanced grammar courses, and there are also special books. One of the principal rules of style is that in a prose passage one should not use "I" except when it is absolutely impossible to avoid it, and *in any case one should never begin two consecutive sentences* with "I". This gives you an idea of what you must do to give some style to your daily report!

20 July 1933

*

French must be written with simplicity and clarity.

29 September 1933

*

French gains by being written with simplicity and clarity; an accumulation of complicated images always renders the style pretentious.

*

218

My dear little smile,

You are absolutely right, and I don't see why, instead of reading interesting things, you should start doing boring exercises.

To learn a language one must read, read, read — and talk as much as one can.

With all my love.

10 July 1935

*

I want to resume my study of French, particularly for speaking. Can I have some hints?

The best is to speak... courageously at every opportunity.

*

Mother, will You tell me the names of some good writers I could read?

If it is to learn French you should take a textbook of French literature to study and read one or two books by each author mentioned in the textbook, beginning at the beginning, that is, with the earliest authors.

22 September 1936

*

If You like, I will take one book that appeals to me and another from the earliest authors, as You advised me.

I did not say that you should read only the earliest authors; I said you should read one or two books by *each author* mentioned in the literature course, *beginning* with the earliest ones.

24 September 1936

*

Mother, I have started to read French books — S has given me a list.

It is good that you read a lot of French, that will teach you how to write.

7 April 1969

*

Today I took class E5 and we continued the reading and explanation of Words of the Mother. *Although I am constantly pointing to the beauty of the language with which* Words *is written, I am also conscious that I am putting more emphasis on the explanation than on the teaching of English.*

It is quite all right because it obliges them to think in English which is the best way to learn a language.

2 May 1946

*

X has asked Your guidance in a difficulty concerning the education of his two young sons. He has put one of them in an Italian missionary school in Bombay where the medium of instruction is English and he also intends to put the other one in the same school shortly. But now, because of the current controversy about the language problem in India, he is feeling puzzled because he finds it difficult to decide whether it is good to give education to his children through the medium of English or whether it should be done through the mother tongue, i.e. Marathi. In the latter case it will be necessary to change the school. He wants to have your guidance in this matter.

The mother tongue is all right. But for those who want to do higher studies, the English is indispensable.

Blessings.

3 November 1967

*

At present many of our Higher Course students do not know sufficiently well any one language in which they could express their thoughts and feelings adequately and sensitively. Is this required or not, Mother? And if so, which language should they learn? Should it be a common or international language[4] *or their vernacular?*

If only *one* language is known this is better.

*

From the point of utility some of our students do not want to learn classical Hindi.

Teach both, the true language and what it has become — that will be very interesting indeed — and more than anything else can cure them of the habit of speaking bad Hindi.

*

Do you want me to continue teaching Hindi in spite of the apathy of the students?

Continue without hesitation....

Amrita says that the situation of his Tamil class is much worse than that of the Hindi one. He says that he will continue even if the students come no more — he will teach to himself!

30 September 1959

*

[4] Mother underlined these words and drew an arrow to them from her answer, thus indicating her preference.

221

Hindi is good only for those who belong to a Hindi-speaking province. Sanskrit is good for all Indians.

*

I have the *deepest respect* for Indian languages and continue to study Sanskrit when I have time.

*

The Sanskrit ought to be the national language of India.
    Blessings.

19 April 1971

*

On certain issues where You and Sri Aurobindo have given direct answers, we (Sri Aurobindo's Action) are also specific, as for instance... on the language issue where You have said for the country that (1) the regional language should be the medium of instruction, (2) Sanskrit should be the national language, and (3) English should be the international language.

Are we correct in giving these replies to such questions?

Yes.
    Blessings.

4 October 1971

*

(Languages to be studied in Auroville)[5]

(1) Tamil
(2) French

---

[5] Written on the occasion of the inauguration of a school in Auroville. The Mother's message for the school was: "A sincere will to know and to progress."

(3) Simplified Sanskrit to replace Hindi as the language of India
(4) English as the international language.

15 December 1970

*

FACSIMILES OF THE MOTHER'S HANDWRITING
IN VARIOUS LANGUAGES

*The following eight pages contain examples of the
Mother's handwriting in these languages:*

Sanskrit (Isha Upanishad, with French translation)
Hebrew
Phoenician
Chinese
Japanese
Bengali

ईशावास्योपनिषत्

हरिः ॐ।

ईशा वास्यमिदꣳ सर्वं यत्किंच जगत्यां जगत्।

Au Seigneur pour qu'il l'habite , tout ceci et chaque chose univers te mouvant dans l'univers mouvant

तेन त्यक्तेन भुञ्जीथा मा गृधः कस्य स्विद्धनम् ॥१॥

retent cela détache toi et jouis - en ne convoite pas aucun bien qui s'approprient les hommes ne convoite

कुर्वन्नेवेह कर्माणि जिजीविषेच्छतꣳ समाः।

Faisant certes ici les oeuvres ici on doit désirer vivre cent ans

एवं त्वयि नान्यथेतोऽस्ति न कर्म लिप्यते नरे ॥२॥

ainsi pour toi et non autrement en est-il. L'action n'englue pas l'homme.

असुर्या नाम ते लोका अन्धेन तमसाऽऽवृताः।

sans soleil s'appellent les mondes enveloppés de ténèbres aveugles

ताꣳ स्ते प्रेत्याभिगच्छन्ति ये के चात्महनो जनाः ॥३॥

où ses là partis vont ceux qui assassinent leur âme gens

अनेजदेकं मनसो जवीयो नैनद्देवा आप्नुवन्पूर्वमर्षत्।

Unique sans mouvement plus prompt les deux mêmes ne peuvent l'atteindre dans sa progression en avant

तद्धावतोऽन्यानत्येति तिष्ठत्तस्मिन्नपो मातरिश्वा दधाति ॥४॥

Cela dans sa stabilité dit tous les autres qui courent En cela les eaux Matariçvan établit

तदेजति तन्नैजति तद्दूरे तद्वन्तिके।

Cela est en mouvement cela est sans mouvement cela est cela aussi est proche lointain

तदन्तरस्य सर्वस्य तदु सर्वस्यास्य बाह्यतः ॥५॥

cela au dedans de ce tout et celui aussi hors de ce tout est

यस्तु सर्वाणि भूतान्यात्मन्येवानुपश्यति ।

Mais celui qui partout les devenirs dans l'Etre perçoit

सर्वभूतेषु चात्मानं ततो न विजुगुप्सते ॥६॥

tous les devenirs et dans l'être celui-là ne se replie plus.

यस्मिन्सर्वाणि भूतान्यात्मैवाभूद्विजानतः ।

Pour qui sont toutes les choses devenues l'être même est devenu pour qui sait

तत्र को मोहः कः शोक एकत्वमनुपश्यतः ॥७॥

... vu douleur ou ... l'Unité ... perçoit

स पर्यगाच्छुक्रमकायमव्रणमस्नाविरꣳ शुद्धमपापविद्धम् ।

lui s'est diffusé, lumineux, incorporel, sans défaut, sans organes, pur, inviolable au mal.

कविर्मनीषी परिभूः स्वयंभूर्याथातथ्यतोऽर्थान्व्यदधा-

Voyant le Penseur celui qui domine, qui existe en soi, a ordonné les choses selon

-च्छाश्वतीभ्यः समाभ्यः ॥८॥

leur loi depuis les ages infinis

अन्धं तमः प्रविशन्ति येऽविद्यामुपासते ।

en d'aveugles ténèbres entrent ceux qui à l'ignorance se vouent

ततो भूय इव ते तमो य उ विद्यायाꣳ रताः ॥९॥

et comme en plus de ténèbres ceux qui à la connaissance sont adonnés.

अन्यदेवाहुर्विद्ययाऽन्यदाहुरविद्यया ।

Bien autre chose a-t-il été dit par la connaissance, bien autre chose a-t-il été dit par l'ignorance

इति शुश्रुम धीराणां ये नस्तद्विचचक्षिरे ॥१०॥

Ainsi avons-nous appris des sages qui nous ont cela révélé.

विद्यां चाविद्यां च यस्तद्वेदोभयꣳ सह ।

Connaissance et ignorance celui qui cela connaît comme les deux à la fois

अविद्यया मृत्युं तीर्त्वा विद्ययाऽमृतमश्नुते ॥११॥

Par l'ignorance la mort ayant franchi par la connaissance de l'immortalité jouit.

अन्धं तमः प्रविशन्ति येऽसंभूतिमुपासते ।

Dans d'aveugles ténèbres entrent ceux qui au non devenir se vouent

ततो भूय इव ते तमो य उ संभूत्यꣳ रताः ॥१२॥

Et comme en plus de ténèbres ceux qui au devenir sont adonnés.

अन्यदेवाऽऽहुः संभवादन्यदाहुरसंभवात् ।

Bien autre chose a-t-il dit par le devenir, bien autre chose a-t-il dit par le non devenir.

इति शुश्रुम धीराणां ये नस्तद्विचचक्षिरे ॥१३॥

Ainsi avons-nous appris des sages qui nous ont cela révélé.

संभूतिं च विनाशं च यस्तद्वेदोभयꣳ सह ।

Devenir et dissolution celui qui cela connaît comme les deux à la fois

विनाशेन मृत्युं तीर्त्वा संभूत्याऽमृतमश्नुते ॥१४॥

par la dissolution la mort ayant franchi par le devenir de l'immortalité jouit

हिरण्मयेन पात्रेण सत्यस्यापिहितं मुखम् ।

de la Vérité

तत्त्वं पूषन्नपावृणु सत्यधर्माय दृष्टये ॥१५॥

Cela toi ôte-le Evolateur pour la loi de la Vérité pour la vision

पूषन्नेकर्षे यम सूर्य प्राजापत्य व्यूह रश्मीन्समूह ।

Evoluteur Unique Rishi Recteur Illuminateur Fils de Père des existences disperse rassemble

तेजो यत्ते रूपं कल्याणतम तत्ते पश्यामि योऽ

La lumière de ton la forme la plus bénie ce que de Toi j'aperçois qui

सावसौ पुरुषः सोऽहमस्मि ॥१६॥

celui et partout à Purusha lui je suis

वायुरनिलममृतमथेदं भस्मान्तं शरीरम् ।

Souffle haleine immortelle voici

ॐ क्रतो स्मर कृतꣳ स्मर क्रतो स्मर कृतꣳ स्मर॥१७॥

Om Pouvoir de faire souviens-toi de ce qui a été fait souviens-toi Pouvoir de faire souviens-toi de ce qui a été fait souviens-toi.

अग्ने नय सुपथा राये अस्मान्विश्वानि देव वयुनानि

Agni par la lumière et la félicité conduis-nous ô dieu toutes les manifestations

विद्वान् ।

qui connaît

युयोध्यस्मज्जुहुराणमेनो भूयिष्ठां ते नमउक्तिं विधेम ॥१८॥

l'égarement à toi notre plus entière nous offrons parole de soumission

इत्युपनिषद् ॥ इति वाजसनेयसंहितोपनिषत्संपूर्णा ॥

ॐ पूर्णमदः ० शिष्यते ॥

ॐ शान्तिः शान्तिः शान्तिः ॥.

א	aleph	a	1
ב	beth	b	2
ג	ghimel	g gh.	3
ד	daleth	d.	4
ה	hé	e hé	5
ו	wav	o ou u	6
ז	zain	z	7
ח	heth	4 hé ch	8
ט	teth	t.	9
י	iod	i.	10
כ	caph	kh	20
ל	lamed	l	30
מ	mem	m	40
נ	noun	n	50
ס	sameik		60
ע	haïn	ho kh	70
פ	phé	ph f	80
צ	tsad	3	90
ק	coph	c k q	100
ר	resch	r	200
ש	shin	sh	300
ת	thao	th	400

Hébreu –

228

Phénicien

Chinois

chariot

planche

flèche

<table>
<tr><td>寒 サム</td><td>喜 ヨロコ</td><td>力 チカラ</td><td>花 ハナ</td><td>圖 ズ</td><td>池 イケ</td></tr>
<tr><td>暖 アタタ</td><td>歌 ウタ</td><td>猿 サル</td><td>原 ハラ</td><td>多 オウ</td><td>供 トモ</td></tr>
<tr><td>笑 ワラ</td><td>雲 クモ</td><td>雑 キジ</td><td>貞 テイ</td><td>皆 ミナ</td><td>村 ムラ</td></tr>
<tr><td>答 コタエ</td><td>天 テン</td><td>外 ソト</td><td>壽 ジュ</td><td>魚 ウオ</td><td>丸 マル</td></tr>
<tr><td>知 シ</td><td>話 ハナシ</td><td>内 ウチ</td><td>金 カネ</td><td>鯉 コイ</td><td>紙 カミ</td></tr>
<tr><td>高 タカ</td><td>書 カ</td><td>恐 オソ</td><td>物 モノ</td><td>頭 アタマ</td><td>神 カミ</td></tr>
<tr><td>風 カゼ</td><td>讀 ヨ</td><td>第 ダイ</td><td>町 マチ</td><td>正 タダ</td><td>岡 オカ</td></tr>
<tr><td>吹 フ</td><td>桃 モモ</td><td>居 イオリ</td><td>習 ナラ</td><td>蟲 ムシ</td><td>河 カワ</td></tr>
<tr><td>強 ツヨ</td><td>流 ナガ</td><td>松 マツ</td><td>次 ツギ</td><td>食 クラ</td><td>銀 ギン</td></tr>
<tr><td>糸 イト</td><td>男 オトコ</td><td>林 ハヤシ</td><td>音 オン</td><td>形 カタチ</td><td>青 アオ</td></tr>
</table>

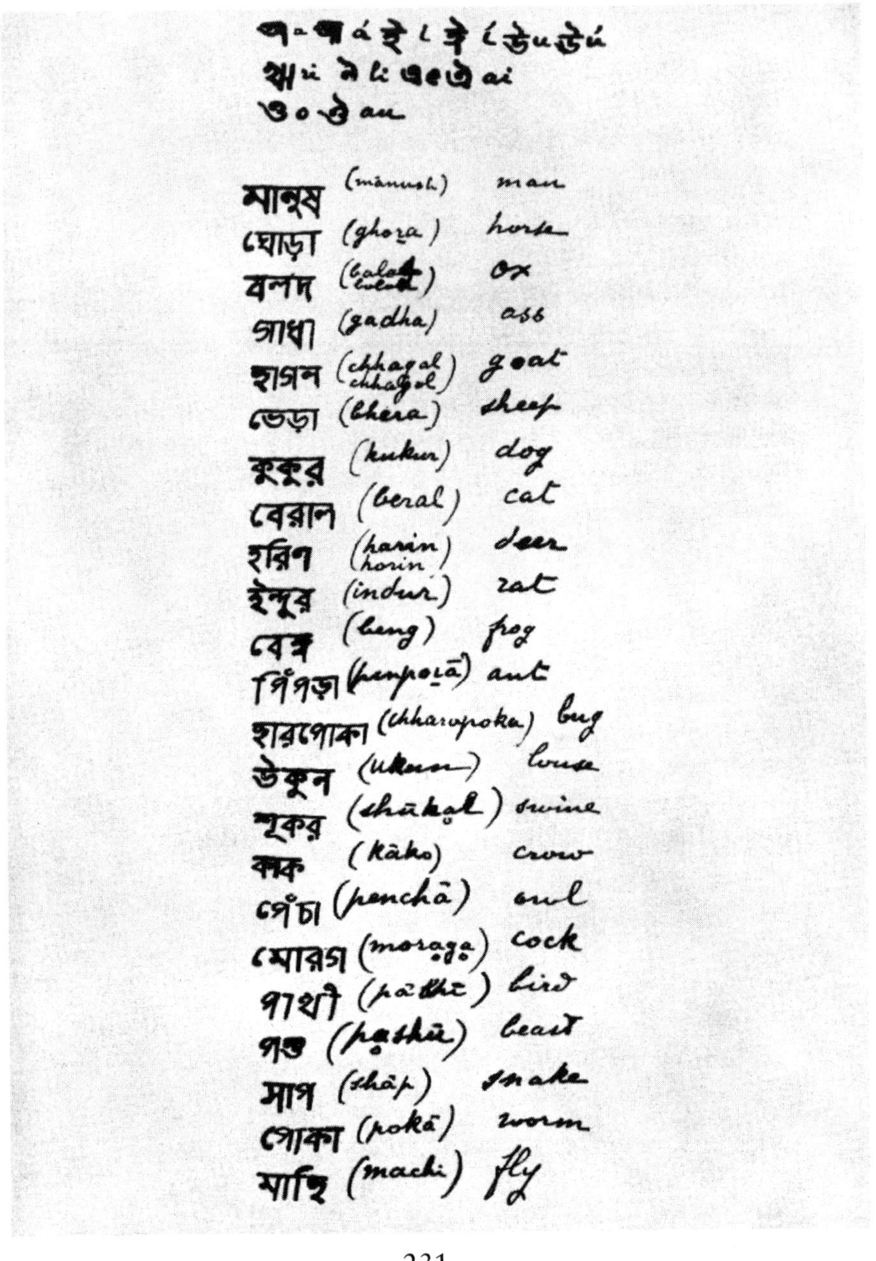

অ a আ á ই i ঈ í উ u ঊ ú
ঋ ri ঌ li এ e ঐ ai
ও o ঔ au

মানুষ	(mānush)	man
ঘোড়া	(ghoṛa)	horse
বলদ	(balad)	ox
গাধা	(gadha)	ass
ছাগল	(chhagal / chhagol)	goat
ভেড়া	(bhera)	sheep
কুকুর	(kukur)	dog
বেরাল	(beral)	cat
হরিণ	(harin / horin)	deer
ইন্দুর	(indur)	rat
বেঙ্গ	(beng)	frog
পিঁপড়া	(pinpoṛā)	ant
ছারপোকা	(chharapoka)	bug
উকুন	(ukun)	louse
শূকর	(shūkar)	swine
কাক	(kāko)	crow
পেঁচা	(penchā)	owl
মোরগ	(moraga)	cock
পাখী	(pākhī)	bird
পশু	(pashu)	beast
সাপ	(shāp)	snake
পোকা	(pokā)	worm
মাছি	(machi)	fly

ARTS

On the physical plane it is in beauty that the Divine expresses Himself.

*

In the physical world, of all things it is beauty that expresses best the Divine. The physical world is the world of form and the perfection of form is beauty. Beauty interprets, expresses, manifests the Eternal. Its role is to put all manifested nature in contact with the Eternal through the perfection of form, through harmony and a sense of the ideal which uplifts and leads towards something higher.

*

Let beauty be your constant ideal.
    The beauty of the soul
    The beauty of sentiments
    The beauty of thoughts
    The beauty of the action
    The beauty in the work
so that nothing comes out of your hands which is not an expression of pure and harmonious beauty.
    And the Divine Help shall always be with you.

*

Supreme art expresses the Beauty which puts you in contact with the Divine Harmony.

*

If art is to manifest something in the divine Life, there also a vast and luminous peace must express itself.

*

Spiritual beauty has a contagious power.

*

Beauty is the joyous offering of Nature.

*

True art means the expression of beauty in the material world. In a world wholly converted, that is to say, expressing integrally the divine reality, art must serve as the revealer and teacher of this divine beauty in life.

*

In art also we must remain on the heights.

*

Good taste is the aristocracy of art.

*

PAINTING

The true painting aims at creating something more beautiful than the ordinary reality.

3 April 1932

*

Would you like me to draw birds or animals sometimes?

If you like — but drawings *from nature* are best for learning.
23 December 1932

*

I tried to copy the drawing You sent me today.

For learning, it would be better to enlarge the drawing so as to bring out the details.

5 January 1933

*

233

I have done this picture without anybody's help. How is it? Will I be able to learn?

To learn means months and months of study before any picture can be done; studies from nature, drawing first for a long time, painting only after.

If you are ready to study hard and regularly, then you can begin, otherwise it is better not to try.

6 January 1933

*

I would like to know if looking at pictures is harmful.

Naturally it depends on what the pictures are. Most often, they are about the things of the ordinary life, and therefore pull down the consciousness towards them.

10 December 1934

*

"Cubism" and Other Ultra-Modernism

If these painters were sincere, if they truly painted what they feel and see, the picture would be the expression of a confused mind and an unruly vital. But, unhappily, the painters are not sincere and then these pictures are nothing else than the expression of a falsehood, an artificial imagination based only on the will to be strange and to bewilder the public in order to attract attention and that has indeed very little to do with beauty.

27 March 1955

*

The largest of the flower-paintings is the best because it is more spontaneous and free. You must feel what you paint and do it with joy.

Copy many beautiful things, but try even more to catch the emotion, the deeper life of things.

12 August 1962

*

To make my difficulty clear to You I am sending You my two latest paintings. One I have completed, but not to my satisfaction. In the other, where the centre is unfinished, I know what I want to do, but I cannot manage it. I want to ask You whether I would make more progress by studying in Paris, or if it is better for me to try here. I shall willingly follow Your decision.

My dear child,

I have seen your paintings — they are almost perfect. But what they lack is not technique — it is *consciousness*. If you develop your consciousness you will spontaneously discover how to express yourself. Nobody, and especially not official teachers, can teach you that.

So to leave here and go anywhere else, to any of the "Art Academies", would be to leave the light and step into a pit of obscurity and unconsciousness.

You cannot learn to be an artist with *tricks* — it is as if you wanted to realise the Divine by imitating religious ceremonies.

Above all and always the most important thing is *Sincerity*.

Develop your inner being — find your soul, and at the same time you will find the true artistic expression.

With my blessings.

25 May 1963

*

Why do you want to do the details? That is not at all necessary. Painting is not done to copy Nature, but to express an impression, a feeling, an emotion that we experience on seeing the beauty of Nature. It is this that is interesting and it is this that

235

has to be expressed, and it is because you have the possibility of doing this that I encourage you to paint.

1963

*

I have seen your paintings and certainly there has been progress over the last year.

Modern art is an experiment, still very clumsy, to express something other than the simple physical appearance. The idea is good — but naturally the value of the expression depends entirely on the value of that which wants to express itself.

At present almost all artists live in the lowest vital and mental consciousness and the results are quite poor.

Try to develop your consciousness, endeavour to discover your soul, and then what you will do will be truly interesting.

This is the programme I am giving you for the year which starts for you today.

12 August 1963

*

I am sorry to have to say that in the paintings, I do not see much improvement on last year. They lack sincerity and spontaneity; it is not *seen*, it is *thought* — and thought in a childish way. What I said last year has yet to be achieved. The consciousness must grow in light and sincerity and the eyes must learn to see artistically.

12 August 1964

*

I was not able to look at your paintings until today. Certainly they represent an effort, and the one which is framed is pleasing to the eye. But you *think* too much and you do not *see* enough. In other words, your vision is not original, spontaneous or direct, which means that your execution is still conventional and lacks originality — an imitation of what others do.

There is, behind all things, a divine beauty, a divine harmony: it is with this that we must come into contact; it is this that we must express.

12 August 1965

*

MUSIC

To all those who took part in today's singing and music: Sri Aurobindo and myself have felt that there was a great progress this time. It was not only from the external point of view of execution, but in the greater aim of the concentration behind and in the inner attitude. May the day bring its benediction to all.

24 April 1932

*

I do not know who is spreading the rumour that I do not like music. That is not true at all — I like music very much, but it should be heard in a small circle, that is, played for five or six people at the most. When there is a crowd it becomes a social gathering, more often than not, and the atmosphere that is created is not good.

*

To keep yourself occupied with music and writing is always good; for your nature finds there its inborn occupation and that helps to maintain the vital energy and keep the balance.

About sadhana I should like to ask you: why not do sadhana through your music? Surely meditation is not the only way of doing sadhana. Through your music bhakti and aspiration can grow and prepare the nature for realisation.

If moments of meditation and concentration come of themselves then it is all right; but there is no need to force it.

23 January 1939

*

Music follows the rule of all things on earth — unless they are turned to the Divine they cannot be divine.

25 May 1941

*

Am I right in saying that when the Mother plays on the organ, certain chords of music create the necessary vibrations for the manifestation of the higher Force which the Mother wants to establish on earth?

When somebody lives in a higher consciousness, the vibrations of this higher consciousness are manifested in whatever this person does, says or thinks. These higher vibrations are manifested by the very fact of the presence of this person upon earth.

Blessings.

*

What is the significance of the tune that goes on repeating itself in your music so often?

You must have noticed that this tune generally comes after some trouble or chaos has been expressed. It comes as a solution to a problem. It means an advancement, a progress, a step forward in consciousness. It comes as an enlightenment. My music resembles the inner movements of the Sadhana. Sometimes a trouble, a chaos, a problem, a wrong movement which seemed conquered returns with a greater force. But then, as an answer or as an aid, the growth, the unveiling of the consciousness — and then the final enlightenment.

This music is very difficult to understand — especially for the Western mind. To people from the West it often means nothing; nor do they easily feel in them the corresponding movements. Mostly those who can appreciate the Indian Ragas can like that music; for there is some resemblance with the Ragas.

But here too from the point of view of form, all conventions of musical laws and notations are broken.

30 October 1957

*

What should one try to do when one meditates with your music at the Playground?

This music aims at awakening certain profound feelings.

To hear it one should make oneself as silent and passive as possible. And if, in the mental silence, a part of the being can take the attitude of the witness who observes without reacting or participating, then one can take account of the effect which the music produces on the feelings and emotions; and if it produces a state of deep calm and of semi-trance, then that is quite good.

15 November 1959

*

Sweet Mother, how can one enter into the feelings of a piece of music played by someone else?

In the same way as one can share the emotions of another person by sympathy, spontaneously, by an affinity more or less deep, or else by an effort of concentration which ends in identification. It is this last process that one adopts when one listens to music with an intense and concentrated attention, to the point of checking all other noise in the head and obtaining a complete silence, into which fall, drop by drop, the notes of the music whose sound alone remains; and with the sound all the feelings, all the movements of emotion can be perceived, experienced, felt as if they were produced in ourselves.

20 October 1959

*

> *X and I play the flute together. We have found a book whose songs have very beautiful, very simple and easy-to-play tunes. We should like to know if the poems of love and death, which do not seem to go with our ideal in the Ashram, have a bad spirit in the tune. Are the Catholic religious pieces of music, which are played in churches, bad to play? If so, we shall not play either the tunes accompanied by vulgar words nor the religious compositions.*

You should eliminate the *words* and keep only the music in both cases.

If you know how to write the music, make copies of the tunes you want to play (without copying the words). If you do not know how to write the music, ask someone who does — Jo for example — to do it for you or to teach you to do it.

Do not keep the books with you, for these books can have a bad influence.

1965

*

> *What is it we should look for in music?*
> *How to judge the quality of a piece of music?*
> *How to develop good taste (for music)?*
> *What do you think of the light music (cinema, jazz, etc.) which our children like very much?*

The role of music lies in helping the consciousness to uplift itself towards the spiritual heights.

All that lowers the consciousness, encourages desires and excites the passions, runs counter to the true goal of music and ought to be avoided.

It is not a question of name but of inspiration — and the spiritual consciousness alone can be the judge there.

22 July 1967

*

(*Concerning a medieval love song*)

The words are ridiculous and even in bad taste. Generally, when we studied a song, if the lyrics were unbecoming they would be changed and only the music retained.

Someone who has a sense of rhythm can do it very easily.

February 1968

*

(*Concerning the words of two Christian canons, "Halleluia" and "Dona Nobis Pacem", inscribed on a programme of vocal music*)

It is all right on condition that it is not exclusive and that other religions are also represented.

March 1968

*

POETRY

Poetry is sensuality of the spirit.

*

For me true poetry is beyond all philosophy and beyond all explanation.

*

PHOTOGRAPHY

Modern photography has become an art and, like all other arts, it can effectively express the inner feelings and the soul, with a true sense of beauty.

*

Photography is an art when the photographer is an artist.

*

241

CINEMA

We see too many films these days and I do not see how they educate us!

When one has the true attitude, everything can be an occasion to learn.

In any case, this excess should make you understand that the imperious desire of certain people to see films is as pernicious as all other desires.

11 May 1963

*

We would like to be able to show the children pictures of life as it should be, but we have not reached that point, far from it. These films have yet to be made. And at present, most of the time, the cinema shows life as it should not be, so strikingly that it makes you disgusted with life.

This too is useful as a preparation.

Films are permitted in the Ashram not as an amusement but as part of education. So we are faced with the problem of education.

If we consider that the child should learn and know only what can keep him pure of every low, crude, violent and degrading movement, we would have to eliminate at a stroke all contact with the rest of humanity, beginning with all these stories of war and murder, of conflict and deception which go under the name of history; we would have to eliminate all present contact with family, relatives and friends; we would have to exercise control over all the vital impulses of their being.

This was the idea behind the enclosed monastic life of convents, or the ascetic life in caves and forests.

This remedy proved to be quite ineffectual and failed to pull mankind out of the mire.

According to Sri Aurobindo, the remedy is quite different.

242

We must face life as a whole, with all the ugliness, falsehood and cruelty it still contains, but we must take care to discover in ourselves the source of all goodness, all beauty, all light and all truth, in order to bring this source consciously into contact with the world so as to transform it.

This is infinitely more difficult than running away or shutting our eyes so as not to see, but it is the only truly effective way — the way of those who are truly strong and pure and capable of manifesting the Truth.

29 May 1968

*

Mother,

How should one see a film? If one identifies oneself with the characters and if it is a tragic or detective film, one is so much involved that one weeps or is frightened. And if one keeps aloof one cannot appreciate it very well. What is to be done then?

It is the vital that is affected and moved.

If you look mentally, the interest is no more the same; instead of being moved or troubled, you can judge quietly the value of the film, whether it is well constructed and well acted and whether the pictures have any artistic value.

In the first case you are "good public", in the second you are more peaceful.

Blessings.

30 January 1970

*

(*Concerning cinema in Auroville*)

Children below fifteen years will see only educational films.

Care should be taken in selecting films to be shown in Auroville.§

243

All that encourages the lower movements and actions must be avoided.[6]

25 February 1972

*

Learn to be silent

The cinema is given for those who like to look at pictures and to listen to the music and the words, and they have a right to look and to hear quietly.

Those who cannot stop talking, chatting, laughing and making a noise or even running about, ought not to be there, because all what they do, they can do elsewhere without spoiling the pleasure of those who are not like them.

So here is the decision: a silent audience — or no cinema.

12 October 1962

*

"The Wizard of Oz"[7]

A short explanation will surely increase the interest of the picture to be shown to you tonight.

This picture is in three sections, two black and one, the most extensive, in colour. The two black sections (first and last) show how things appear in the physical world; the coloured one expresses a similar sequence of events and similar characters in the vital world, the world where one can go when the body is in deep sleep, when one gets out of the body. So long as you have a physical body, no true harm can happen to you in the vital world, for the physical body acts as a protection, and you

---

[6] The first two paragraphs are based upon the Mother's comments; when the notation was shown to her, she wrote the final paragraph.

[7] The Mother made this statement over the loudspeaker when this film was shown at the Ashram playground.

can always return into it at will. This is shown in the picture in a classical way. You will see that the little girl wears on her feet some magic ruby-red slippers, and so long as she keeps the slippers on her feet nothing wrong can happen to her. The ruby-red slippers are the sign and the symbol of the connection with the physical body, and as long as the slippers are on her feet, she can, at will, return to her body and find shelter therein.

Two other details can be noted with interest. One is the snow shower that saves the party from the influence of the wicked witch who by her black magic has stopped their advance towards the emerald castle of beneficent vitality. In the vital world, snow is the symbol of purity. It is the purity of their feelings and intentions that saves them from the great danger. Note also that to go to the castle of the good wizard they must follow the broad path of golden bricks, the path of luminous confidence and joy.

The second is: when Dorothy throws water on the straw man to save him from burning, some water falls on the face of the wicked witch who lit the fire and at once she gets dissolved and dies. The water is the symbol of the power of purification and no hostile being or force can resist this power handled with goodwill and sincerity.

Finally, when the good fairy teaches the little girl how to go back home by knocking her red slippers one against the other, she says that nothing is better than home; by "home" she means the physical world which is the place of protection and realisation.

As you see, the subject of this picture is interesting and not altogether devoid of knowledge. Unhappily the rendering is not as beautiful and harmonious as it could have been. In the setup there are some serious faults of taste and many regrettable vulgarities.

14 September 1952

*

OTHER SUBJECTS

To know how to read and write, to speak at least one language correctly, to know a little general geography, have an overall view of modern science and know some rules of conduct — this is indispensable for living in a group or a community.

*

It seems to me that psychology without yoga is lifeless.

The study of psychology must necessarily lead to yoga, at least to practical yoga if not theoretical.

23 December 1960

*

Do not divide what is one. Both science and spirituality have the same goal — the Supreme Divinity. The only difference between them is that the latter knows it and the other not.

December 1962

*

Sweet Mother,

There are some things which are good for my progress but seem to me very uninteresting. For example, mathematics is a good subject but it does not appeal to me. Please tell me, how can I take interest in the things to which I am not drawn?

There are a lot of things that we need to know, not because we find them specially interesting but because they are useful and even indispensable; mathematics is one of them.

It is only when we have a strong background of knowledge that we can face life successfully.

*

246

History and geography can only become interesting to minds that are eager to know the earth on which they live.

Before one can take an interest in these two subjects, one must widen the horizons of one's thirst for knowledge as well as one's field of consciousness.

*

How can mathematics, history or science help me to find you?

They can help in several ways:

1. To become capable of receiving and bearing the light of the Truth, the mind must be made strong, wide and supple. These studies are a very good way to achieve this.

2. If you study science deeply enough, it will teach you the unreality of appearances and thus lead you to the spiritual reality.

3. The study of all the aspects and movements of physical Nature will bring you into contact with the universal Mother, and so you will be closer to me.

17 December 1966

*

As for arithmetic, I am much more in favour of *practical* than of written arithmetic, with an emphasis on the development of the faculty of mental arithmetic. It is more difficult, but it greatly increases the capacity for inner visualisation and reasoning. It is a very effective way of developing true intelligence instead of memorised knowledge.

When one knows mental arithmetic and *understands* arithmetic, it then takes very little time to learn written arithmetic.

With the help of similar objects — you can begin with the children themselves for small numbers and then take pebbles and counters when it comes to tens and hundreds.

247

In this way, by taking a little trouble, you can teach them all the operations *logically* and so they become for the children something real and living which has a concrete meaning.

National Education

Our aim is not a national system of education for India, but an education for the world at large.

*

Sublime Mother,

Our aim is no exclusive national system of education for India but an essential and fundamental education for all mankind. But, is it not true, Mother, that this education, because of India's special fitness (by virtue of its past cultural striving and attainment), is India's privilege and special responsibility towards herself and the world? At any rate, this essential education is India's national education to my mind. In fact, I regard this as the national education of each great country with characteristic differentiations peculiar to each nation.

I wonder whether this is correct and Mother would endorse it.

Yes, this is quite correct and part of what I would have said if I had had time to answer your questions.

India has or rather *had* the knowledge of the Spirit, but she neglected matter and suffered for it.

The West has the knowledge of matter but rejected the Spirit and suffers badly for it.

An integral education which could, with some variations, be adapted to all the nations of the world, must bring back the legitimate authority of the Spirit over a matter fully developed and utilised.

This is in short what I wanted to say.

With blessings.

26 July 1965

BASIC ISSUES OF INDIAN EDUCATION[1]

1. In view of the present and the future of national and international living, what is it that India should aim at in education?

Prepare her children for the rejection of falsehood and the manifestation of Truth.

2. By what steps could the country proceed to realise this high aim? How can a beginning in that direction be made?

Make matter ready to manifest the Spirit.

3. What is India's true genius and what is her destiny?

To teach to the world that matter is false and impotent unless it becomes the manifestation of the Spirit.

4. How does the Mother view the progress of Science and Technology in India? What contribution can they make to the growth of the Spirit in man?

Its only use is to make the material basis stronger, completer and more effective for the manifestation of the Spirit.

5. The country feels much concerned about national unity. What is the Mother's vision of things? How will India do her duty by herself and by the world?

The unity of all the nations is the compelling future of the world.

---

[1] In August 1965 an Education Commission of the Government of India visited the Ashram to evaluate the ideals and educational methods of the Centre of Education. At that time a group of teachers submitted this series of questions to the Mother.

But for the unity of all nations to be possible, each nation must first realise its own unity.

6. The language problem harasses India a good deal. What would be our correct attitude in this matter?

Unity must be a living fact and not the imposition of an arbitrary rule. When India will be one, she will have spontaneously a language understood by all.

7. Education has normally become literacy and a social status. Is it not an unhealthy trend? But how to give education its inner worth and intrinsic enjoyability?

Get out of conventions and insist on the growth of the soul.

8. What illusions and delusions is our education today beset with? How could we possibly keep clear of them?

a) The almost exclusive importance given to success, career and money.
b) Insist on the paramount importance of the contact with the Spirit and the growth and manifestation of the Truth of the being.

5 August 1965

*

1. How to prepare children for the rejection of false-hood (a) when the falsehood is still within the blood and every cell of my body? (b) when attachment to falsehood is becoming stronger and stronger by the egoistic and possessive nature?

2. How can the unity of each nation be realised (a) when there is no unity within the individual? (b) when

251

there is no unity between two members of a family? (c)
when there is no unity in one organisation or institution?
   3. How to get out of conventions and insist on the
growth of the soul when even an Ashramite spreads the
infection of social status to satisfy personal wants?
   4. How not to give an almost exclusive importance
to success, career and money when everyone is running
after money for the exhibition and satisfaction of one's
ego and self-importance?[2]

To each one a *body* has been given to do that work, because it
is in realising these things in *oneself* that one helps humanity to
realise them upon earth.
   The teacher must absolutely possess the qualities and the
consciousness he wants his students to acquire.

*

I would like them (the Government) to recognise Yoga as education, not so much for ourselves, but it will be good for the
country.
   Matter will be transformed, that will be a solid base. Life
will be divinised. Let India take the lead.

*

MESSAGE FOR THE INAUGURATION OF
A FRENCH INSTITUTE AT PONDICHERRY

In any country the best education that can be given to children
consists in teaching them what the true nature of their country is
and its own qualities, the mission their nation has to fulfil in the
world and its true place in the terrestrial concert. To that should

---

[2] These four questions, asked by a teacher, are based upon the Mother's replies to the
series of questions in the previous letter (5 August 1965).

be added a wide understanding of the role of other nations, but without the spirit of imitation and without ever losing sight of the genius of one's own country. France meant generosity of sentiment, newness and boldness of ideas and chivalry in action. It was that France which commanded the respect and admiration of all: it is by these virtues that she dominated the world.

An utilitarian, calculating, mercantile France is France no longer. These things do not agree with her true nature and in practising them she loses the nobility of her world position.

This is what the children of today must be made to know.

4 April 1955

253

II

Sri Aurobindo Ashram
Department of Physical Education

Founded in May 1945, the Sri Aurobindo Ashram Department of Physical Education organises the physical education programme for the students and teachers of the Centre of Education and for the members of the Ashram. Its activities are coordinated and supervised by a group of instructors called captains, who give training in athletics (track and field events), aquatics, gymnastics, games, combative sports and asanas. The yearly schedule is divided into four seasons: during the first three, there is a period of training followed by competitions; at the end of the year, participants prepare an annual demonstration of physical culture which is presented on December 2nd at the Ashram sportsground. Facilities of the department include a library, gymnasium, playground, sportsground, swimming pool, judo hall and tennis courts.

The Mother took active interest in the development of the Physical Education Department and helped to shape its programme. For years she spent her late afternoon and evening hours with those who took part in the various physical activities.

Youth

YOUTH does not depend on the small number of years one has lived, but on the capacity to grow and progress. To grow is to increase one's potentialities, one's capacities; to progress is to make constantly more perfect the capacities that one already possesses. Old age does not come from a great number of years but from the incapacity or the refusal to continue to grow and progress. I have known old people of twenty and young people of seventy. As soon as one wants to settle down in life and reap the benefits of one's past efforts, as soon as one thinks that one has done what one had to do and accomplished what one had to accomplish, in short, as soon as one ceases to progress, to advance along the road of perfection, one is sure to fall back and become old.

One can also teach the body that there is almost no limit to its growth in capacities or its progress, provided that one discovers the true method and the right conditioning. This is one of the many experiments which we want to attempt in order to break these collective suggestions and show the world that human potentialities exceed all imagination.

2 February 1949

Concentration and Dispersion

IN SPORTING activities those who want to be successful choose a certain line or subject which appeals more to them and suits their nature; they concentrate on their choice and take great care not to disperse their energies in different directions. As in life a man chooses his career and concentrates all his attention upon it, so the sportsman chooses a special activity and concentrates all his efforts to achieve as much perfection as he can in this line. This perfection comes usually by a building up of spontaneous reflex which is the result of constant repetition of the same movements. But this spontaneous reflex can be, with advantage, replaced by the faculty of concentrated attention. This faculty of concentration belongs not only to the intellectual but to all activities and is obtained by the conscious control of the energies.

It is well known that the value of a man is in proportion to his capacity of concentrated attention, the greater the concentration the more exceptional is the result, to the extent that a perfect and unfailing concentrated attention sets the stamp of genius on what is produced. There can be genius in sports as in any other human activity.

Shall we then advise a limit to one action in order to achieve perfection in concentration?

The advantages of limitation are well known, but it has also its inconvenience, bringing narrowness and incapacity for any other line than the one chosen. This is contrary to the ideal of a perfectly developed and harmonised human being. How to conciliate these two contrary tendencies?

There seems to be only one solution to the problem. In the same way as an athlete develops methodically his muscles by a scientific and gradual training, the faculty of concentrated attention can be developed scientifically by a methodical training —

developed in such a way that concentration is obtained at will and on whatever subject or activity is chosen. Thus the work of preparation instead of being done in the subconscient by a slow and steady repetition of the same movements, is done consciously by a concentration of will and a gathered attention centred on one point or another according to plan and decision. The chief difficulty seems to be to obtain this power of concentration independent from all inner and outer circumstances — difficult perhaps but not impossible for him who is determined and persevering. Moreover, whatever method of development is chosen, determination and perseverance are indispensable to obtain success.

The aim in the training is to develop this power of concentrating the attention at will on whatever subject or activity one chooses from the most spiritual to the most material, without losing anything of the fullness of the power, — for instance, in the physical field, transferring the use of the power from one game to another or one activity to another so as to succeed equally in all.

This extreme attention concentrated on a game or a physical activity like lifting, vaulting, punching, running, etc., focusing all energies on any of these movements which bring about in the body the thrill of an exhilarating joy is the thing which carries with it perfection in execution and success. Generally this happens when the sportsman is especially interested in a game or an activity and its happening escapes all control, decision or will.

Yet by a proper training of concentrated attention one can obtain the phenomenon at will, on command, so to say, and the resulting perfection in the execution of any activity follows inevitably.

This is exactly what we want to try in our Department of Physical Education. By this process the result may come more slowly than by the usual method, but the lack of rapidity will surely be compensated by a fullness and richness in the expression.

Bulletin, April 1949

Our Flag and Our Cover

THE FLAG that is shown on the cover of our *Bulletin* represents the symbol of a full-blown golden lotus with two rows of petals, four inside and twelve outside, at the exact centre of a silver-blue square.

This blue is the blue of the spirit and the gold is the colour of the Supreme Mother. The red of the cover surrounding the flag signifies the illumined physical consciousness.

This flag was originally chosen as the flag of the J.S.A.S.A.;[1] but later, when we celebrated India's Independence Day (15 August 1947), we found that it also expressed the spiritual mission of the whole of India. So for us it is the symbolic flag of a resurgent, united and victorious India rising above the torpor of the centuries, having cast off the shackles of enslavement and undergone all the pangs of a new birth to emerge once more as a great and united nation and lead the world and humanity towards the highest ideal of the spirit.

We therefore consider ourselves very fortunate to have a flag with such a symbol and we cherish it deeply.

Bulletin, April 1949

---

[1] Jeunesse Sportive de l'Ashram de Sri Aurobindo.

Energy Inexhaustible

ONE OF the most powerful aids that yogic discipline can provide to the sportsman is to teach him how to renew his energies by drawing them from the inexhaustible source of universal energy.

Modern science has made great progress in the art of nourishment, which is the best known means of replenishing one's energies. But this process is at best precarious and subject to all kinds of limitations. We shall not speak about it here, for the subject has already been discussed at great length. But it is quite obvious that so long as the world and men are what they are, food is an indispensable factor. Yogic science knows of other ways of acquiring energy, and we shall mention two of the most important.

The first is to put oneself in relation with the energies accumulated in the terrestrial material world and to draw freely from this inexhaustible source. These material energies are obscure and half unconscious; they encourage animality in man, but, at the same time, they establish a kind of harmonious relationship between the human being and material Nature. Those who know how to receive and use these energies are usually successful in life and succeed in everything they undertake. But they are still largely dependent on their living conditions and their state of bodily health. The harmony created in them is not immune from all attack; it usually vanishes when circumstances become adverse. The child spontaneously receives this energy from material Nature as he expends all his energies without calculating, joyfully and freely. But in most human beings, as they grow up, this faculty is blunted by the worries of life, as a result of the predominant place which mental activities come to occupy in the consciousness.

However, there is a source of energy which, once discovered, is never exhausted, whatever the outer circumstances and physical conditions of life may be. It is the energy that can be described as spiritual, and is received no longer from below, from the inconscient depths, but from above, from the supreme origin of the universe and man, from the all-powerful and eternal splendours of the superconscient. It is there, all around us, permeating everything; and to enter into contact with it and to receive it, it is enough to aspire sincerely for it, to open oneself to it in faith and trust, to widen one's consciousness and identify it with the universal Consciousness.

At the outset, this may seem very difficult, if not impossible. Yet by examining this phenomenon more closely, one can see that it is not so alien, not so remote from the normally developed human consciousness. Indeed, there are very few people who have not felt, at least once in their lives, as if lifted up beyond themselves, filled with an unexpected and uncommon force which, for a time, has made them capable of doing anything whatever; at such moments nothing seems too difficult and the word "impossible" loses its meaning.

This experience, however fleeting it may be, gives a glimpse of the kind of contact with the higher energy that yogic discipline can secure and maintain.

The method of achieving this contact can hardly be given here. Besides, it is something individual and unique for each one, which starts from where he stands, adapting itself to his personal needs and helping him to take one more step forward. The path is sometimes long and slow, but the result is worth the trouble one takes. We can easily imagine the consequences of this power to draw at will and in all circumstances on the boundless source of an energy that is all-powerful in its luminous purity. Weariness, exhaustion, illness, old age and even death become mere obstacles on the way, which a persistent will is sure to overcome.

Bulletin, August 1949

Correct Judgment

ONE OF the great problems in sports competitions is equity of judgment.

To avoid the clashes and quarrels which would otherwise be inevitable, it has been decided once and for all that the competitors would submit without argument to the judges' decision. This may solve the problem for those who are being judged, but not for those who judge; for, if they are sincere, the more trust they are shown, the more care they should take to be absolutely correct in their judgments. That is why, to begin with, I eliminate all the cases in which the judgment is made beforehand, so to say, for reasons of policy or for any other reason. For although unfortunately this happens all too often, everyone agrees that it is vile and that human dignity demands that it should not be done.

As a rule, everything is thought to be all right when judgments are based on a thorough technical knowledge and on a sufficient degree of impartiality. These judgments rely on sense-perception, which is normally considered incontrovertible. In fact, however, this mode of perception is in itself uncertain. The sense-organs are directly under the influence of the psychological state of the individual who uses them, and thus the sense-perceptions are altered, falsified, distorted in one way or another by the perceiver's feelings towards the thing perceived.

For example, those who belong to a group or an association are either too lenient or unduly severe towards the members of this group. From the point of view of truth, neither leniency nor severity is worth more than the other, for in both cases the judgment is based on a feeling and not on the objective and disinterested perception of the facts. This is a very obvious case, but even without going to this extreme, no human being, unless he is a Yogin, is free from these attractions and repulsions, which are rarely perceived by the active consciousness, but which nonetheless exert a great influence on the functioning of the senses.

Only one who is above all likes and dislikes, all desires and preferences, can regard all things with perfect impartiality; the purely objective perception of his senses becomes like that of an extremely delicate and faultless mechanism which benefits from the light of a living consciousness.

Here too yogic discipline will come to our aid by helping us to build characters of such nobility that they can become instruments of the truth.

Bulletin, November 1949

The Olympic Rings

IT HAS been officially stated that the five rings of the symbol
of the Olympic Games represent the five continents, but no
special significance has been attached to the colour of the
rings, nor has there been any intention of allotting a specific
colour to each continent.

Nevertheless, it is interesting to study these colours and to
find out what meaning they may have and what message they
may convey.

It is quite well known that each colour has its significance,
but the meanings attached to the various colours by different
interpreters vary and are often conflicting. There does not seem
to exist any universally accepted classification of these signif-
icances. This is because these colours are considered from a
mental standpoint, or at least because the vision is influenced by
the mind of the interpreter. But if one rises above the mind to
the truly occult regions beyond, the real meaning of each colour
is the same for all those who can read it directly. This is true
not only in this particular case but for all occult and spiritual
experience. There is a remarkable similarity in the experiences
of mystics of all times and places.

Consequently, if the colours of the rings in the Olympic
Symbol are viewed from this standpoint, we shall be able to find
their real esoteric meaning and see how they apply to the five
continents.

Green denotes a vast peaceful feeling with a direct contact and a very harmonious relationship with Nature. It could
represent a continent with vast open spaces and an unspoiled
population living close to the soil and Nature.

Red is the colour of the physical and material world. The
red ring could therefore be allotted to a people that has achieved
a great mastery over the physical world. This colour would also

indicate that material success has given it predominance over the others. In any case, it represents a people that stresses physical and material things.

Blue, on the other hand, indicates a young continent with its whole future before it and great possibilities, but still new and growing.

Black is a very unfortunate choice of colour as it can only represent a continent which is fast falling into deep obscurity — the descent of a declining people into dark oblivion.

On the contrary, yellow is the most glorious colour of all. It is the golden colour of Light — the Light which comes from the Source and Origin of all things and which, with its helping hand, will lead evolving humanity back to its divine Origin.

The arrangement of the rings also has a significance. Black is the central colour upholding all the others, and this is indeed an indication of the black chaos which now governs the world and of the blindness of those who are at present struggling to guide the ship of humanity on the dark sea of ignorance.

It is our hope that in the future this black ring will be replaced by a white one, when there comes a turn in the tide of human affairs, when the shades of ignorance are dispelled by the dawn of a new light, the bright, white, self-luminous light of the new Consciousness, and when at the helm of the ship stand those who will face this brilliant radiance and set course towards the Promised Land.§

Bulletin, November 1949

The Championship Badge

DURING the Athletic Championships of the J.S.A.S.A. which were held this quarter, the champion of each sub-group received as a prize a badge of championship. This badge is in the form of a golden tortoise with a full circle of red in the centre from which radiate twelve white rays.

The form and colour of the badge have an occult significance and may be interpreted as follows:

The tortoise is the symbol of terrestrial immortality, that is, the immortality of the physical body on this earth. The red centre symbolises the illumined physical and from this radiate the twelve white rays of the integral Light of Truth. The rays are curved to indicate that the Light is dynamic in its nature and its action.

The golden colour of the tortoise itself shows that it is the Supramental which supports this terrestrial immortality and which alone can bring about the transformation.§

Bulletin, November 1949

Tournaments

JANUARY, February, March and April are for us the months of tournaments. Small and big, all participate with the same ardour, but, I must say, not in the spirit of the ordinary competitors. For we always strive, not to win, but to play the best we can and open thus the way to a new progress.

We are not aiming at success — our aim is perfection.

We are not seeking fame or reputation; we want to prepare ourselves for a Divine manifestation. That is why we can boldly say: It is better to be than to seem. We need not appear to be good if our sincerity is perfect. And by perfect sincerity we mean that all our thoughts, feelings, sensations and actions should express nothing but the central Truth of our being.

Bulletin, April 1950

Replies to Prayers of the Physical Education Groups[1]

GROUP A

Sweet Mother, for us Thou hast kept the path free from all dangers and difficulties, the path that surely leads to the goal; and when the final victory will be won, it will reach out to infinity.

Mother, keep us always green, so that we may advance without stop on the road Thou hast with such labour prepared for us.

My little ones, you are the hope, you are the future. Keep always this youth which is the faculty to progress; for you the phrase "it is impossible" will have no meaning.

22 April 1949

*

GROUP B

Sweet Mother, we want to be Thy faithful soldiers to fight for Thy final victory.

Victory to Sweet Mother.

Call to Victory

I salute you, my brave little soldiers, I give you my call to the rendezvous with Victory.

3 April 1949

*

[1] The groups are listed here as they were originally formed; since then, they have been reorganised.

GROUP C

Lord, free from all ignorance Thy supreme workers and guide their standard of purity by the shortest way towards the Realisation.
May Thy will be done and not ours.

The Lord will name "supreme" only those of his workers who will have wholly surmounted and overpassed in them all animality. Let us be at the outset his faithful and sincere workers and when this more modest programme is accomplished we shall prepare ourselves for greater realisations.

23 April 1949

*

GROUP D

Sweet Mother, we want to be Thy valiant warriors, we will follow Thee to the final Victory.

With a single sincere heart we all will for Victory, but it is by stages that it can be achieved. A scrupulous discipline is the first step. Let your new uniform be the symbol of its fulfilment.

17 April 1949

*

GROUP DG

Sweet Mother, we are Thy little children aspiring for Thy all-powerful Light. And Thou, Sweet Mother, hast given us the assurance of the final Victory; it is Thy will that we should be Thy faithful, sincere, brave and disciplined soldiers.

Sweet Mother, here is our pledge. We are determined to be so, and above all, to place ourselves, without reserve, in Thy hands. Give us the power to do it.

I accept your pledge and you can rely upon my help to realise it. Age exists only for those who choose to become old.

Forward, ever forward, without fear and without hesitation.

22 April 1949

*

GROUP DK

Mother Divine, here is our prayer:
   Grant that we may always be Thy obedient and sincere soldiers, may Thy force enable us to fight the hostile powers and win Thy victory.
   Victory to the Mother!

Be always faithful and persevering and you will have your share of the realisation.

22 April 1949

*

GROUP E

We want to be what Thou wantest us to be.

I have full trust in your goodwill. Trust in my help.

*

CAPTAINS' GROUP

All you Captains of Physical Education:

You can and must be the élite. I was thinking that, in the Ashram, there should be a nucleus around which all will be organised. The Captains of Physical Education can be the nucleus of Physical Education. They need not be many in number, but a good selection, first class people, true candidates for supermanhood, ready to give themselves entirely, unreservedly to the big divine work. This is what is expected from you. This must be your programme.

March 1961

*

Sweet Mother,
We aspire to work all together towards the goal that Thou hast proposed to us.
Grant us the rectitude, the courage, the perseverance and the goodwill necessary to accomplish this sublime task.
Kindle in us the flame which will burn out all resistance and make us fit to be Thy faithful servants.

My children,
We are united towards the same goal and for the same accomplishment — for a work unique and new, that the divine Grace has given us to accomplish. I hope that more and more you will understand the exceptional importance of this work and that you will sense in yourselves the sublime joy that the accomplishment will give you.

The divine force is with you — feel its presence more and more and be careful never to betray it.

Feel, wish, act, that you may be new beings for the realisation of a new world and for this my blessings shall always be with you.

24 April 1961

Messages for Competitions

ATHLETICS COMPETITION 1959

Behind the appearances that the physical eyes can see, there is a reality much more concrete and lasting. It is in this reality that I am with you today and will be during all the athletic season. The force, the power, the light and the consciousness will be in your midst constantly to give to each one, according to his receptivity, the success in his endeavour and the progress which is the crowning result of all sincere effort.

19 July 1959

*

GYMNASTICS COMPETITION 1959

What I told you at the opening of the athletics stands good for the Gymnastic Competition; I will be with you all through, helping you in your effort and enjoying your performances.

With my blessings.

16 October 1959

*

ATHLETICS COMPETITION 1960

In joy and confidence, let all do their best, with my force, my help and my blessings.

21 August 1960

*

ATHLETICS COMPETITION 1962

Replace the ambition to be first by the will to do the best possible. Replace the desire for success by the yearning for progress.

Replace the eagerness for fame by the aspiration for perfection.

Physical Education is meant to bring into the body, consciousness and control, discipline and mastery, all things necessary for a higher and better life.

Keep all that in mind, practise sincerely and you will become a good athlete; this is the first step on the way to be a true man.

Blessings.

15 July 1962

*

ATHLETICS COMPETITION 1963

To all those who want to make their body fit for a Divine Life, I say, do not miss this excellent opportunity of the athletic competition and never forget that whatever we do we must aspire for perfection. For it is this yearning for perfection which will, in spite of all difficulties, lead us to our Goal.

Blessings.

21 August 1963

*

ATHLETICS COMPETITION 1964

We are here to lay the foundations of a new world.

All the virtues and skills required to succeed in athletics are exactly those the physical man must have to be fit for receiving and manifesting the new force.

I expect that with this knowledge and in this spirit you will enter this athletic competition and go through it successfully.

My blessings are with you.

24 August 1964

*

24 - 8 . 64

We are here to lay the foundations of a new world.

All the virtues and skill required to succeed in athletics are exactly those the physical man must have to be fit for receiving and manifesting the new force.

I expect that with this knowledge and in this spirit you will enter this athletic competition and go through it successfully.

My blessings are with you

GYMNASTICS COMPETITION 1964

The 18th October is a good day.
Gymnastics is a good art.
And you will be good gymnasts.
Blessings.

18 October 1964

*

275

COMPETITIONS 1966

It might be better to remind you that we are here for a special work, a work which is done nowhere else.

We want to come in contact with the supreme consciousness, the universal consciousness, we want to bring it down in ourselves and to manifest it. But for that we must have a very solid base; our base is our physical being, our body. Therefore we have to build up a body solid, healthy, enduring, skilful, agile and strong, ready for everything. There is no better way to prepare the body than physical exercise: sports, athletics, gymnastics, and all games are the best means to develop and strengthen the body.

Therefore I call you to go through the competitions beginning today, full-heartedly with all your energy and all your will.

1 April 1966

*

COMPETITIONS 1967

On this occasion of our physical education and sportive activities:

I must tell you once more that for us spiritual life does not mean contempt for Matter but its divinisation. We do not want to reject the body but to transform it. For this physical education is one of the means most directly effective.

So I invite you to participate in the programme beginning today with enthusiasm and discipline — discipline, because it is the indispensable condition of order; enthusiasm, because it is the essential condition of success.

Blessings.

1 April 1967

*

1 . 4 . 68

The first condition
for acquiring power is
to be obedient.

The body must learn
to obey before it can
manifest power; and
physical education is
the most thorough discipline
for the body.

So be eager and sincere in
your efforts for physical education
and you will acquire a powerful body.
my blessings are with you

COMPETITIONS 1968

The first condition for acquiring power is to be obedient.

The body must learn to obey before it can manifest power; and physical education is the most thorough discipline for the body.

So be eager and sincere in your efforts for physical education and you will acquire a powerful body.

My blessings are with you.

1 April 1968

*

COMPETITIONS 1969

Since the beginning of this year a new consciousness is at work upon earth to prepare the men for a new creation, the superman. For this creation to be possible the substance that constitutes man's body must undergo a big change, it must become more receptive to the consciousness and more plastic under its working.

These are just the qualities that one can acquire through physical education.

So, if we follow this discipline with such a result in view, we are sure to obtain the most interesting result.

My blessings to all, for progress and achievement.

1 April 1969

*

COMPETITIONS 1970

What better offering can we make to the Divine, than to offer the skill of our growing bodies?

Let us offer our efforts towards perfection, and physical education will take for us a new meaning and a greater value.

The world is preparing for a new creation, let us help through physical education, by making our bodies stronger,

278

more receptive and more plastic, on the way to physical transformation.

1 April 1970

*

COMPETITIONS 1971

We are at one of these "Hours of God", when the old bases get shaken, and there is a great confusion; but it is a wonderful opportunity for those who want to leap forward, the possibility of progress is exceptional.

Will you not be of those who take advantage of it?

Let your body be prepared through physical education for this great change!

My blessings to all.

1 April 1971

*

COMPETITIONS 1972

This year, let us offer all the activities of our body in consecration to Sri Aurobindo.

1 April 1972

Messages for the Annual Demonstration of Physical Culture

DEMONSTRATION 1960

Bravo! To all those who participated in yesterday's performance![1] It was excellent. My congratulations to everybody. Everything was well planned and well executed.

With love and blessings to all.

November 1960

*

DEMONSTRATION 1963

Yesterday I was with you all the time, with all the force and all the consciousness to help you and uphold you, I knew that the rain was a test which had to be overcome.

You have done it victoriously and I am very happy about it. Let everyone know of my entire satisfaction.

With my blessings.

3 December 1963

*

DEMONSTRATION 1964

My blessings for all those who will take part in the demonstration so that they may be at the summit of their capacities.

2 December 1964

*

---

[1] A rehearsal of the demonstration.

The prayer of the cells
in the body.

Now that, by the effect
of the Grace, we are slowly
emerging out of inconscience
and waking to a conscious
life, an ardent prayer
rises in us for more light,
more consciousness,
" O Supreme Lord of the universe,
we implore Thee, give us the
strength and the beauty, the
harmonious perfection needed
to be Thy divine instruments
upon earth. "

꒡

281

DEMONSTRATION 1966

Be courageous, enduring, vigilant; above all, be sincere, with perfect honesty.

Then you will be able to face all difficulties. And victory will be yours.

2 December 1966

*

DEMONSTRATION 1967

The prayer of the cells in the body

Now that, by the effect of the Grace, we are slowly emerging out of inconscience and waking to a conscious life, an ardent prayer rises in us for more light, more consciousness,

"O Supreme Lord of the universe, we implore Thee, give us the strength and the beauty, the harmonious perfection needed to be Thy divine instruments upon earth."

2 December 1967

General Messages and Letters

Become Master of your body — this will lead you to Freedom.

*

Physical culture is the best way of developing the consciousness of the body, and the more the body is conscious, the more it is capable of receiving the divine forces that are at work to transform it and give birth to the new race.

*

(Concerning a room to be used for gymnastics)

Does this room have air and light? Without air and light exercises do more harm than good.

5 October 1945

*

It is an urgent and indispensable lesson to be learned. Nothing useful can be won without a team-spirit and a sporting discipline.

15 January 1947

*

In what spirit should we take and do the sports competitions and games that we are doing now?

Read the enclosed booklet[1] — it will give you an answer and read also Sri Aurobindo's message in the first *Bulletin*.[2]

2 June 1949

*

---

[1] *Code of Sportsmanship.*
[2] Message to the Jeunesse Sportive de l'Ashram de Sri Aurobindo; see *The Supramental Manifestation*, Cent. Vol. 16, pp. 1-4.

283

If I understand well what you have written, you mean that by concentrating one's attention on the physical activity one is doing, it automatically stops all mental activity and this increases the efficiency of the body. This is true provided the concentration is total which is rather rare.

Blessings.

2 June 1949

*

(*A captain, who had begun teaching athletics to a group of children ten to eleven years of age, asked Mother if he should make a plan of activities. She replied:*)

A plan is good, but more for yourself than for the children. I mean to say that you must know exactly what you want to do and you must organise your work. But do not enforce too rigidly your method because the children like to be free and spontaneous in their movements, and this freedom is good for their growth.

My love and blessings.

6 June 1950

*

To the Soviet Gymnasts[3]

We salute you, brothers already so far on the way to the physical perfection for which we all aspire here.

Be welcome in the Ashram, amongst us. We feel sure that today one step more is taken towards unity of the great human family.

3 April 1956

*

[3] Message to the Soviet Gymnasts who gave demonstrations at the Ashram sportsground on 2 and 3 April 1956.

Build in yourself the total harmony, so that when the time comes Perfect Beauty can express itself through your body.

1959

*

ABOUT HATHA YOGA

From our experience we have found that a particular system of exercises cannot be stamped as the only yogic type of exercises and we cannot definitely say that participation in those exercises only will help to gain health because they are yogic exercises.

Any rational system of exercises suited to one's need and capacity will help the participant to improve in health. Moreover it is the attitude that is more important. Any well-planned and scientifically arranged programme of exercises practised with a yogic attitude will become yogic exercises and the person practising them will draw full benefit from the point of view of physical health and moral and spiritual uplift.

Bulletin, April 1959

*

I simply want to be beautiful.

Do sincerely some physical culture and you will succeed.

1965

*

It does not seem to me quite wise to take children below six years to sea bathing; the sea water is too strong for them.

8 February 1966

*

285

(*A captain wrote that she had told some children that Mother would be happy if they followed the discipline of their group. Mother commented:*)

Your reply is correct.

When one is incapable of conforming to a discipline, one is also incapable of doing anything of lasting value in life.

16 February 1967

*

(*A captain informed Mother that he felt mentally and physically "pulled down". She wrote:*)

Do not worry — with some good and regular exercises and my blessings it will be all right.

Love and blessings.

14 March 1967

*

Thrice I have been injured in my right knee and thrice I have recovered from it.

Ma, grant that I may not be injured once again and miss my group activities.

Be *more conscious* and you will no more be injured.

8 July 1968

*

Mother, I have seen that I am not able to force my physical body to do a little better than my actual capacity. I would like to know how I can force it. But, Mother, is it good to force one's body?

No.

The body is capable of progressing and gradually it can learn to do what it could not do. But its capacity for progress is much slower than the vital desire for progress and the mental will for progress. And if the vital and the mental were left as masters of action, they would simply harass the body, destroy its poise and upset its health.

Therefore, one must be patient and follow the rhythm of one's body; it is more reasonable and knows what it can do and what it cannot.

Naturally, there are tamasic bodies and they need some encouragement for progressing.

But in everything and in all cases, one must keep one's balance.

Blessings.

13 October 1969

*

Mother, why should one take part in competitions and demonstrations in sports?

Because it is an occasion to put in a greater effort and therefore to make a rapid progress.

Blessings.

16 November 1969

*

(*Concerning accidents in sports*)

I do not think there are more accidents here than outside. Certainly there should be less. But for that, children who are here must take care to grow in consciousness (a thing which they can do here more easily than anywhere else). Unfortunately, however, very few among them take the trouble to do it. So they lose the good chance given to them.

22 December 1969

*

Mother, what is the difference between sports and physical education?

Sports are all the games, competitions, tournaments, etc., all the things based on contests and ending in placings and prizes.

Physical education means chiefly the combination of all exercises for the sake of the growth and upkeep of the body.

Naturally, here we have the two together. But it is particularly so because human beings, especially in their young age, still require some excitement in order to make an effort.

Blessings.

14 January 1970

*

Sports help the body to prepare for the Transformation.

30 September 1972

*

(Concerning the sketch on the Games Tournament Award Card for the winner)

The drawing on the winner's card is an adaptation from a Greek bronze and is meant to express our will to use the physical strength for mastery over the black bull of passion.

*

(Concerning the sketch on the Games Tournament Award Card for the runner-up)

This *Penseur* of Rodin on the Runner-up Cards signifies the necessity of reflection to perfect means for a better result.

*

(*Concerning the painting "Oedipus and the Sphinx" by Gustave Moreau, reproduced on the Gymnastics Competition Award Card*)

The Riddle of the World

If you can solve it, you will be immortal, but if you fail you will perish.

To Women about Their Body

(Answers to Some Questions)

1. For God's sake can't you forget that you are a girl or a boy and try to become a human being?

2. Each idea (or system of ideas) is true in its own time and place. But if it tries to be exclusive or to persist even when its time is over, then it ceases to be true.

The Mother

While handling children in the Group for Physical Education we meet certain problems with girl students. Most of these are suggestions put upon them by their friends, older girls, parents and the doctor. Please throw your light on the following questions so that we may be better equipped in our knowledge to execute our responsibilities more efficiently.

1. *What attitude should a girl take towards her monthly periods?*
2. *Should a girl participate in her normal programme of Physical Education during her periods?*
3. *Why are some girls completely run down during their periods and suffer from pains in the lower back and abdomen while others may have slight or no inconvenience at all?*
4. *How can a girl overcome her suffering and pains during periods?*
5. *Do you think there should be different types of exercises for boys and girls? Will a girl bring harm on*

her genital organs by practising the so-called manly sports?

6. *Will a girl's appearance change and become muscular like a man and make her look ugly if she practises vigorous exercises?*
7. *Will the practice of vigorous types of exercises bring difficulties in child-birth if the girls want to marry and have children afterwards?*
8. *What should be the ideal of Physical Education for a girl from the point of view of her sex?*
9. *What roles should man and woman play in our new way of life? What shall be the relation between them?*
10. *What should be the ideal of a woman's physical beauty?*

Before answering your questions I wish to tell you something which you know no doubt, but which you must never forget if you wish to learn how to lead a wise life.

It is true that we are, in our inner being, a spirit, a living soul that holds within it the Divine and aspires to become it, to manifest it perfectly; it is equally true, for the moment at least, that in our most material external being, in our body, we are still an animal, a mammalian, of a higher order no doubt, but made like animals and subject to the laws of animal Nature.

You have been taught surely that one peculiarity of the mammal is that the female conceives the child, carries it and builds it up within herself until the moment when the young one, fully formed, comes out of the body of its mother and lives independently.

In view of this function Nature has provided the woman with an additional quantity of blood which has to be used for the child in the making. But as the use of this additional blood is not a constant need, when there is no child in the making, the surplus blood has to be thrown out to avoid excess and congestion.

This is the cause of the monthly periods. It is a simple natural phenomenon, result of the way in which woman has been made and there is no need to attach to it more importance than to the other functions of the body. It is not a disease and cannot be the cause of any weakness or real discomfort. Therefore a normal woman, one who is not ridiculously sensitive, should merely take the necessary precautions of cleanliness, never think of it any more and lead her daily life as usual without any change in her programme. This is the best way to be in good health.

Besides, even while recognising that in our body we still belong dreadfully to animality, we must not therefore conclude that this animal part, as it is the most concrete and the most real for us, is one to which we are obliged to be subjected and which we must allow to rule over us. Unfortunately this is what happens most often in life and men are certainly much more slaves than masters of their physical being. Yet it is the contrary that should be, for the truth of individual life is quite another thing.

We have in us an intelligent will more or less enlightened which is the first instrument of our psychic being. It is this intelligent will that we must use in order to learn to live not like an animal man, but as a human being, candidate for Divinity.

And the first step towards this realisation is to become master of this body instead of remaining an impotent slave.

One most effective help towards this goal is physical culture.

For about a century there has been a renewal of a knowledge greatly favoured in ancient times, partially forgotten since then. Now it is reawakening, and with the progress of modern science, it is acquiring quite a new amplitude and importance. This knowledge deals with the physical body and the extraordinary mastery that can be obtained over it with the help of enlightened and systematised physical education.

This renewal has been the result of the action of a new power and light that have spread upon the earth in order to prepare it for the great transformations that must take place in the near future.

292

We must not hesitate to give a primary importance to this physical education whose very purpose is to make our body capable of receiving and expressing the new force which seeks to manifest upon earth.

This said, I now answer the questions you put to me.

1. What attitude should a girl take towards her monthly periods?

The attitude you take towards something quite natural and unavoidable. Give it as little importance as possible and go on with your usual life, without changing anything because of it.

2. Should a girl participate in her normal programme of Physical Education during her periods?

Certainly if she is accustomed to physical exercise, she must not stop because of that. If one keeps the habit of leading one's normal life always, very soon one does not even notice the presence of the menses.

3. Why are some girls completely run down during their periods and suffer from pain in the lower back and abdomen while others may have slight or no inconvenience at all?

It is a question of temperament and mostly of education. If from her childhood a girl has been accustomed to pay much attention to the slightest uneasiness and to make a big fuss about the smallest inconvenience, then she loses all capacity of endurance and anything becomes the occasion for being pulled down. Especially if the parents themselves get too easily anxious about the reactions of their children. It is wiser to teach a child to be a bit sturdy and enduring than to show much care for these small inconveniences and accidents that cannot always be avoided in life. An attitude of quiet forbearance is the best one can adopt for oneself and teach to the children.

It is a well-known fact that if you expect some pain you are bound to have it and, once it has come, if you concentrate upon it, then it increases more and more until it becomes what is usually termed as "unbearable", although with some will and courage there is hardly any pain that one cannot bear.

4. How can a girl overcome her suffering and pain during periods?

There are some exercises that make the abdomen strong and improve the circulation. These exercises must be done regularly and continued even after the pains have disappeared. For the grown-up girls, this kind of pain comes almost entirely from sexual desires. If we get rid of the desires we get rid of the pain. There are two ways of getting rid of desires; the first one, the usual one, is through satisfaction (or rather what is called so, because there is no such thing as satisfaction in the domain of desire). That means leading the ordinary human-animal life, marriage, children and all the rest of it.

There is, of course, another way, a better way, — control, mastery, transformation; this is more dignified and also more effective.

5. Do you think there should be different types of exercises for boys and girls? Will a girl bring harm on her genital organs by practising the so-called manly sports?

In all cases, as well for boys as for girls, the exercises must be graded according to the strength and the capacity of each one. If a weak student tries at once to do hard and heavy exercises, he may suffer for his foolishness. But with a wise and progressive training, girls as well as boys can participate in all kinds of sports, and thus increase their strength and health.

To become strong and healthy can never bring harm to a body, even if it is a woman's body!

6. Will a girl's appearance change and become muscular like a muscular man's and make her look ugly if she practises vigorous exercises?

Weakness and fragility may look attractive in the view of a perverted mind, but it is not the truth of Nature nor the truth of the Spirit.

If you have ever looked at the photos of the women gymnasts you will know what perfectly beautiful bodies they have; and nobody can deny that they are muscular!

7. Will the practice of vigorous types of exercises bring difficulties in child-birth if the girls want to marry and have children afterwards?

I never came across such a case. On the contrary, women who are trained to strong exercises and have a muscular body go through the ordeal of child-formation and child-birth much more easily and painlessly.

I heard the authentic story of one of these African women who are accustomed to walk for miles carrying heavy loads. She was pregnant and the time of delivery came during one of the day's marches. She sat on the side of the track, under a tree, gave birth to the child, waited for half an hour, then she rose and adding the new-born babe to the former luggage, went on her way quietly, as if nothing had happened. This is a splendid example of what a woman can do when she is in full possession of her health and strength.

Doctors will say that such a thing cannot occur in a civilised world with all the so-called progress that humanity has achieved; but we cannot deny that, from the physical point of view, this is a more happy condition than all the sensitiveness, the sufferings and the complications created by the modern civilisations.

Moreover, usually doctors are more interested in the abnormal cases, and they judge mostly from that point of view. But for us, it is different; it is from the normal that we can rise to the supernormal, not from the abnormal which is always a sign of perversion and inferiority.

8. What should be the ideal of physical education for a girl from the point of view of her sex?

I do not see why there should be any special ideal of physical education for girls other than for boys.

Physical education has for its aim to develop all the possibilities of a human body, possibilities of harmony, strength, plasticity, cleverness, agility, endurance, and to increase the control over the functioning of the limbs and the organs, to make of the body a perfect instrument at the disposal of a conscious will. This programme is excellent for all human beings equally, and there is no point in wanting to adopt another one for girls.

9. What roles should man and woman play in our new way of life? What shall be the relation between them?

Why make at all a distinction between them? They are all equally human beings, trying to become fit instruments for the Divine Work, above sex, caste, creed and nationality, all children of the same Infinite Mother and aspirants to the one Eternal Godhead.

10. What should be the ideal of a woman's physical beauty?

A perfect harmony in the proportions, suppleness and strength, grace and force, plasticity and endurance, and above all, an excellent health, unvarying and unchanging, which is the result of a pure soul, a happy trust in life and an unshakable faith in the Divine Grace.

One word to finish:

I have told you these things, because you needed to hear them, but do not make of them absolute dogmas, for that would take away their truth.

Published in September 1960

III

The New Age Association

The New Age Association was founded in 1964 as a forum of expression for the Higher Course students of the Sri Aurobindo International Centre of Education.

The reader will please note the meaning of the following signs which have been placed after the subjects of the quarterly seminars and the seventh and ninth annual conferences:

* * = *subject* given *by the Mother*;

* ‡ = *subject* chosen *by the Mother from a list of proposed topics;*

* † = *subject* approved *by the Mother.*

The New Age Association

A free talk where each one is able to express what he thinks or feels.

1964

*

INAUGURAL SESSION: *12 July 1964*

> Never believe that you know.
> Always try to know better.
> Blessings.

12 July 1964

*

FIRST SEMINAR: *9 August 1964*

> What is the best way of surmounting the ordinary mental activity?*

My answer: Keep silent.

*

SECOND SEMINAR: *22 November 1964*

> How to be steady and sincere in our aspiration for the Divine Life.*

Consider the Divine Life as the most important thing to obtain.

*

THIRD SEMINAR: *14 February 1965*

> How to discriminate between Truth and falsehood in the impulses of action.*

Those who wish to help the Light of Truth to prevail over the forces of darkness and falsehood, can do so by carefully observing the initiating impulses of their movements and actions, and discriminating between those that come from the Truth and those that come from the falsehood, in order to obey the first and to refuse or reject the others.

This power of discrimination is one of the first effects of the Advent of the Truth's Light in the earth's atmosphere.

Indeed it is very difficult to discriminate the impulses of Truth from the impulses of falsehood, unless one has received this special gift of discrimination that the Light of Truth has brought.

However, to help at the beginning, one can take as a guiding rule that all that brings with it or creates peace, faith, joy, harmony, wideness, unity and ascending growth comes from the Truth; while all that carries with it restlessness, doubt, scepticism, sorrow, discord, selfish narrowness, inertia, discouragement and despair comes straight from the falsehood.

22 January 1965

*

FOURTH SEMINAR: *25 April 1965*

> How to make one's studies a means of one's sadhana?‡

*

FIFTH SEMINAR: *8 August 1965*

How to turn one's difficulties into opportunities for progress?‡

*

SIXTH SEMINAR: *21 November 1965*

1. What is the best way of making humanity progress?†
2. What is true freedom and how to attain it?†

1. To progress oneself.
2. a) Freedom from the ego.
   b) Get rid of the ego.

13 October 1965

*

SEVENTH SEMINAR: *20 February 1966*

How to serve the Truth?[1]†

*

EIGHTH SEMINAR: *14 August 1966*

What is the destiny of Man?‡

*

---

[1] This subject is related to the Mother's New Year message for 1966: "Let us serve the Truth."

NINTH SEMINAR: *27 November 1966*

What is true love and how to find it?‡

Do *you* know what is true love?
     There is only *one* true love, the love *from* the Divine, which, in human beings, turns into love *for* the Divine.
     Shall we say that the nature of the Divine is Love.

*

TENTH SEMINAR: *19 February 1967*

Why is the Choice imperative?[2]‡

Because we are at one of the "hours of God" as Sri Aurobindo puts it — and the transforming evolution of the world has taken a hastened and intensified movement.

*

ELEVENTH SEMINAR: *30 April 1967*

What is the need of the hour?‡

Sincerity.
     Do not try to deceive the Divine.

*

TWELFTH SEMINAR: *13 August 1967*

Sri Aurobindo and the New Age.‡

*

[2] This subject is related to the New Year message for 1967:
"Men, countries, continents! The choice is imperative: Truth or the abyss."

Do you know what
is true love?

There is only one true
love, the love from
the Divine, which, in
human beings, turns
into love for the Divine.

Shall we say that
the nature of the Divine
is Love,

305

FOURTH ANNUAL CONFERENCE: *10 September 1967*

To break away from the old traditions and not to obey the old rules is good — but on condition that one discovers in oneself a higher and truer consciousness which manifests Harmony, Peace, Beauty and a superior Order, vast and progressive.

26 August 1967

*

THIRTEENTH SEMINAR: *26 November 1967*

The new outlook on education.‡

What should be the guiding principles of the new ideal of education?

Truth, Harmony, Liberty.

*

FOURTEENTH SEMINAR: *25 February 1968*

What we expect from the Mother.*

What is the right thing that we should expect from You?

Everything.

What have You been expecting from us and from humanity in general for the accomplishment of Your Work upon earth?

Nothing.

From Your long experience of over sixty years, have You found that Your expectation from us and from humanity has been sufficiently fulfilled?

As I am expecting nothing I cannot answer this question.

Does the success of Your Work for us and for humanity depend in any way upon the fulfilment of Your expectation from us and from humanity?

Happily not.

20 February 1968

*

FIFTEENTH SEMINAR: *28 April 1968*

1. How to remain young?‡
2. What is the secret of perpetual progress?[3]‡

1. Since the process of decline and disintegration which brings old age is really the beginning of death, is it possible to prevent getting old without conquering death?
Is it possible to keep the body constantly young without complete transformation of its material cells by the supramental Ananda?

How can these questions be answered before the supramental is manifested upon earth? It is only after that manifestation that we may know how it came and how it manifests.

25 April 1968

---

[3] These subjects are related to the New Year message for 1968:
"Remain young, never stop striving towards perfection."

2. Does Your answer mean that the supramental is not yet manifested upon earth? Or are You referring to its full manifestation down to the roots of inconscient Matter? 29th February 1956 has been declared by You as the beginning of the supramental manifestation. So Your answer may be referring to its complete manifestation. Will You please clarify this point?

I am speaking of a supramental manifestation evident to all, even the most ignorant — as the human manifestation has been evident to all when it happened.

26 April 1968

*

SIXTEENTH SEMINAR: *23 February 1969*

1. The God of the Religions and the ONE Divine.‡
2. Asceticism and true austerity.‡

What should be the attitude of the sadhak of Sri Aurobindo's yoga towards the various forms of God worshipped by different religions in the past and the present? If he continues to worship them, will it create an obstacle to his progress and prevent his realisation of his aim?

A benevolent goodwill towards all worshippers.

An enlightened indifference towards all religions.

As for the relation with the beings of the Overmind, if this relation exists already, each case must have its own solution.

What will be the role of the different gods of the religions

*in the supramental age? Can they help in the establish-
ment of the supramental Truth upon earth and in the
work of the transformation of Matter?*

It is too soon to put such a question.

19 February 1969

*

SEVENTEENTH SEMINAR: *27 April 1969*

    1. Why is our yoga an adventure?‡
    2. The power of faith.‡

1. In what sense is our yoga an adventure?

It can be called an adventure because it is the first time that
a yoga aims at transformation and divinisation of physical life
instead of escape from it.

2. Why is faith so supremely important in yoga?

Because we are aiming at something quite new that has never
been done before.

3. What is its determining power due to?

Your faith puts you under the protection of the Supreme who is
all-powerful.

26 April 1969

*

SIXTH ANNUAL CONFERENCE: *17 August 1969*

Above all words, above all thoughts, in the luminous silence of
an aspiring faith give yourself totally, unreservedly, absolutely

309

to the Supreme Lord of all existences and He will make of you what He wants you to be.

With love and blessings.[4]

*

EIGHTEENTH SEMINAR: *23 November 1969*

Here is the subject.

The salvation of the world lies in union and harmony. How do you conceive this union and this harmony?

Blessings.*

*

NINETEENTH SEMINAR: *22 February 1970*

What is the big change for which the world is preparing? How can one help it?[5]†

1. What is the big change for which the world is preparing?

A change of consciousness. And when our consciousness will change we will know what the change is.

2. How can one help this change to come?

The change does not need our help to come, but we need to open ourselves to the consciousness so that its coming is not in vain for us.

19 February 1970

---

[4] This statement, written to a sadhak on another occasion, was approved by the Mother as the message for this conference.

[5] This subject is related to the New Year message for 1970:
"The world is preparing for a big change. Will you help?"

Is the aim of life to be happy?

This is just putting things topsy-turvy.
The aim of human life is to discover the Divine and to manifest It. Naturally this discovery leads to happiness; but this happiness is a consequence, not an aim in itself. And it is this mistake of taking a mere consequence for aim of life that has been the cause of most of the miseries which are afflicting human life.

TWENTIETH SEMINAR: *26 April 1970*

Is the aim of life to be happy?‡

Is the aim of life to be happy?
    This is just putting things topsy-turvy.

The aim of human life is to discover the Divine and to manifest It. Naturally this discovery leads to happiness; but this happiness is a consequence, not an aim in itself. And it is this mistake of taking a mere consequence for aim of life that has been the cause of most of the miseries which are afflicting human life.

28 March 1970

*

SEVENTH ANNUAL CONFERENCE: *16 August 1970*

India of Sri Aurobindo's Dream.†

You have said in one of Your messages:
  "The number one problem for India is to find back and manifest her soul."
How to find back India's soul?

Become conscious of your psychic being. Let your psychic being become intensely interested in India's Soul and aspire towards it, with an attitude of service; and if you are sincere you will succeed.

15 June 1970

*

TWENTY-FIRST SEMINAR: *21 November 1970*

The solution of the world's problems lies in a change of consciousness. What is your conception of this change and how to bring it about?‡

The consciousness that has to be manifested is already in the earth atmosphere. It is now only a question of receptivity.

19 November 1970

*

TWENTY-SECOND SEMINAR: *28 February 1971*

How to take a leap towards the future?[6]‡

In one of Your previous New Year messages You had asked us to make an "imperative choice". Now this year You have asked us to take "a leap". What is the difference between that "choice" and this "leap"?

The choice is mental. The leap is made by the whole being.

How is this leap to be taken?

Each one in his own way.

Why have You used the Biblical term "Blessed" in this year's message? Has it any significance?

"Blessed" is not the exclusive property of the Bible.

24 February 1971

*

TWENTY-THIRD SEMINAR: *25 April 1971*

What is our ideal of integral perfection?‡

Conscious union with the Divine.

28 March 1971

*

---

[6] This subject is related to the New Year message for 1971: "Blessed are those who take a leap towards the future."

EIGHTH ANNUAL CONFERENCE: *22 August 1971*

> Have faith and be sincere.
> Blessings.

22 August 1971

*

TWENTY-FOURTH SEMINAR: *28 November 1971*

> Sri Aurobindo's call to the youth.‡

What is Sri Aurobindo's call to the youth?

To become the builders of a better future in the light of the Supramental consciousness.

27 November 1971

*

TWENTY-FIFTH SEMINAR: *27 February 1972*

> How to be worthy of Sri Aurobindo's Centenary?[7]†

On the 1st of January this year You said: "A special help has come on to the earth for Sri Aurobindo's centenary year."

> *Will You please indicate the nature and action of this help and also what we should do to avail ourselves of it?*

Those who will be able to become receptive by the mastery of the psychic upon their ego, will know what this help is and will have the full benefit of it.

24 February 1972

---

[7] This subject is related to the New Year message for 1972:
"Let us all try to be worthy of Sri Aurobindo's centenary."

314

*

Twenty-Sixth Seminar: *23 April 1972*

Education and Yoga.‡

What should be the spirit and character of education when it is undertaken as a part of the discipline of Yoga?

Read Sri Aurobindo.

19 April 1972

*

Ninth Annual Conference: *12 August 1972*

Sri Aurobindo reveals the future.*

In Your message of 2 January 1972, You have said:
   "In this year of his centenary, his help will be stronger still. It is up to us to be more open and to take advantage of it.
   "The future is for those who have the soul of a hero."
   Will You please explain what You mean by "a hero" in the above message?

A hero fears nothing, complains of nothing and never gives way.

*

Twenty-Seventh Seminar: *25 February 1973*

How to collaborate in all sincerity in showing to the

315

world that man can be a true servant of the Divine?[8]‡

By being a true servant of the Divine.

24 February 1973

*

TWENTY-EIGHTH SEMINAR: *22 April 1973*

How to reconcile the individual's claim for freedom with
the collectivity's need for unity and order?†

Freedom is far from meaning disorder and confusion.

It is the inner liberty that one must have, and if you have it
nobody can take it away from you.

28 March 1973

*

(*In October 1967, some students were reluctant to speak
at the seminars, indicating the difficulties of mental inertia, and shyness and nervousness in speaking before an
audience. These difficulties were referred to the Mother
who wrote the following reply.*)

The chief meaning of this kind of activity is just to solve the
difficulties they speak of — inertia, shyness, laziness, etc., etc.

And it is just for that I asked you to do it four times a
year.

The students are not here to have an easy life but to prepare
themselves for the Divine Life.

How can they expect to get ready if they shun an effort,
remain lazy and "tamasic"?

30 October 1967

---

[8] This subject is related to the Christmas message of 1972:
"We want to show to the world that man can be a true servant of the Divine. Who will
collaborate *in all sincerity*?"

IV

A Glimpse of Mother's Work
in the School

(1)

FRENCH IN THE ASHRAM AND THE SCHOOL

(Two or three teachers were having a discussion about the language of instruction in the school. Their discussion was submitted to Mother with the remark:) Sri Aurobindo says in his book on education that the child should be taught in his mother-tongue.

Sri Aurobindo did say that, but he also said many other things which complete his advice and abolish all possibility of dogmatism. Sri Aurobindo himself has often repeated that if one affirms one thing, one should be able to affirm its opposite; otherwise one cannot understand the Truth.

(In the same letter, one of the teachers wondered about the future of French in the Ashram.)

French will continue to be taught in the Ashram, at least so long as I am here, because Sri Aurobindo, who loved French very much and knew it very well, considered it to be an essential part of the knowledge of languages.

23 August 1965

*

(In the course of a conversation about French, a disciple pointed out to Mother that now many French people, especially newcomers, speak in English, even to people who know French perfectly well. Mother concentrated for a moment and said: "So much the worse for them." The disciple then asked whether it would be helpful if she gave a message on this matter. She wrote the following message and suggested that it should be put up in the

319

Ashram and in the school, and that a copy should be put up in the "Bibliothèque Choisie". Photocopies were made for this purpose.)

Sri Aurobindo loved French very much. He used to say that it was a clear and precise language, whose use encouraged clarity of mind. From the point of view of the development of the consciousness, that is precious. In French, one can say exactly what one wants to say.
    Blessings.

19 October 1971

(2)

THE ORGANISATION OF WORK IN FRENCH CLASSES

(A group of teachers were considering a reorganisation of certain classes. One of them asked Mother whether she had any objection.)

No objection, these are things which you should arrange freely among yourselves.

January 1961

*

(Two teachers had a rather heated discussion about the work. One of them presented the problem to Mother and asked for her opinion. Mother replied:)

Truly speaking, *I have no opinion.* According to the truth-vision, everything is still terribly mixed, a more or less fortunate combination of light and darkness, of truth and falsehood, of knowledge and ignorance, and so long as decisions are made and action is carried out according to opinions, it will always be like that.

We want to give the example of an action that is carried out according to the truth-vision, but unfortunately we are still very far from realising this ideal; and even if the truth-vision is expressed, it is immediately distorted in its implementation.

So, in the present state of things, it is impossible to say: this is true and this is false, this leads us away from the goal, this leads us nearer to the goal.

Everything can be used for the sake of progress; *everything* can be useful if one knows how to use it.

The important thing is never to lose sight of the ideal you want to realise and to make use of every circumstance for this purpose.

After all, it is always preferable not to make any decision for or against things, but to watch events as they develop, with the impartiality of a witness, relying on the divine Wisdom which will decide for the best and do what is needful.

July 1961

*

(A teacher had passed on to several colleagues a personal answer from Mother to some questions about the work. Regretting this indiscretion, she immediately spoke to Mother about it.)

There is no harm in having said what you did, because, you see, to each person I can say, in all sincerity, that "I agree." In fact, it is a thing that is rather difficult for all of you to understand, since the mind can hardly approve of it. But behind each one's point of view there is an aspect, sometimes a very small aspect of *truth*, and I always agree with this aspect — on condition, of course, that it does not want to be exclusive by trying to eliminate the others.

And I am seeking for a method in action by which all these aspects can be expressed, each one in its own place, without interfering with one another. The day I find this means, I shall

321

begin to reorganise the school. In the meantime, you can always air ideas; it is healthy, so long as it is neither dogmatic, nor exclusive, nor aggressive, and so long as you *never* quarrel.

August 1961

(3)

TEACHING FRENCH TO INDIAN TEACHERS WHO TEACH IN FRENCH

Selecting a Text for Study

(While choosing a text to study with a young Indian teacher who wanted to improve her French, the French teacher asked Mother for her opinion on La Peste *by Albert Camus.)*

Reading certain things can be good for Europeans who have a rather thick skin, to arouse in them a feeling of true compassion; but here in India it is not necessary. And it is not good to give an even darker picture of a life that is already dark enough in itself.

(Mother suggested Recherche d'une église *by Jules Romains, and sent her own copy for the French teacher to look at. The teacher was "shocked" by certain chapters of the book and reported her feelings to Mother in rather strong terms. Mother replied:)*

Recherche d'une église was the book of my choice. Jules Romains is a great writer and his French is of the highest order. When I mentioned cuts,[1] it was because certain passages are not quite suitable for a young woman's mind. But it would have been easy to make these cuts, and the rest is very good.

---

[1] In a preceding letter Mother had written: "With certain cuts, some of Jules Romains' books would also be good, especially *Recherche d'une église.*"

(The French teacher continued her search for texts and suggested La France d'aujourd'hui *by Marc Blancpain.)*

I have just been looking at the book, with interest. This time, it is very good.

May 1960

*

FINDING A PROGRAMME OF WORK

(The French teacher outlined a study course on the history of civilisation for one of her students, a young Indian teacher, and submitted the project to Mother.)

Yes, this work would be of interest, but only if it is based on Sri Aurobindo's *The Human Cycle* (it has been published in the *Bulletin*). For in this book, not only are all the problems of human evolution posed, they are also solved. Each time that Sri Aurobindo mentions a civilisation or a country, the corresponding historical facts could be studied, and this work would be really interesting.

September 1960

*

In one French class for Indian teachers, several students wanted to read the works of contemporary authors, because the language in them is more up-to-date than in classical writings. What does Mother think?

What I know of modern authors has taken away any wish I might have had to read more of them.

Why step deliberately into the mire? What is to be gained by it? The knowledge that the Western world is wallowing in the mud? It is hardly necessary. Selected passages, carefully selected, seem to be the solution.

May 1963

*

(Concerning a young teacher who had to learn French intensively in order to be able to teach in French and had at the same time to keep up with a rather heavy time-table in the school.)

I fully agree. X should have the time to learn French thoroughly and her hours of work and teaching should be organised in such a way that she has the time to continue her lessons with you, until she feels that they are no longer necessary.

September 1966

(4)

TEACHING FRENCH TO THE STUDENTS

How can we improve the children's spelling?

Generally, for spelling, one must take the help of the eyes. Each word should have its *own form*, which the eye remembers. *Visual memory* is more useful than mental memory. One should *read* a lot — see, see, see, on the blackboard, in books, on pictures.

And as for style, gender, and grammar too, the best thing is to read, to read a great deal. In this way all this goes into the subconscient. It is the best way to learn.

January 1962

*

ABOUT TESTS

Tests may be useful in giving you the *academic* worth of a child, but not his *real* worth.

As for the real worth of a child, something else is to be found, but that will be for later on, and will be of a different nature.

324

I am not *opposing real* worth to *academic* worth; they can coexist in the same individual, but it is a rather rare phenomenon which produces exceptional types of people.

1962

*

(Mother's comments in the margin of a letter from a teacher about French in the school. The students were using work-sheets.)

One of the reasons why the children do not make any progress in French is that the teachers do not correct them.

Very true.

Working with the work-sheets will be effective only if corrections are strict.

Very true.

I have begun to prepare corrected versions of all the exercises for the benefit of the teachers and the students.

Very good.

The teachers should read these corrected versions at least once...

Certainly more than once.

... so that they can become aware of their own mistakes.

Yes, they need that very much.

325

It would be good for the child to have this corrected version in hand so that he can compare it with his own work.

Yes, that is very useful.

Merely to underline the mistakes teaches the children nothing.

True.

I am afraid that the corrected versions I am making for the teachers may remain piously in a drawer.

Heaven forbid!

If so, by the end of the year the children will have done a considerable amount of work to no purpose.

You are right. It is the teachers, almost all of them, with only a few exceptions, who are lazy — more than the students.

I think I am bothering you with this French.

No, you are not bothering me, you are quite right.

It seems to me that so much goodwill is wasted. The goodwill of the children is wasted because, although the atmosphere in the classes is good, the work is ineffective and the work that is needed is not done.

Yes.

25 December 1962

(5)

THE "BIBLIOTHÈQUE CHOISIE"[2]

(*A teacher noticed that the "Bibliothèque Choisie" contained a rather high proportion of books which should not be there if the library is to be worthy of its name. She spoke of this to Mother in the course of several interviews. This was the outcome:*)

Mother's advice about the composition of the "Bibliothèque Choisie".[3]

Remove all modern novels.

Include only scholarly works, on philosophy, art, the sciences.

The best thing would be to bring the list of books to Mother, a little at a time, so that she can see what they contain.

This is an important matter.

(*The teacher asked Mother what she meant by "scholarly works". She replied:*)

All books that aim to teach.

The aim of the "Bibliothèque Choisie" is to teach the students good French and the best in French thought.

It should include mainly scholarly works, that is, works which aim to teach: books on philosophy, art, the sciences, etc.

There should be very few novels (the students read only too many novels), and no modern novels, unless they are of particularly good quality.

---

[2] Library of Selected Works.
[3] This note was taken down as Mother was speaking. It was immediately read out to her and she wrote on it "Approved" and signed it.

Literature has its place in the "Bibliothèque Choisie", so that the students can learn what literature is.

The most important thing to be taken into consideration when selecting books, is the quality of the language and style,[4] something "splendid" as in Flaubert. No translations, or very few, and only if they are of famous works — one cannot say "masterpieces" because there are so few of them![5]

> (*About the bad books which are to be withdrawn from the "Bibliothèque Choisie", Mother said:*)

They should be put in a special place, in a special room called "Bad Books", so that those who want to study what they contain may do so.

Great care must be taken when ordering books.

The question of the "Bibliothèque Choisie" is an important one.

MESSAGE FOR THE "BIBLIOTHÈQUE CHOISIE"

The aim of the "Bibliothèque Choisie" is to teach French well.

1. The books should be well written.
2. Preference should be given to those that are interesting from the point of view of learning.
3. Include novels only if they are remarkably well written.
4. Very few translations — only those of famous books.
5. Send all the rest to the Big Library with the note: "Not to be recommended."[6]

1971

*

[4] As this sentence was being read out, Mother showed particular approval.
[5] This note was taken down after a conversation between Mother and the same teacher. It was read to Mother, who wrote "Approved" and signed it.
[6] This message was dictated by Mother, then checked by her and signed.

(The teacher read out to Mother a letter in which she had written, among other things: "I think it is possible to change most of the books in the "Bibliothèque Choisie" and to raise its standard a little. Please tell me if you approve of this and if I may try to realise it." Mother replied orally, with force:)

Completely, I approve completely. It is indispensable. We have fallen to such a level! In everything! Ah, I agree completely.

1972

(6)

MOTHER'S ACTION IN A CLASS OF CHILDREN AGED TEN TO ELEVEN

How should we teach French to the young children?

The best thing would be to tell them a story, using very simple words and phrases so that they can understand (a little story, short and interesting or amusing), and then afterwards ask them to write down in class what they have heard.

Yes, but the children are very noisy.

A minimum of silence is necessary. I know that the most undisciplined children are usually the most intelligent. But to be tamed they must feel the pressure of an intelligence that is more powerful than their own. And for that, one must be able not to come down to their level, and above all know how to remain unaffected by what they do. In fact, it is a yogic problem.

Can calm in the teacher provide the solution to all these problems?

Yes, but for that the calm must be perfect in all parts of the being so that the power can express itself through him.

(The children's notebooks had been sent to Mother for her assessment.)

I have put marks in the children's notebooks without making any classification. Is this classification really necessary? Each one has different merits and it is difficult to grade them.

June-July 1960

＊

(Extract from one of the teacher's letters:) I trust You and I trust the children because of You; as for myself, I know nothing and I want nothing, except what You want for us. Only show me at every step what should be done and how to answer. Lead us, and may we follow You silently in the depths of our hearts, whatever the outer results may be. Only let the children grow and flower in Your Peace and Love and let us all live together for You.

The relationship that has really been established between the class, you, the children and me, is certainly the most important thing and it must be preserved at all costs. But that depends on an *inner attitude* much more than on an outer framework or material organisation. In fact, this same *attitude* should be present throughout the whole school and all the classes, in all the teachers and all the students. This is what must be obtained and what we must strive for.

(There was a considerable improvement in the class. The teacher wrote:) All this, which has so completely changed, is the result of Your work in us, isn't it?

Yes, certainly.

(The teacher asked whether, because of the experiment which was going on with Mother, it would not be better to keep the same children the following year, rather than to take another group.)

An experiment should be flexible and plastic enough to be applicable and adapted to all the children, with any changes in detail that their different characters may require. So you may rest assured that the experiment will continue. Only the children may not be the same ones.

(The teacher had organised work-groups with the children. The results were uneven and the class was noisy. The teacher asked whether they should continue.)

Let them continue with the experiment. Little by little things will settle down and the results will improve.

(After an excellent period, the work with the children became more difficult.)

This slackening is no doubt due to the approach of the holidays.

October 1960

(7)

MOTHER'S ACTION IN A CLASS OF CHILDREN AGED SEVEN TO NINE

(Mother gave the name "Arbre Ensoleillé" ["Sunlit Tree"] to the class according to ideas expressed by the children themselves. She explained:)

The tree is life that aspires and grows. The sun is the light of Truth.

It is not the cold light of reason that helps life to grow and blossom, it is the warm and life-giving light of Truth; it is the sun, when it pours its joyful rays on the world.

(The teacher introduced activities such as doing odd jobs, gardening, making a zoo out of cardboard, observing a chrysalis, etc. The children enjoyed these activities but afterwards were reluctant to go on from there to do more "scholastic" work.)

A good beginning. It will evolve quite naturally towards more intellectual activities, and meanwhile any work that is done with care is an opportunity to learn something.

(Reply to some practical questions)

1. It is better not to lock the children up in the classroom, even to play.
2. A moment of silence and concentration is always good for *all the children*. But the prayer *should not be compulsory*. Those who want to do it will be encouraged. I suggest that you put up a notice-board in the classroom with these words written on it in large letters:

"Mother is always here amongst us to help us and guide us."

Most of the children will understand, and some are capable of *feeling*.

December 1960

*

(The teacher found the children turbulent, rather lazy and as talkative as parrots. She asked:) Is it like this because their real interest is not turned towards study?

Yes.

What can we do to obtain calm and quietness in the class and get the children to do some work?

The only effective thing is to create or awaken in them a *real* interest in study, *the need to learn and to know*, to awaken their *mental curiosity*.

(The teacher complained of a lack of results.)

It is only after months, and even years of assiduous, regular and obstinate effort that one can rightfully say (and even then!) that it has been useless and fruitless.

What should be done?

Compulsion is neither the best nor the most effective principle of education.

True education must *reveal* what is already present in the developing beings and make it blossom. Just as flowers blossom in the sun, children blossom in joy. It goes without saying that joy does not mean weakness, disorder and confusion. But a luminous kindliness which encourages the good and does not severely insist on the bad.

Grace is always much closer to Truth than justice.

What should be done so that Mother can act in the class?

There is nothing, no method, no process, which is bad in itself; everything depends on the spirit in which it is done.

If you want my help, it is not by accepting one principle of action and rejecting another that you can have it, but by concentrating before the class, by establishing silence and peace in your hcart (and in your head too, if possible) and *by calling my presence* with a sincere aspiration that I should be behind all your actions, not in the way you think that I would act (for

333

that can only be an arbitrary opinion and therefore necessarily wrong), but in silence and calm and inner spontaneity. This is the only true way of getting out of your difficulty.

And until you are able to achieve this, do your best quietly and perseveringly, according to your own capacities and the circumstances, with simplicity and without tormenting yourself.

The Grace is always there with anyone who wishes to do well.

What does Mother call "persevering" where work with the children is concerned?

What I meant to say in the notebook, was that it is always preferable to continue quietly with what one is doing until an *inner psychological change* brings about the outer change smoothly. This is what I call *persevering*.

January 1961

*

The work and the discipline are becoming slack. Is it because of a "vital strike" on the teacher's part?

Certainly. It is a weakening of the force due to the non-collaboration of the vital which causes the slackening. Children do not live in their minds enough to obey spontaneously a mental will that is not sustained by a vital force which influences them by its mere presence, without requiring any outer expression. When the vital collaborates, my force works through it and automatically maintains order simply by its presence in the vital.

Young children are not very sensitive to a mental power that is not clothed with vital power. And in order to have vital power you yourself must be *perfectly calm*.

(The teacher proposed to start with the children a course

of study in the subjects which interested them.)

Yes, it is a good idea. An atmosphere of friendly collaboration is always best.

February 1961

*

A difficult period is beginning. What would be the true attitude for the teacher?

The psychic inspiration alone is true. All that comes from the vital and the mind is necessarily mixed with egoism and is arbitrary. One should not act in *reaction* to outer contact, but with an immutable vision of love and goodwill. Everything else is a mixture which can only have confused and mixed results, and perpetuate the disorder.

> (*Extract from one of the teacher's letters:*) *It seems that it is merely mental impulses that are making me act, and that they miss the mark. That is why although I intervene very little, I feel that it is still too much, because it is not the real thing. And I think I have learnt from You that true calm is much more effective than any external intervention.*
>
> *It also seems that if I am going through an experience, perhaps the same thing may be true for the children, and in fact we are going through this experience together, we have embarked on the same boat; the Divine alone knows its meaning and its outcome.*[7]

The problem is more far-reaching than it appears at first sight. It is in fact a revolt of the vital forces of the children against all discipline and all constraint. The normal ordinary method would have been to expel all the undisciplined children from

---

[7] Mother underlined this extract and wrote in the margin: "This is correct."

the school and to keep only those who are "good". But this is a defeat and an impoverishment.

If, by transmitting the inner force, *in absolute calm*, one can finally control this revolt, it becomes a conversion and a true enrichment. That is what I want to try and I hope that it will be possible for you to go on collaborating with my action. And now that you have understood not only what I want to do, but also the mechanism and the process of this action, I am confident that we shall succeed. We must expect relapses and not be discouraged by them.

Vital forces, especially in children whose reason is not very well developed, fight desperately before accepting the light and allowing themselves to be converted by it. But success is certain in the end, and we must know how to endure and wait.

(The teacher prayed for light, love, flexibility and all that is necessary in order to collaborate with Mother's work in the class.)

All this is constantly with you. Remain open and let it work.

March 1961

*

(The teacher planned to let the children work in groups. Should she form the groups herself, according to their standards, or should she let the children group themselves according to their affinities?)

Let the children group themselves according to their spontaneous sympathies.

Does calm in the teacher necessarily bring about calm in the class, that is to say, "a quiet atmosphere where each one can work according to his own rhythm and capacities, without noise or restlessness, without impatience or laziness...?"

If your calm is integral, that is, both inner and outer, founded on the perception of the Divine Presence, and unchanging, that is to say, constant and unvarying in all circumstances, it will undoubtedly be all-powerful, and the children will necessarily be influenced by it and the class will certainly become, spontaneously and almost automatically, what you want it to be.[8]

April 1961

*

(*The teacher thought that a liking for work and the joy of working should be developed in the children. Mother replied:*)

You are quite right in everything you say about the school, the class and work, and I fully approve the effort of organisation that you want to make.

(*Mother also sent these two messages to the children:*)

If one does not love work, one is always unhappy in life.

In order to be truly happy in life, *one must love work.*

July 1961

*

SOME OTHER MESSAGES OF MOTHER TO THE CHILDREN OF THIS CLASS

My dear children, love work and you will be happy. Love to learn and you will progress.

---

[8] From the time of this message, calm was definitively reestablished in the classroom.

(The children decided with their teacher on a programme for the year: to speak in French, to read correctly, to write French without mistakes, to count properly, to understand arithmetic problems, to learn how to add, subtract, multiply and divide. Mother replied in the class notebook:)

My dear children, I have read your letter and I agree that it would be very good if by the end of the year you knew all the things that you have listed here.

But there is one point on which I want to draw your attention, because it is the central point and the most important one: it is your attitude in class and the state of mind in which you come to school.

To benefit from your daily attendance in class, you must go there with a sincere will to learn, to be attentive and concentrated, to listen to what your teacher tells you and to work quietly and seriously.

If you spend your time shouting, fidgeting and upsetting everything like unconscious and ill-mannered children, you are wasting your time, you are wasting the teacher's time and you will learn nothing at all. And at the end of the year I will have to say that you are bad students and do not deserve to move up into a higher class.

You must come to your class with the will to learn, otherwise it is a waste of time, because even if only one of you misbehaves all the others will be disturbed. So this is the decision I want you to take: to be good, quiet, attentive, and to work hard. This is what you must promise me to do in this notebook.

And when each of you has written, with all his goodwill, then send the notebook back to me so that I can give you my blessings.

Beginning of 1961

*

(The children do not sit up straight and their handwriting is bad. Mother wrote:)

It is no more tiring to hold yourself straight than to hold yourself badly. When you hold yourself straight, the body grows harmoniously. When you hold yourself badly, the body becomes misshapen and ugly.

It is no more tiring to write neatly than to scrawl. When your work is neatly written, it is read with pleasure. When it is too badly written, it cannot be read at all.

To do with care all that one does is the basis of all progress.

1961

*

The days pass, the weeks pass, the months pass, the years pass and time fades into the past. And later on, when they have grown up, those who no longer have the immense advantage of being children regret the time that they have wasted and that they could have used to learn all the things which are needed to know how to live.

March 1961

(8)

MOTHER'S ACTION IN A CLASS OF CHILDREN AGED SIXTEEN TO EIGHTEEN

In 1968, while a reorganisation of the school was taking place, Mother declared that she was ready to reply to any questions that the students wished to ask her about interesting subjects of study. When someone asked her to choose a subject, she replied: "Death."

This offer was made to all the students. The following work represents the response of a French class to Mother's offer.

In the course of each session, the questions were formulated by each student individually and sent together to Mother.

(The students wrote to Mother, asking to be allowed to work with her on a study on death. Mother gave these instructions orally to the teacher.)

The subject is: What is death?

How should you begin? You must look into yourself, look inside; do not try to know by reading books or to find out what is happening in the vital and the mind: what you feel, what you think about death.

The research should be carried out exclusively on a material plane: what is death, from the physical point of view?

You must concentrate and find the answers in yourself. Don't make any speeches. Say only one sentence. The more intelligent you are, the less words you need to express yourself.

27 April 1968

*

(The students' replies to the question, "What is death, from the physical point of view?":

"All circulation of blood in the brain cells stops."

"When the brain stops functioning and the decomposition of the body begins, that is death."

"The cessation of all physical activity due to the absence of the energy source, or soul."

"The actual fact of death makes me think of an experience in which one is projected with increasing force into space."

Mother wrote to the class:)

I read what you sent with interest. And here is my reply:

Death is the phenomenon of decentralisation and dispersion of the cells which make up the physical body.

The consciousness is, by its very nature, immortal, and in order to manifest in the physical world, it assumes more or less lasting material forms.

The material substance is in course of transformation in order to become a multiform and increasingly perfect and lasting mode of expression for this consciousness.

18 May 1968

*

(This time, Mother gave separate replies to the questions and sent them to the teacher:)

Here are my replies to your students' questions. I hope they will be able to understand.

If a cell becomes conscious of its own personality, is it not liable to act only in its own self-interest, taking no account of the collective interest?

What is the self-interest of a cell!

*

Does the decentralisation occur all at once or by degrees?

Everything does not disperse all at once; it takes a long time.

The central will of the physical being abdicates its will to hold all the cells together. That is the first phenomenon. It accepts dissolution for one reason or another. One of the strongest reasons is the sense of an irreparable disharmony; the other is a kind of disgust with continuing the effort of coordination and harmonisation. In fact, there are innumerable reasons, but unless there is a violent accident, it is above all this will to maintain cohesion which abdicates for one reason or another, or without reason. It is this which inevitably precedes death.

341

Must each cell be conscious of its oneness with the centre?

It is not like that. It is still a semi-collective consciousness, it is not an individual consciousness of the cells.

*

Does decentralisation always occur after death, or can it start before?

It often starts before.

Do the cells disperse in space or in the body itself? If they disperse in space, the body must surely disappear with the cells?

Naturally, the body dissolves after death, but that takes a long time.

In the expression "dispersion of the cells", doesn't the word "dispersion" have a special meaning? If so, what is it?

I used the word dispersion of the cells in its most concrete sense.

When the concentration which forms the body comes to an end and the body dissolves, all the cells that have been especially developed and have become conscious of the divine Presence within them, are scattered and enter other combinations in which they awaken, by contagion, the consciousness of the Presence that each one has had. And in this way, by this phenomenon of concentration, development and dispersion, all matter evolves and learns by contagion, develops by contagion, has the experience by contagion.

Naturally, the cell dissolves with the body. It is the consciousness of the cells that enters other combinations.

5 June 1968

*

When the will of the physical being abdicates without reason, is it without any physical reason or without any reason at all?

The physical consciousness is conscious only physically; the will of the physical being can abdicate without any reason of which it is aware.

What causes the physical being's disgust with continuing the effort of coordination and harmonisation?

Usually, this disgust occurs when there is, in one part of the being (an important part, either vital or mental), an absolute refusal to progress. And so, physically, this is manifested as a refusal to strive against the deterioration which comes with time.

Where is the connection between the central will of the physical being and the cells established? And how?

The cells have an inner composition or structure which corresponds to the structure of the universe. So the link is established between identical external and internal states.... It is not "external", but it is external for the individual. That is, the cell, in its internal composition, receives the vibration of the corresponding state in the composition of the whole. Each cell is composed of different radiances, with a wholly luminous centre, and the connection is established between light and light. That is, the will, the central light, acts on the cell by touching the corresponding lights, by an inner contact of the being. Each cell is a world in miniature corresponding to the whole.

15 July 1968

*

343

Is the will for progress enough to prevent the deterioration that comes with time? How can the physical being prevent this deterioration?

That is precisely what the transformation of the body is: the physical cells not only become conscious, but receptive to the true Consciousness-Force; that is, they allow the working of this higher Consciousness. That is the work of transformation.

How does the will, the central light, which is not material, act on the gross matter of the cell?

It is just like asking, "How does the will act on matter?" All life is like that. You should explain to these children that their whole existence is the result of the action of the will, that without will, matter would be inert and immobile and that it is precisely the fact that the vibration of will acts on matter that makes life possible. Otherwise there would be no life. If they want a scientific answer and want to know how, it is more difficult, but the fact is there, it is a fact that can be seen at every second.

20 July 1968

*

How does one become conscious of the physical being?

Mankind, nearly all of mankind, is conscious only of the physical being. With education, the number of men who are conscious of their vital and mind is increasing. As for the human beings who are conscious of their psychic being, they are relatively few.

If you mean, "How does one awaken the consciousness of the physical being?", that is precisely the aim of physical education. It is physical education that teaches the cells to be conscious. But for the development of the brain, it is study, observation, intelligent education, above all observation and reasoning. And naturally, for the whole education of the consciousness from the point of view of character, it is yoga.

344

Does the central will of the physical being have a particular location in the body?

It is the brain.

Can one experience death without dying?

Certainly. One can experience death yogically; one can even experience it materially, if death is short enough so that the doctors do not have time to pronounce you dead.

After death, which part of the being becomes aware that one is dead?

Any part of the being that survives can become aware that the body is no longer there. It depends.

How can one tell for certain that the physical body is dead?

Only when it decomposes.

How can one control or prevent the process of disintegration?

By carefully maintaining the physical balance.

When one dies, does one necessarily feel physical pain?

Not necessarily.

28 September 1968

*

What should we do in our daily lives to stop the process of death?

The method is to detach one's consciousness from the body and to concentrate it on the deeper life, so as to bring this deeper consciousness into the body.

If the sense of "self" has identified itself more with the mind in life, is this the same sense of "self" that has all the experiences after death, that is, that retains at the same time the memories of life? I am asking this about the mind, for it remains formed a little longer than the other parts after death.

It is not true that the mind is more durable. The psychic consciousness which has identified itself with the little physical part leaves this little physical person. Insofar as this consciousness has shaped the life, it remembers what it has shaped and the memory is closely linked to the psychic consciousness in the events. Wherever the psychic consciousness has not taken part in events, there is no memory. And only the psychic consciousness can continue; it is not the mind that retains memories, that is quite incorrect.

1 February 1969

*

(A few days later, during a conversation with the teacher about this student, Mother said, by way of conclusion:)

In fact, there is no death.

V

Answers to a Monitress

Sutras

1. Have no ambition, above all never lay claim to anything, but be at each moment the utmost that you can be.

25 February 1957

2. As for your place in the universal manifestation, the Supreme alone will show it to you.

2 May 1957

3. The Supreme Lord has ineluctably decreed the place you occupy in the world concert, but whatever that place may be, you have the same equal right as everyone else to scale the supreme heights as far as the supramental realisation.

17 May 1957

4. What you are in the truth of your being is ineluctably decreed and nothing and no one can prevent you from being it; but the path you will take to attain it is left to your own free choice.

19 May 1957

5. On the path of ascending evolution, each one is free to choose the direction he will take: the swift and steep ascent towards the summits of Truth, the supreme realisation, or, turning his back to the peaks, the easy descent towards the interminable meanderings of endless rebirths.

23 May 1957

6. In the course of the ages and even in the course of your present life you can make your choice once and for all, irrevocably, and then you have only to confirm it at each new occasion; or else, if you have not taken the final decision at the outset, at each

moment you will have to make a new choice between falsehood and truth.

23 May 1957

7. But even supposing that you have not taken the irrevocable decision at the outset, if you have the good fortune to be alive at one of those extraordinary moments in universal history when the Grace is present, incarnate on earth, It will give you once again, at certain exceptional moments, the possibility of making a final choice that will lead you straight to the goal.

23 May 1957

Correspondence

Why are no diplomas and certificates given to the students of the Centre of Education?

For the last hundred years or so mankind has been suffering from a disease which seems to be spreading more and more and which has reached a climax in our times; it is what we may call "utilitarianism". People and things, circumstances and activities seem to be viewed and appreciated exclusively from this angle. Nothing has any value unless it is useful. Certainly something that is useful is better than something that is not. But first we must agree on what we describe as useful — useful to whom, to what, for what?

For, more and more, the races who consider themselves civilised describe as useful whatever can attract, procure or produce money. Everything is judged and evaluated from a monetary angle. That is what I call utilitarianism. And this disease is highly contagious, for even children are not immune to it.

At an age when they should be dreaming of beauty, greatness and perfection, dreams that may be too sublime for ordinary common sense, but which are nevertheless far superior to this dull good sense, children now dream of money and worry about how to earn it.

So when they think of their studies, they think above all about what can be useful to them, so that later on when they grow up they can earn a lot of money.

And the thing that becomes most important for them is to prepare themselves to pass examinations with success, for with diplomas, certificates and titles they will be able to find good positions and earn a lot of money.

For them study has no other purpose, no other interest.

To learn for the sake of knowledge, to study in order to

351

know the secrets of Nature and life, to educate oneself in order to grow in consciousness, to discipline oneself in order to become master of oneself, to overcome one's weaknesses, incapacities and ignorance, to prepare oneself to advance in life towards a goal that is nobler and vaster, more generous and more true... they hardly give it a thought and consider it all very utopian. The only thing that matters is to be practical, to prepare themselves and learn how to earn money.

Children who are infected with this disease are out of place at the Centre of Education of the Ashram. And it is to make this quite clear to them that we do not prepare them for any official examination or competition and do not give them any diplomas or titles which they can use in the outside world.

We want here only those who aspire for a higher and better life, who thirst for knowledge and perfection, who look forward eagerly to a future that will be more totally true.

There is plenty of room in the world for all the others.

17 July 1960

Sweet Mother, in the Physical Education Section, you have made all the necessary arrangements so that by physical training we may be able to develop our body in every possible way and thus become ready to participate in the great work of integral transformation.

We have been teaching games, sports and all sorts of physical activities for several years, but we find that most of our students cannot grasp the fundamental spirit. They are usually distracted by amusement, excitement, impulsive moods and all kinds of likes and dislikes. In consequence, the discipline, the will, the resolution, the hard work and the true attitude which ensure our progress are lacking on the whole. A football match or an exciting game arouses a lot of enthusiasm but a conscientious and concentrated work which will help

us to master certain physical qualities and set right cer-
tain defects is always done without much eagerness. The
great majority of students, big and small, suffer from this
malady. Very few approach physical education with the
right attitude. How shall we learn to make it our normal
practice?

The contents of the consciousness must change, the level of the consciousness must be raised, the quality of the consciousness must progress.

Things are as you have described them, because most children have their consciousness centred in the physical which is tamasic and reluctant to make any effort. They want an easy life, and only the excitement or the rivalry of a game or a competition awakens enough interest in them so that they consent to make an effort. For this, a vital passion has to be aroused to intensify the will.

The idea of progress belongs to the intelligent will which is active only in very few who are in contact with their psychic being; later on, in those who are mentally more developed and begin to understand the need to develop and control themselves.

I said that the remedy is to raise the consciousness to a higher level. But, naturally, one must start with the level of the consciousness of the captains and instructors themselves.

First of all, they should have a clear conception of what they want to obtain from those for whom they are responsible; and not only that, but they should also have realised in themselves the qualities which they demand from others. Over and above these qualities, they should have developed in their character and action a great deal of patience, endurance, kindness, understanding and impartiality. They should have no likes or dislikes, no attractions or repulsions.

That is why the new group of captains must really be an élite group in order to set a good example to the pupils and students, if we want them in their turn to adopt the true attitude.

Therefore I say to all: set to work sincerely and sooner or later the obstacles will be overcome.

5 July 1961

Sweet Mother,
Some activities in our programme of physical edu-
cation are of a more serious nature than others and call
for more concentration; these activities tend to become
boring for the children. Should the captains organise
their groups in such a way that everything they teach is
interesting and amusing, or should the children try to
create an interest in themselves?

Both are indispensable and should, as far as possible, be always present.

With a little imagination and inventive flexibility, the instructors should give charm and novelty to what they teach.

On their part, the children, by cultivating in themselves the will and inclination for progress, should create a constant interest in what they do.

In the meanwhile, the captains can partly entrust to the children the responsibility for organising their own exercises, using as much as possible whatever ingenious ideas may occur to them.

If the sense of collaboration and responsibility is awakened in the children, then they will take an interest in what they do and do it with pleasure.

21 July 1961

Sweet Mother,
We have a minute of concentration before and after
group every day. What should we try to do during this
concentration?

Before, make an offering to the Divine of what you are going to do, so that it may be done in a spirit of consecration.

Afterwards, ask the Divine to increase the will for progress in us, so that we may become instruments that are more and more capable of serving Him.

You may also, before starting, offer yourselves to the Divine in silence.

And at the end, give thanks to the Divine in silence.

I mean a movement of the *heart* without any words in the head.

24 July 1961

In human life the cause of all difficulties, all discords, all moral sufferings, is the presence in everyone of the ego with its desires, its likes and dislikes. Even in a disinterested work which consists in helping others, until one has learned to overcome the ego and its demands, until one can force it to keep calm and quiet in one corner, the ego reacts to everything that displeases it, starts an inner storm that rises to the surface and spoils all the work.

This work of overcoming the ego is long, slow and difficult; it demands constant alertness and sustained effort. This effort is easier for some and more difficult for others.

We are here in the Ashram to do this work together with the help of Sri Aurobindo's knowledge and force, in an attempt to realise a community that is more harmonious, more united, and consequently much more effective in life.

As long as I was physically present among you all, my presence was helping you to achieve this mastery over the ego and so it was not necessary for me to speak to you about it individually very often.

But now this effort must become the basis of each individual's existence, more especially for those of you who have a responsible position and have to take care of others. The leaders must always set the example, the leaders must always practise the virtues they demand from those who are in their care; they

355

must be understanding, patient, enduring, full of sympathy and warm and friendly goodwill, not out of egoism to win friends for themselves, but out of generosity to be able to understand and help others.

To forget oneself, one's own likings and preferences, is indispensable in order to be a true leader.

That is what I am asking of you now, so that you can face your responsibilities as you should. And then you will find that where you used to feel disorder and disunity, they have vanished, and harmony, peace and joy have taken their place.

You know that I love you and that I am always with you to sustain you, help you and show you the way.

Blessings.

26 August 1969

Sweet Mother,
Some children ask me what is the best way of spending their holidays here.

It is an excellent opportunity to do some interesting work, to learn something new or develop some weak point in their nature or their studies.

It is an excellent opportunity to choose some occupation freely and thus discover the true capacities of their being.

Blessings.

1 November 1969

Sweet Mother,
Do you approve of students going to spend their holidays at home or elsewhere?

Rather, one could say that what the children do during their holidays shows what they are and how far they are capable of profiting from their stay here. Thus, the case is different for each one and the quality of his reaction indicates the quality of his character.

Truly speaking, those who would rather stay here than do anything else, are ready to take full advantage of their education here and are capable of fully understanding the ideal they are taught.

Blessings.

2 November 1969

Sweet Mother,
Does this mean that those who go out are incapable of fully understanding the ideal they are taught, or are we unable to make them understand the ideal?

I do not say that the teaching here is perfect and exactly what it should be. But it is certain that a good number of students are very interested and understand very well that there is something here which is not to be found elsewhere.

So, it is those students who should remain here, and as we do not have enough room to meet all demands, the choice would be easier.

Blessings.

3 November 1969

Sweet Mother,
Is it possible to teach the ideal to those who do not understand it, and how can it be taught to them? Are we, instructors and teachers, worthy of this formidable task?

What we want to teach is not only a mental ideal, it is a new idea of life and a realisation of consciousness. This realisation is new to all, and the only true way to teach others is to live according to this new consciousness oneself and to allow oneself to be transformed by it. There is no better lesson than that of an example. To tell others: "Do not be selfish," is not much use, but if somebody is free from all selfishness, he becomes a wonderful example to others; and someone who sincerely aspires to act in accordance with the Supreme Truth, creates a kind of contagion for the people around him. So the first duty of all those who are teachers or instructors is to give an example of the qualities they teach to others.

And if, among these teachers and instructors, some are not worthy of their post, because by their character they give a bad example, their first duty is to become worthy by changing their character and their action; there is no other way.

Blessings.

4 November 1969

Sweet Mother,
What qualifications do you consider essential for an instructor or a teacher in the Ashram? Isn't it better not to do this work if one feels incapable of doing it well? For then it is the children who suffer because of us, isn't that so?

Whatever imperfections the teachers and instructors here may have, they will always be better than those from outside. For all who work here do so without remuneration and in the service of a higher cause. It is clearly understood that each one, whatever his worth or capacity, can and must progress constantly to realise an ideal which is still much higher than the present realisation of humanity.

But if one is truly eager to do one's best, it is by doing the work that one progresses and learns to do it better and better.

Criticism is seldom useful, it discourages more than it helps.

And all goodwill deserves encouragement, for with patience and endurance, there is no progress which cannot be made.

The main thing is to keep the certitude that whatever may have been accomplished, one can always do better if one wants to.

The ideal to attain is an unflinching *equality* of soul and conduct, a patience that never fails and, of course, the absence of any preference or desire.

It is obvious that for one who teaches, the essential condition for the proper fulfilment of his task is the absence of all egoism; and no human being is exempt from the necessity of this effort.

But, I repeat, this effort is easier to make here than anywhere else.

Blessings.

5 November 1969

Sweet Mother,
Should those who are much attracted by the plea-sures of ordinary life, such as cinemas, restaurants, social life, etc., come to study in our school? For, as a rule, one feels that this is why most of our students go out during the holidays, and every time they come back they need quite a long time to readjust themselves here.

Those who are strongly attached to ordinary life and its agitation should not come here, for they are out of their element and create disorder.

But it is difficult to know this before they come, for most of them are very young, and their character is not yet well formed.

But as soon as they are caught in the frenzy of the world, it would be better, for themselves and for others, that they return to their parents and their habits.

Blessings.

14 November 1969

Sweet Mother,
    There are several children here who are sent by their parents just for their education. The idea that they are only students and that they will go away from here after their studies, is already firmly fixed in their minds.
    Once we know that these children have a clear idea of what they want to do, is it not better to advise them officially to go and study elsewhere? Or, because they have already been accepted, should we allow them to continue their studies and finish them here?

Unfortunately, there are many parents who send their children here not because they think that they will have a special education here but because the Ashram does not ask money for their studies; and consequently parents need to spend much less money here than elsewhere.

But the poor children are not responsible for this transaction, and we must give them a chance to develop fully if they are capable of it. Therefore, we accept them if we see a possibility in them. And it is only when they clearly show that they are incapable of benefiting from their education here that we are ready to let them go if they want to.

Blessings.

15 November 1969

Sweet Mother,
    For the students who know that they will go away from here after their studies, is it not necessary for them to go out from time to time in order to be able to adjust themselves later to ordinary life?

There is no difficulty in adapting to ordinary life, it is a bondage to which one is subjected from birth, for all carry it in themselves by atavism, and even those who are born to be freed need to

360

struggle seriously and continuously to get rid of this atavism in order to be truly free.

Blessings.

16 November 1969

Sweet Mother,
What do you expect of those students who are going to leave after their studies here? Surely there must be a great difference between them and ordinary people. What is the difference?

Often, as soon as they find themselves in the midst of ordinary life, many of them realise the difference and regret what they have lost. Few of them have the courage to give up the comforts they find in their ordinary surroundings, but even the others no longer face life with the same unconsciousness as those who have never been in contact with the Ashram.

The work we do is not done with the expectation of something in return, but simply to help the progress of humanity.

Blessings.

18 November 1969

Sweet Mother,
How far do you consider it the duty of a teacher or an instructor to impose discipline on the students?

To prevent the students from being irregular, rude or negligent is obviously indispensable; unkind and harmful mischief cannot be tolerated.

But as a general and absolute rule, the teachers and especially the physical education instructors must be a constant living example of the qualities demanded from the students; discipline, regularity, good manners, courage, endurance, patience in effort, are taught much more by example than by words. And as an absolute rule: never to do in front of a child what you forbid him to do.

For the rest, each case implies its own solution, and one must act with tact and discernment.

That is why to be a teacher or an instructor is the best of all disciplines, if one knows how to comply with it.

Blessings.

20 November 1969

A child ought to stop being naughty because he learns to be ashamed of being naughty, not because he is afraid of punishment.[1]

In the first case, he makes true progress.

In the second, he falls one step down in human consciousness, for fear is a degradation of consciousness.

21 November 1969

Sweet Mother,

Do the responsibilities of a teacher or an instructor cease after his working hours at school or at the playground?

I am asking this because our children usually behave very badly in the streets. They walk where they like, they talk in the middle of the road, and the most difficult problem is when they ride their bicycles without lights or brakes, or double. None of us take any notice of all that because it is outside our working hours.

And as nothing is being done to put a stop to this, indifference to the law has become so widespread that one even sees responsible people disregarding these laws.

---

[1] Later Mother added: "This is the first step. When he has come so far, he can then make further progress and learn the joy of being good."

The best remedy for this sorry state of affairs would be, when all the children are assembled (probably at the playground), to give them a short lesson on how to behave in the street — what one may do and what one ought not to do. Someone who knows how to speak to them and tell them this in an interesting, and even if possible an amusing way, could no doubt obtain a result.

Blessings.

21 November 1969

Sweet Mother,
   Does this mean that once we have explained properly to the children how to behave in the street, we no longer have any responsibility for what they do outside our working hours?

It is difficult to interfere in an incident one has not witnessed. Gossip is always suspect. But if one of the instructors personally witnesses the bad behaviour of one of his students, then it is appropriate for him to intervene, on condition, of course, that his relation with the student is friendly and affectionate.

Blessings.

22 November 1969

Sweet Mother,
   Don't you think that in our programme of education children should be taught to do some disinterested work for the Ashram, at least once a week?

It is always good to do disinterested work. But it becomes much better if the work becomes an enjoyment and not a boring task.

Blessings.

26 November 1969

363

Sweet Mother,
Every year we give a special prize to the best students
of groups A1 and A2. This year there is a boy who has
worked very well throughout the year, but now he has
gone home for the holidays and hasn't taken part in the
Demonstration of December 2. Do you think he should
still be given the prize for this year?

All depends on how he left: whether it was to obey his parents or
whether he wanted to go himself. If he wanted to leave, whatever
his outer merit, it would perhaps be better not to give him the
prize, because that would mean that we attach no importance
to the inner attitude and to the student's understanding of the
aim we pursue, that is, to prepare the men of tomorrow for the
new creation.
Blessings.

9 December 1969

Sweet Mother,
Is it good to give prizes to the children or reward
them in order to make them work or to create some sort
of interest?

It is obvious that for the children it is better to study in order to
develop their consciousness and learn a little of all they do not
know; but to give prizes to those who have been particularly
studious, disciplined and attentive, is not bad.
Blessings.

17 December 1969

Sweet Mother,
Don't you think that to become a teacher or an in-
structor here, especially for the little ones, it is necessary

364

to have lived in the Ashram for a certain length of time?

It is a certain attitude of consciousness which is necessary — and unfortunately, living even several years in the Ashram does not always lead to this right attitude.

Truly speaking, teachers should be taken *on trial* to see if they can acquire this right attitude and adapt themselves to the needs of their task.

Blessings.

18 December 1969

Sweet Mother,
What do you mean by "a certain attitude of consciousness"?

The attitude of consciousness which is required is an inner certitude that, in comparison with all that is to be known, one knows nothing; and that at every moment one must be ready to learn in order to be able to teach. This is the first indispensable point.

There is a second one. It is that outer life, as we know it, is a more or less illusory appearance and that we must constantly keep a living aspiration for the Truth.

Blessings.

19 December 1969

Sweet Mother,
What is the role of parents or guardians in the Ashram? How should they contribute to a better education of their children?

Here, the first duty of the parents or guardians is not to contradict either by word or example the education that is given to their children.

In a positive way, the best thing they can do is to encourage the children to be docile and disciplined.

Blessings.

24 December 1969

Sweet Mother,
What is Your opinion about fashion, dress and ornaments?
What do You consider to be of good taste in our Ashram life?

Thank God, I have no opinions.

For me good taste means being simple and sincere.

Blessings.

4 January 1970

Sweet Mother,
How are we to teach the children to organise the freedom that You give us here?

Children have everything to learn. This should be their main preoccupation in order to prepare themselves for a useful and productive life.

At the same time, as they grow up, they must discover in themselves the thing or things which interest them most and which they are capable of doing well. There are latent faculties to be developed. There are also faculties to be discovered.

Children must be taught to like to overcome difficulties, and also that this gives a special value to life; when one knows how to do it, it destroys boredom for ever and gives an altogether new interest to life.

We are on earth to progress and we have everything to learn.

14 January 1972

Sweet Mother,
Yesterday You wrote: "There are latent faculties to be developed. There are also faculties to be discovered."
What is the role of the teacher or the instructor in the discovery of these faculties?

The teacher should not be a book that is read aloud, the same for everyone, no matter what his nature and character. The first duty of the teacher is to help the student to know himself and to discover what he is capable of doing.

For that one must observe his games, the activities to which he is drawn naturally and spontaneously and also what he likes to learn, whether his intelligence is awake, the stories he enjoys, the activities which interest him, the human achievements which attract him.

The teacher must find out the category to which each of the children in his care belongs. And if after careful observation he discovers two or three exceptional children who are eager to learn and who love progress, he should help them to make use of their energies for this purpose by giving them the freedom of choice that encourages individual growth.

The old method of the seated class to which the teacher gives the same lesson for all, is certainly economical and easy, but also very ineffective, and so time is wasted for everybody.

15 January 1972

Sweet Mother,
You have written: "If after careful observation, he (the teacher) discovers two or three exceptional children who are eager to learn and who love progress, he should help them to make use of their energies for this purpose by giving them the freedom of choice that encourages individual growth."
Do You mean that freedom of choice should be given

only to exceptional children? What about the others?

I said we should give freedom of choice to exceptional children because for them it is absolutely indispensable if we truly want to help them to develop fully.

Of course this freedom of choice can be given to all the children, and after all it is a good way to find their true nature; but most of them will prove to be lazy and not very interested in studies. But, on the other hand, they may be skilful with their hands and be willing to learn to make things. This too should be encouraged. In this way the children will find their true place in society, and will be prepared to fulfil it when they grow up.

Everyone should be taught the joy of doing well whatever he does, whether it is intellectual, artistic or manual work, and above all, the dignity of all work, whatever it may be, when it is done with care and skill.

16 January 1972

Sweet Mother,
    For the exceptional children, do You think that we should turn their energies towards their special talent or is it better to direct them towards a total development?

It depends entirely on the child and his capacities.

18 January 1972

Sweet Mother,
    Once I asked You whether, in our programme of education, we should teach the children to do some disinterested work for the Ashram, at least once a week. And You answered:
    "It is always good to do disinterested work. But this

368

becomes much better if the work becomes an enjoyment and not a boring task."
Could You suggest how we could introduce this into our programme?

If the children could see the different kinds of work they can do, the inclination to do one thing or another would awaken and it would become as interesting as a game for them — if they are really intelligent.

18 January 1972

Sweet Mother,
When You said that we should observe the games of the children,[2] what age did You have in mind?

It depends entirely on the child. Some are already awake at the age of seven, some take longer.
What is important is to give the children the chance to see and judge for themselves.

Mother, from seven to what age?[3]

One could say about eighteen. It depends on the case. Some children are fully developed at the age of fourteen or fifteen. It is different for each one. It depends on the case.

18 January 1972

Sweet Mother,
You have written: "The teacher must find out the category to which each of the children in his care belongs."

[2] Letter of 15 January 1972.
[3] Oral question and reply.

369

How can we distinguish the categories of children?

By watching them live.

To be able to classify the children one must find out about their nature by observing their habits and reactions.

The teacher must not be a machine for reciting lessons, he must be a psychologist and an observer.

19 January 1972

Sweet Mother,
Should we put the children of each category together?

That has both advantages and disadvantages. The grouping of students should be made according to the resources at our disposal and the facilities we have. The arrangement should be flexible so that it can be improved upon if necessary.

To be a good teacher one must have the insight and knowledge of a Guru with an unfailing patience.

19 January 1972

Sweet Mother,
You have said: "The first duty of the teacher is to help the student to know himself."
How can we help a student to know himself? For that, isn't it necessary for us to have attained a higher level of consciousness ourselves?

Oh, yes indeed![4]

The attitude of the teacher must be one of a constant will to progress, not only in order to know always better what he

---

[4] Oral reply (this sentence only).

wants to teach the students, but above all in order to be a living example to show them what they can become.

(*After five minutes' meditation*) The teacher should be the living example of what he asks the students to become.

19 January 1972

Sweet Mother,
  Is that the only way of teaching the students to know themselves?[5]

It is the only right way. You see, a teacher who tells them, "You must not lie" and yet lies himself; "You must not lose your temper" and loses it himself — what would the result be? The children will not only lose confidence in the teacher but also in what he teaches.

Mother, every day I type out what You write, and P takes it to the School to show it to the other teachers, and they like it very much. And now some teachers are giving me questions to ask You.[6]

(*Laughing*) Good! It is very good!

19 January 1972

Sweet Mother,
  When we attempt to organise the children into categories based on their capacity for initiative, we see that there is a mixture of levels of achievement in various subjects. That makes the work very difficult for certain teachers who are in the habit of taking ordinary classes in the old classical way.

[5] Oral question and reply.
[6] Oral comment and reply.

371

We are here to do difficult things. If we repeat what others do, it is not worth the trouble; there are already many schools in the world.

Men have tried to cure the ignorance of the masses by adopting the easiest methods. But now we have passed that stage and humanity is ready to learn better and more fully. It is up to those who are in the lead to show the way so that others can follow.

21 January 1972

Sweet Mother,
How do You conceive the organisation of our education, to enable the children to discover their capacities and then follow the path of their individual development?

That is what we are trying to do here. It depends on the teacher. I do not have a theory one could put down on paper...[7]

This is what we are trying to do here. But doing it well depends on the teacher, on the trouble he takes, and on his power of psychological understanding. He must be capable of recognising the character and possibilities of the student, so that he can adapt his teaching to the needs of each individual.

22 January 1972

Sweet Mother,
Should the teachers be classified by subject? Is that the best way?

Classification by subject is important when one wants to study one or several subjects in depth, once an overall grounding that is useful for everyone has already been provided equally to all:

---

[7] Oral reply (this paragraph only).

372

for example, reading and writing, speaking at least one language correctly, a little general geography, a general outline of modern science and a few indispensable rules of conduct for group or communal living.

For a detailed and thorough study of one subject the appropriate age depends on the child and his capacity to learn.

The precocious ones can start at the age of twelve. For most it will be more like fifteen and even seventeen or eighteen.

And when one wants to master a particular subject, especially a scientific or philosophical subject, one must be prepared to spend one's whole life learning; one must never stop studying.

22 January 1972

Sweet Mother,
I come back to the same question. What do You mean exactly by "categories of children"?
Do these categories correspond only to their character or also to their interests?

The categories of character.

In assessing the possibilities of a child, ordinary moral notions are not of much use. Natures that are rebellious, undisciplined, obstinate, often conceal qualities that no one has known how to use. Indolent natures may also have a great potential for calm and patience.

It is a whole world to discover and easy solutions are not much use. The teacher must be even more hard-working than the student in order to learn how to discern and make the best possible use of different characters.

23 January 1972

Sweet Mother,
Yesterday You mentioned rules of conduct.

What are the rules of conduct You consider indispensable in our community?

Patience, perseverance, generosity, broad-mindedness, insight, calm and understanding firmness, and control over the ego until it is completely mastered or even abolished.

Mother, this is not exactly what I wanted to ask. What I understand by "rules of conduct" was "manners".

Manners belong to the moral rules of ordinary life and have no value from our point of view.

23 January 1972

Sweet Mother,
You have spoken of arranging students according to categories of character. In our present state of ignorance, if we try to impose a classification, would it not be something very arbitrary and even a dangerous game for the growing child?

Naturally, it is better not to take arbitrary and ignorant decisions. It would be disastrous for the children.
What I have said is for those who are capable of recognising characters and assessing them rightly, otherwise the result would be awful and more harmful than the usual mechanical teaching.

24 January 1972

Sweet Mother,
To be able to do what You have asked of us, isn't it the teacher's first duty to do an intense and sincere yoga instead of acting in a hasty and arbitrary manner?

374

Certainly![8]

What I have written is an ideal to be realised; you must prepare yourselves to be able to do it.

To be able to adopt this method, the teacher must be a discerning psychologist and that requires time and experience.

24 January 1972

Sweet Mother,

You have said that the teacher must be a discerning psychologist, a Guru. You know very well that we are far from being all that. The teachers being what they are, how should the system of education be organised in order to improve our way of teaching?

By doing what they can, knowing that they have everything to learn. In this way they will gain experience and do things better and better. That is the best way to learn, and if they do it in all sincerity, in two or three years they will become experts and will be truly useful.

Naturally, work done in this way becomes really interesting and makes the teachers as well as the students progress.

25 January 1972

Sweet Mother,

Should we also have categories for the teachers as we do for the children — according to their way of teaching, of seeing things, and their affinity for certain subjects?

For that, the teacher who organises the studies must be a discerning psychologist, observant and full of goodwill, knowing that he too has to learn and progress.

[8] Oral reply (this sentence only).

The true attitude is to take life as a field of perpetual study, where one must never stop learning and think that one knows everything there is to know. One can always know more and understand better.

25 January 1972

> *Sweet Mother,*
> *If the children want to do practical work from the age of nine in the field of electronics or technology, should they be encouraged?*

Yes, of course.

25 January 1972

> *Sweet Mother,*
> *In this method of work, the teacher must devote sufficient time to each one individually. But the teachers are few in number. How can we respect the needs of each one as fully as possible and at the same time satisfy all those who ask for help?*

One cannot make a theory. It depends on each case, the possibilities and circumstances. It is an attitude which the teacher must have and apply as well as he can, and better and better if possible.

26 January 1972

> *Sweet Mother,*
> *You said the other day that there were teachers who were not capable, and that they should stop teaching. What is the criterion for assessing the capacity of a teacher?*

376

First, he must understand, he must know what we want to do and understand well how to do it.

Secondly, he must have a power of psychological discernment in dealing with the students, he must understand his students and what they are capable of doing.

Naturally, he must know the subject he is teaching. If he is teaching French, he must know French. If he is teaching English, Geography, Science, he must know what he is teaching.

But the most important thing is that he must have psychological discernment.[9]

31 January 1972

Sweet Mother,
    Nowadays in schools elsewhere, especially in the West, much importance is given to "sex-education".

What is "sex-education"? What do they teach?

For myself, I don't like people to be preoccupied with these things. In my time we were never preoccupied with these things. Now children talk about them all the time — it is in their minds, in their feelings. It is disgusting. It is difficult, very difficult.

But if they talk about it elsewhere, we have to talk about it here too. They should be told the consequences of these things. Especially the girls ought to be told that the consequences can be disastrous. When I was young, in those days, people never spoke about all that, they never paid attention to these things. In those days, people did not talk about all that. Here, I did not want this subject to be discussed. That is why we do physical culture. In that way the energies are used to develop strength, beauty, skill and all that; and one is more capable of control. You will see, the ones who do a lot of physical culture, they are much more capable of mastering their impulses.[10]

---

[9] Oral reply.   [10] Oral reply (the above paragraphs only).

(*After meditation*) The energies that are used in human beings for reproduction and which take such a predominant place in their existence should on the contrary be sublimated and used for progress and higher development, to prepare the advent of the new race. But first the vital and the physical must be freed from all desire, otherwise there is a great risk of disaster.

1 February 1972

Sweet Mother,
What is the essential difference between the behaviour and responsibility of a teacher with regard to young children and with regard to older students (over fourteen or fifteen, for instance)?

Naturally, as the consciousness and intelligence develop in the children, it is more and more through them that we can deal with the children.

3 February 1972

Sweet Mother,
Should one punish a child?

Punish? What do you mean by punish? If a child is noisy in class and prevents the others from working, you must tell him to behave himself; and if he continues, you can send him out of the class. That is not a punishment, it is a natural consequence of his actions. But to punish! To punish! You have no right to punish. Are you the Divine? Who has given you the right to punish? The children too can punish you for your actions. Are you perfect yourselves? Do you know what is good or what is bad? Only the Divine knows. Only the Divine has the right to punish.[11]

---

[11] Oral reply (this paragraph only).

The vibrations that you emit bring you into contact with corresponding vibrations. If you emit harmful and destructive vibrations, quite naturally you draw corresponding vibrations towards yourselves and that is the real punishment, if you want to use that word; but it does not correspond at all to the divine organisation of the world.

Every action has its consequences, good or bad, but the idea of reward and punishment is a purely human idea and does not at all correspond to the way in which the Truth-Consciousness acts. If the Consciousness that rules the world had acted according to human principles of punishment and reward, there would have been no men left on earth for a long time.

When men become pure enough to transmit the divine vibrations without distorting them, then suffering will be abolished from the world. That is the only way.

3 February 1972

Some teachers have written to me that they have read what I wrote for you and that it had done them a lot of good. So you can continue showing them.[12]

This prayer, Mother?

Yes, if you type this out on a piece of paper:
    "We want to be true servitors of the Divine."
And then the prayer:
    "Supreme Lord, Perfect Consciousness, You alone truly know what we are, what we can do, the progress we must make in order to become capable and worthy of serving You as we want to do. Make us conscious of our capacities, but also of our difficulties, so that we may be able to surmount them and serve You faithfully."

---

[12] All the material for this date (14 February) is oral.

379

And then this — the conclusion:
> "The supreme happiness is to be true servitors of the Divine."

There are people whom it helps. Did you show them your notebook?

I don't show this [meditation] notebook to everyone. I type out the questions on education from the other notebook and give them to the school. But I don't show this notebook to everybody.

No, that one is for you. But you can copy things like this which are for everybody. You can show it to all those who have good-will. I have received several letters telling me that it had done them a lot of good. So you can continue.

Yes, Mother, I don't show this notebook to everyone because l thought that You wanted to use it immediately for the Bulletin.

Not all of it. For example, I wouldn't put this in the *Bulletin*.

14 February 1972

Sweet Mother,
> *Concerning the categories You have mentioned for the school, should there also be similar categories for physical education?*

For physical exercises, it all depends on the body and its capacities. Easy exercises that are not tiring can be given to everyone.

Afterwards, it all depends on the body, on its strength, its health, its resistance to fatigue, etc., etc.

Exercises should be given according to capacity and the children should be grouped according to these capacities. It is a matter of experience and observation.

To be a good teacher of physical culture one must know anatomy, the various functions of the body, their development and their functioning.

16 February 1972

Sweet Mother,
Could you write something on discipline for us?

Discipline is indispensable to physical life. The proper functioning of the organs is based on a discipline. It is precisely when an organ or a part of the body does not obey the general discipline of the body that one falls ill.

Discipline is indispensable to progress. It is only when one imposes a rigorous and enlightened discipline on oneself that one can be free from the discipline of others.

The supreme discipline is integral surrender to the Divine and to allow nothing else either in one's feelings or in one's activities. Nothing should ever be omitted from this surrender — that is the supreme and most rigorous discipline.

17 February 1972

Sweet Mother,
Yesterday You wrote on discipline. But what attitude
should we take towards the imposed discipline to which
we must conform in communal life?

Communal life must necessarily have a discipline so that the weaker are not bullied by the stronger; and this discipline must be respected by all those who want to live in that community.

But for the community to be happy, this discipline should be set by the most broad minded person or persons, if possible the person or persons who are conscious of the Divine Presence and are surrendered to it.

For the world to be happy, power should only be in the hands of those who are conscious of the Divine Will. But for the time being that is impossible because the number of those who are *truly* conscious of the Divine Will is very small, and because they necessarily have no ambition.

In fact, when the time comes for this realisation, it will take place quite naturally.

The duty of each one is to prepare himself for it as completely as he can.

18 February 1972

Mother,
    Some people criticise the fact that we have too many rules in our physical education and that we impose too much discipline on the children.

There can be no physical education without discipline. The body itself could not function without a strict discipline. Actually, the failure to recognise this fact is the principal cause of illness.

Digestion, growth, blood-circulation, everything, everything is a discipline. Thought, movement, gestures, everything is a discipline, and if there is no discipline people immediately fall ill.[13]

18 February 1972

Sweet Mother,
    The students, especially the adolescents, often complain that they have to do even the physical exercises that they do not like and do not find interesting. Would you reply to this, Mother?

We are not on earth to follow our own sweet will but to progress.

[13] Oral reply (this paragraph only).

382

Physical exercises are not done for fun or to satisfy one's whims, but as a methodical discipline to develop and strengthen the body.

True wisdom is to take pleasure in everything one does and that is possible if one takes everything one does as a way to progress. Perfection is difficult to attain and there is always a great deal of progress to be made in order to achieve it.

To seek pleasure is certainly the best way to make yourself miserable.

If you truly want peace and happiness, your constant pre-occupation should be:

"What progress must I make to be able to know and serve the Divine?"[14]

Show this to C. She ought not to have listened to what the children say. She has been here a long time. She ought to know that.

That ["To seek pleasure is certainly the best way to make yourself miserable"] is an absolute truth. It affirms that if you want to satisfy your little ego, you are sure to be unhappy. For sure! It is the best way to make yourself miserable. To say: "Oh, it is boring; oh, I must do what I like; oh, that person is unkind to me; oh, life does not bring me what I want." Ouah!!!

"Am I what I ought to be?

"Am I doing what I ought to be doing?

"Am I progressing as much as I should?"

Then it becomes interesting.

"What should I learn in order to make my next progress? What infirmity must I cure? What shortcoming must I overcome? What weakness must I get rid of?"

And then, naturally, the next moment: "How can I become capable of understanding and serving the Divine?"

---

[14] Written question and reply. The comment following is oral.

I have written it down specially so that you can show it to C.

Yes, Mother, she knows, but she wanted to know how to explain to the children.

Yes, that is all there is to say.

19 February 1972

VI

Answers to a Monitor

Answers to a Monitor

Here our activities are so varied that it is difficult to stick to one thing and perfect it. Perhaps that is the reason why we are not able to go beyond a mediocre average. Or is it because of our lack of solid concentration?

The cause of mediocre work is neither the variety nor the number of activities, but lack of the power of concentration.

One must learn to concentrate and do everything with full concentration.

4 July 1961

It really is a problem to know how to create interest in the students, whether in games, athletics or gymnastics. Even our enthusiasm dwindles when we see their lack of interest in everything.

The interest of the students is proportionate to the *true capacity* of the teacher.

12 July 1961

(Regarding a message to the Physical Education Captains) We are very far from what you ask of us, at least I am. It is an arduous task and will take time, a very long time, but what can be done at present? To change our consciousness and become an élite will take a great deal of time. At present, we are on the same level as our students, so the immediate problem is not solved. How can we awaken interest in them for each thing and each day?

It is even more impossible than to change and become an élite.

Therefore, the best thing is to start to work immediately. The rest is simply an excuse that our laziness gives to itself.

15 July 1961

We speak very often of the psychic and the soul, but I understand nothing about them. What are these two things and how can one experience them?

Sri Aurobindo has written a lot on this subject (in his letters) and I too have explained everything in the book on *Education*. One must read, study and *above all practise*.

4 October 1961

I want you to look attentively into yourself and try to explain to me what exactly it is that you enjoy in detective stories.

16 October 1961

I read them as a relaxation. In detective stories (especially Perry Mason), there is always a courtroom scene in which the lawyer Perry Mason seems certain to lose his case, his client is accused of murder, all the proofs are against him, but the master stroke of the lawyer Perry Mason changes the situation. Right through the story there are mysteries and the trial is like the mental gymnastics of a master gymnast. But each time, when I have finished the book, I feel that I have gained nothing, learnt nothing new, that it was a waste of time.

It is not *absolutely* useless. You have doubtless a great deal of *tamas* in your mind and the mental acrobatics of the author shake up this *tamas* a little and awaken the mind. But this cannot last long and soon you must turn to higher things.

16 October 1961

Sweet Mother,
    I have noticed something which applies to all of us:
it is that we take part in as many items as possible in the
2nd December programme.[1] *Is it not better to choose*
one or two items and give a very good demonstration in
these rather than do several in a mediocre way?

Each one does according to his or her nature and if he (or she)
follows courageously and sincerely the law of the nature, he
or she acts according to truth. Thus it is impossible to judge
and decide for others. One can know only for oneself, and
even then one has to be very *sincere* in order not to deceive
oneself.

4 November 1961

Sweet Mother,
    You have often told us that our activities must be an
offering to the Divine. What does it mean exactly, and
how to do it? For instance, when one plays tennis or
basketball, how does one do that as an offering? Mental
formations are not enough, naturally!

It means that what you do should not be done with a personal,
egoistic aim, for success, for glory, for gain, for material profit
or out of vanity, but as a service and an offering, in order to
become more conscious of the divine will and to give oneself
more entirely to it, until one has made enough progress to know
and *feel* that it is the Divine who acts in you, His force that
animates you and His will that supports you — not only a mental
knowledge, but the sincerity of a state of consciousness and the
power of a living experience.

---

[1] The annual demonstration of physical culture.

For that to be possible, all egoistic motives and all egoistic reactions must disappear.

20 November 1961

Sweet Mother,
We have had a discussion with friends concerning the problem and possible methods of physical education. The fundamental problem is this: how to establish a programme which will please everyone and which will be as effective as possible for all members in general? Are tournaments necessary? Should we have no compulsion whatsoever? And if complete freedom is given, will that be practical? etc.... It is a subject to which it is not easy to find a solution which sufficiently satisfies everyone, except when Mother Herself intervenes.

It is impossible. Each has his own taste and his own temperament. One can do nothing without *discipline* — the whole of life is a discipline.

20 September 1962

In a discussion with a friend about our physical education programme and the other innumerable activities we have here, he asked me: "Can you give me a valid example of at least one person who takes part in so many activities and maintains a fairly high standard — one single person in the whole world?"

Do not forget — all of you who are here — that we want to realise something which does not yet exist on the earth; so it is absurd to seek elsewhere an example of what we want to do.

He told me this also: "Mother says that there is all freedom and all facilities for those who are gifted for a particular subject and want to pursue it to the full. But where is this freedom to become, for instance, a great musician, etc.?" Sweet Mother, can you please say a few words on the subject of this freedom?

The freedom of which I speak is the freedom to follow the soul's will and not that of mental and vital whims and fancies.

The freedom of which I speak is an austere truth which tends to surmount all the weaknesses and desires of the lower, ignorant being.

The freedom of which I speak is the freedom to consecrate oneself entirely and without reserve to one's highest, noblest and most divine aspiration.

Who amongst you follows sincerely that path? It is easy to judge, but it is more difficult to understand and still much more difficult to realise.

18 November 1962

Girls are always at a disadvantage: they cannot do what they want, like boys.

Why not?

One has hundreds of proofs to the contrary.

31 May 1963

I have too much "grey matter" in my head which prevents me from thinking clearly and grasping new ideas quickly. How can I free myself from this?

By studying much, by reflecting much, by doing intellectual exercises. For instance, enunciate a general idea clearly and then enunciate the opposite idea, and seek the synthesis of both these ideas, that is to say, find a third idea which harmonises the other two.

25 June 1963

391

Why do you read novels? It is a stupid occupation and a waste of time. It is certainly one of the reasons why your brain lacks clarity and is still in a muddle.

27 June 1963

Sweet Mother,

A few days ago I noticed something very curious in the children of group A2: the boys do not want to work with the girls; they do not even want to remain at their side or together with them. How did this idea of a difference come to these little children who are barely eleven years old! It is strange.

It is atavistic and comes from the subconscient.

This instinct is based both on masculine pride, the foolish idea of superiority, and the still more foolish fear caused by the idea that a woman is a dangerous being who entices you into sin. In children, all this is still subconscious, but it influences their actions.

3 July 1963

Sweet Mother,

You have explained that this separation of girls and boys is atavistic, but it is still necessary to ask You what we, the captains, should do. Personally, I think it is better to close one's eyes to it, but there are others who prefer to give advice or even to scold. I think that by closing one's eyes to it, one minimises the importance of the problem and so this idea of difference between girls and boys will be less striking. What do You think?

One cannot make a general rule, everything depends on the case and the circumstances. Both methods contain good and bad elements, advantages and disadvantages. For the captains, the main thing is to have tact and sufficient inner perception to intervene when necessary or to close one's eyes when it is preferable not to see.

15 July 1963

Would it not be better to have a basic discipline here instead of so much liberty from which we are not capable of profiting?

You say this, but you are one of those who revolt (at least in thought) against the minimum discipline demanded when it is absolutely indispensable, as in the physical education, for example.

21 July 1963

Our teacher X gave us a talk in a serious and significant tone: "Be prepared to go through hard tests, we are on the eve of something very difficult and dangerous." But he did not explain.

It is a pity he did not explain his thought, because I do not know what he is referring to — probably he wanted to caution you against your frivolity, your thoughtlessness, your negligence and your carelessness.

All you young people here have had a very easy life, and instead of taking advantage of it to concentrate your efforts on spiritual progress, you have amused yourselves as much as you could, without creating too much scandal, and so your vigilance has been lulled.

Doubtless X spoke like that in order to re-awaken it.

27 August 1963

I am not properly prepared for the performance of the 1st December, and, moreover, I do not feel at all enthusiastic.

393

When one has decided and accepted to do something, it must be done as well as one can.

Everything can be an occasion to progress in consciousness and self-mastery. And this striving to progress immediately renders the thing, no matter what it is, interesting.

26 September 1963

Sri Aurobindo writes in one of his Aphorisms: "Those who are deficient in the free, full and intelligent observation of a self-imposed law, must be placed in subjection to the will of others."[2] I Mother, I am one of those. Will You take me and discipline me?

My child, it is exactly what I have been trying to do for quite a long time, especially since I have been receiving your notebook and correcting it.

It is with that disciplinary aim that I asked you to write one single sentence each day — it need not have been long, but it ought to have been *without mistakes* — alas!

Up to now, I have never succeeded — your sentences are often long and ambiguous, others are short — but all contain mistakes and often, very often, the *same mistakes* of gender, agreement and conjugation that I have corrected numerous times.

One would think that even if you re-read your notebook when I send it back to you, you do not study it and do not try to profit by it to make progress.

To discipline one's life is not easy, even for those who are strong, severe with themselves, courageous and enduring.

But before trying to discipline one's whole life, one must at least try to discipline *one* activity, and persist until one succeeds.

13 October 1963

---

[2] More Answers from the Mother, Cent. Vol. 17, p. 99.

It seems that a list of books (English classics) was sent to You for Your approval, but that You wish only the works of the Mother and Sri Aurobindo to be read. You have even remarked that to read these old classics is to lower the level of one's consciousness.

Mother, is it only for those who are practising yoga that You advise this or is it for everybody?

First of all, what has been reported is not correct. Secondly, the advice is adapted to each case and cannot be generalised.

12 November 1963

I am very irregular in my studies, I do not know what to do.

Shake off your "tamas" a little, otherwise you will become a blockhead!

27 December 1963

One is often afraid of doing what is new; the body refuses to act in a new way, like trying a new gymnastic figure or another way of diving. From where does this fear come? How can one free oneself of it? And again, how can one encourage others to do the same?

The body is afraid of anything new because its very base is inertia, *tamas*; it is the vital which brings the dominance of *rajas* (activity). That is why, generally, the intrusion of the vital in the form of ambition, emulation and egotism, obliges the body to shake off tamas and make the necessary effort to progress.

Naturally, those in whom the mind predominates can lecture their body and provide it with all the necessary reasons to enable it to overcome its fear.

395

The best way for everybody is self-giving to the Divine and confidence in His infinite Grace.

13 May 1964

While waiting to become ready for a spiritual discipline, what should I do, apart from aspiring that the Mother may pull me out of the slumber and awaken my psychic consciousness?

To develop your intelligence read regularly and very attentively the teachings of Sri Aurobindo. To develop and master your vital, observe attentively your movements and reactions with the will to overcome desires, and aspire to find your psychic being and unite yourself with it. Physically, continue to do as you are doing, develop and control your body methodically, make yourself useful by working in the Playground and in the place you work, and try to do it in as selfless a way as possible.

If you are sincere and scrupulously honest, my help is certainly with you and one day you will become conscious of it.

22 July 1964

There are times when I feel like abandoning all my activities — the Playground, the band, studies, etc., and devote all my time to the work. But my logic does not accept this. From where does this idea come and why?

In this case your logic is right. In the outer nature there is often a tamasic tendency to simplify the conditions of life in order to avoid the effort of organising more complicated circumstances. But when one desires to progress in the integrality of the being, this simplification is not at all advisable.

19 August 1964

*Often, when I read Sri Aurobindo's works or listen to
His words, I am wonderstruck: how can this eternal
truth, this beauty of expression escape people? It is really strange that He is not yet recognised, at least as a
supreme creator, a pure artist, a poet* par excellence! *So
I tell myself that my judgments, my appreciations are influenced by my devotion for the Master — and everyone
is not devoted. I do not think this is true. But then why
are hearts not yet enchanted by His words?*

Who can understand Sri Aurobindo? He is as vast as the universe
and his teaching is infinite...

The only way to come a little close to him is to love him
sincerely and give oneself unreservedly to his work. Thus, each
one does his best and contributes as much as he can to that
transformation of the world which Sri Aurobindo has predicted.

2 December 1964

*Sri Aurobindo has said somewhere that if one surren-
ders to the Divine Grace, it will do everything for us.
Therefore, what value has tapasya?*

If you want to know what Sri Aurobindo has said on a given
subject, you must at least read all that he has written on that
subject. You will then see that he has apparently said the most
contradictory things. But when one has read everything, and
understood a little, one perceives that all the contradictions
complement each other and are organised and unified into an
integral synthesis.

Here is another quotation from Sri Aurobindo which will
show you that your question is based on ignorance. There are
many others which you can read with interest and which will
make your intelligence more supple:

"If there is not a complete surrender, then it is not possible
to adopt the baby cat attitude; it becomes mere tamasic passivity

calling itself surrender. If a complete surrender is not possible in the beginning, it follows that personal effort is necessary."

16 December 1964

How to increase concentration (single-mindedness) and will-force — they are so necessary for doing anything.

Through regular, persevering, obstinate, unflagging exercise — I mean exercise of concentration and will.

7 April 1965

Are mental indifference and lack of curiosity a sort of mental inertia?

Usually they are due to mental inertia, unless one has obtained calm and indifference through a very intense sadhana resulting in a perfect equality for which the good and bad, the pleasant and unpleasant no longer exist. But in that case, mental activity is replaced by an intuitive activity of a much higher kind.

25 May 1966

How can one get out of this mental laziness and inertia?

By wanting to, with persistence and obstinacy. By doing daily a mental exercise of reading, organisation and development.

This must alternate in the course of the day with exercises of mental silence in concentration.

1 June 1966

VII

Conversations

5 April 1967

(*Mother writes a note.*) It is an answer to a question. Do you know what I told the teachers of the school? I have been asked another question. Here is the beginning of my reply:

"The division between 'ordinary life' and 'spiritual life' is an outdated antiquity."

Did you read his question? Read it again to me.

> "We discussed the future. It seemed to me that nearly all the teachers were eager to do something so that the children could become more conscious of why they are here. At that point I said that in my opinion, to speak to the children of spiritual things often has the opposite result, and that these words lose all their value."

"Spiritual things" — what does he mean by spiritual things?

Obviously, if the teachers recite them like a story...

Spiritual things... They are taught history *or* spiritual things, they are taught science *or* spiritual things. That is the stupidity. In history, the Spirit is there; in science, the Spirit is there — the Truth is everywhere. And what is needed is not to teach it in a false way, but to teach it in a true way. They cannot get that into their heads.

> He adds: "I have suggested that it might be better to meet and listen to Mother's voice,[1] for even if we don't understand everything, your voice would accomplish its own inner work, which we are not in a position to evaluate. About this, I would like to know what is the best

[1] Tape-recordings of Mother's classes during the 1950s.

way of bringing the child into relation with you. For all the suggestions, including mine, seemed arbitrary to me and without any real value.

"Mother, wouldn't it be better if the teachers were to concentrate solely on the subjects they are teaching, for you are taking care of the spiritual life?"

I shall give him this reply: There is no "spiritual life"! It is still the old idea, still the old idea of the sage, the sannyasin, the... who represents spiritual life, while all the others represent ordinary life — and it is not true, it is not true, it is not true at all.

If they still need an opposition between two things — for the poor mind doesn't work if you don't give it an opposition — if they need an opposition, let them take the opposition between Truth and Falsehood, it is a little better; I don't say it is perfect, but it is a little better. So, in all things, Falsehood and Truth are mixed everywhere: in the so-called "spiritual life", in sannyasins, in swamis, in those who think they represent the life divine on earth, all that — there also, there is a mixture of Falsehood and Truth.

It would be better not to make any division.

(Silence)

For the children, precisely because they are children, it would be best to instil in them the will to conquer the future, the will to always look ahead and to want to move on as swiftly as they can towards... what will be — but they should not drag with them the burden, the millstone of the whole oppressive weight of the past. It is only when we are very high in consciousness and knowledge that it is good to look behind to find the points where this future begins to show itself. When we can look at the whole picture, when we have a very global vision, it becomes interesting to know that what will be realised later on has already been announced beforehand, in the same way that

Sri Aurobindo said that the divine life will manifest on earth, because it is *already* involved in the depths of Matter; from this standpoint it is interesting to look back or to look down below — not to know what happened, or to know what men have known: that is quite useless.

The children should be told: There are wonderful things to be manifested, prepare yourself to receive them. Then if they want something a little more concrete and easier to understand, you can tell them: Sri Aurobindo came to announce these things; when you are able to read him, you will understand. So this awakens the interest, the desire to learn.

> *I see very clearly the difficulty he is referring to: most people — and in all the things that are written, or in the lectures they give — use inflated speech, without any truth of personal experience, which has no effect, or rather a negative effect. That is what he is referring to.*

Yes, that is why they should do as I have said.

Ah! But not so long ago, most of the teachers were saying, "Oh! But we must do this, because it is done everywhere." (*Smiling*) They have already come a little distance. But there is much more to be covered.

But above all, what is most important is to eliminate these divisions. And every one of them, all of them have it in their minds: the division between leading a spiritual life and leading an ordinary life, having a spiritual consciousness and having an ordinary consciousness — there is only one consciousness.

In most people it is three-quarters asleep and distorted; in many it is still completely distorted. But what is needed, very simply, is not to leap from one consciousness into another, but to open one's consciousness (*upward gesture*) and to fill it with vibrations of Truth, to bring it in harmony with what must be here — there it exists from all eternity — but here, what must be here: the "tomorrow" of the earth. If you weigh yourself down with a whole burden that you have to drag behind you, if you drag behind you everything that you must abandon, you will not be able to advance very fast.

Mind you, to know things from the earth's past can be very interesting and very useful, but it must not be something that binds you or ties you to the past. If it is used as a spring-board, it is all right. But really, it is quite secondary.

(Silence)

It would be interesting to formulate or to elaborate a new method of teaching for children, to take them very young. It is easy when they are very young. We need people — oh! we would need remarkable teachers — who have, first, an ample enough documentation of what is known so as to be able to answer every question, and at the same time, at least the knowledge, if not the experience — the experience would be better — of the true intuitive intellectual attitude, and — naturally the capacity would be still more preferable — at least the knowledge that the true way of knowing is mental silence, an attentive silence turned towards the truer Consciousness, and the capacity to receive what comes from there. The best would be to have this capacity; at least, it should be explained that it is the true thing — a sort of demonstration — and that it works not only from the point of view of what must be learned, of the whole domain of knowledge, but also of the whole domain of what should be done: the capacity to receive the exact indication of *how* to do it; and as you go on, it changes into a very clear perception of what must be done, and a precise indication of when it must be done. At least the children, as soon as they have the capacity to think — it starts at the age of seven, but at about fourteen or fifteen it is very clear — the children should be given little indications at the age of seven, a complete explanation at fourteen, of how to do it, and that it is the only way to be in relation with the deeper truth of things, and that all the rest is a more or less clumsy

404

mental approximation to something that can be known directly.

The conclusion is that the teachers themselves should at least have a sincere beginning of discipline and experience, that it is not a question of accumulating books and retelling them like this. One can't be a teacher in this way; let the outside world be like that if it likes. We are not propagandists, we simply want to show what can be done and try to prove that it *must* be done.

When you take the children very young, it is wonderful. There is so little to do: it is enough to *be*.

Never make a mistake.

Never lose your temper.

Always understand.

And to know and see clearly why there has been this movement, why there has been this impulse, what is the inner constitution of the child, what is the thing to be strengthened and brought forward — this is the only thing to do; and to leave them, to leave them free to blossom; simply to give them the opportunity to see many things, to touch many things, to do as many things as possible. It is great fun. And above all, not to try to impose on them what you think you know.

Never scold them. Always understand, and if the child is ready, explain; if he is not ready for an explanation — if you are ready yourself — replace the false vibration by a true one. But this... this is to demand from the teachers a perfection which they rarely have.

But it would be very interesting to make a programme for the teachers and the true programme of study, from the very bottom — which is so plastic and which receives impressions so deeply. If they were given a few drops of truth when they are very young, they would blossom quite naturally as the being grows. It would be beautiful work.

11 November 1967[1]

So?

A: The reply you gave to B's recent letter[2] has been interpreted in two different ways.

Some lay emphasis on the first sentence which says, "It would be infinitely preferable that the division should disappear immediately," and think that we should try to do away with this division at once, right down to the practical level, by adopting a single organisation for the whole school, that is, either a generalisation of the existing free-progress classes or a compromise.

The others think that we should first clear up the psychological differences and spread the spirit of free progress. On the basis of the second part of your reply, they think that a period of transition is needed for the classes that have followed the traditional pattern so far, and then we would decide what to do.

First of all, before I reply, I would like to know exactly, in a very, very practical and material way, what the difference is.

This is what I think: in the free-progress system, there are no classes with all the students sitting down, with the teacher on his dais lecturing the whole time; there are students sitting down here and there, at their tables. They do the work they want to do and the teacher is simply there, anywhere, either in a room or in a special place; they go to him and ask him questions. This is how I understand it, quite...

---

[1] A conversation with five teachers of the Centre of Education.
[2] See this volume, pages 175-176.

A: *That's exactly how it is, Mother.*

So now, in order to continue the old system, all the students would have to go on sitting in a row, with the teacher sitting on his dais, that is, a completely ridiculous situation. I remember very well when I used to go to the Playground, I was glad when I could sit with everyone around me and we were free.... But a table, a dais, the students tied to... I am speaking very materially, not at all from the psychological point of view; so if that changes, it will already be a great improvement.

Not all the students coming in, like that, almost in a line, and then sitting down, each one in his place, and then the teacher coming and sitting down.... Then, if they are well-mannered, all the students stand up (*laughter*), the teacher sits down and begins his lecture. The students think about anything whatever, all their thoughts wander off in every direction and they pay attention if they feel like it. Well, that is a waste of time, that's all.

That is very, very, very material and practical; it can change at once. The teacher can choose either a corner or a place or a little room — I don't know what, it's all the same to me — any place where the students can come and ask for his guidance, either in the room or in a room nearby. He can busy himself in an interesting way, preparing the answers he will give to his students, not thinking about something else.

That can be done at once, eh?

Now, it is not necessary that they should all call themselves by the same name. That is where...There is, in man, a kind of spirit of — ah! we can give it a polite name — well, a sheep-like spirit.... All the time they need... they need someone to lead them.

The student should come to school not like someone going to his daily grind because he cannot avoid it, but because it would be possible for him to do something interesting. The teacher should not be in school, come to school with the idea that for half an hour or three-quarters of an hour he is going to recite something which he has more or less well prepared and which is boring even for him, and that therefore he cannot amuse the students, but instead to try to come into contact mentally — and if possible more deeply — with a number of little developing individualities who, we hope, have some curiosity about things, and in order to be able to satisfy this curiosity. So he himself must be aware, very modestly, that he does not know enough and that he has a lot to learn; but not to learn from books — by trying to understand life.

So there you have another framework for your work. I don't know...You distribute things to the students....

> A: *Mother, I shall tell you in a minute how we are going to work: there is total freedom...*

Good, good. So now, go on. Your question.

> A: *In any case, in our new way of seeing things, and even for practical reasons, a single monolithic organisation for several hundred students is difficult to imagine, especially if we want to establish the intimate atmosphere that the child needs in order to flourish. When we discussed this problem with C, we thought of forming families, that is, parallel groups of one hundred and eighty to two hundred children at the very maximum, and while the organisation of these groups would certainly be inspired by the same ideal and include all the facilities required for a child's development during the so-called secondary stage, each one would retain a certain originality.*
>
> *These groups would of course still have every possibility of mutual exchange and multiple contacts, perhaps even occasionally certain common activities which could be more and more frequent up to the end of the secondary stage. Then comes another organisation which is adapted to the specialisation of university life.*

While manifesting an overall unity of purpose, we would in this way maintain a living diversity. What do you think about that?

All right. That will do. It is good. That is the principle, isn't it?

A: Yes, Mother.

That is the principle and now, to come down to practice, you have a certain number of rooms and all that... How are you going to...

A: Now, Mother, I shall speak about our classes, that is, about the continuation of what already exists.

All right.

At this point, A gives a long report on the organisation of the free-progress classes.

That is good, that is good. So then what do you want?... It is good. But this can be made general, surely!

A: Mother, we have a few hesitations because, in the traditional classes, there are some children — the older ones, of course — who have not learnt to work in this way. So we thought, according to what you wrote in your last letter, that there would be a period of transition, and if, for example, as you suggested, in three months' time the situation favoured a more rapid evolution, well, we would make the change.

(*To B*) But you, for example, what do you suggest to replace what you used to do?

409

B: In principle, it is the same thing as A has suggested.

Yes.

B: The only difference is that in the afternoon the teachers want to see the students at a fixed time as before.

At a fixed time? The students come to school at a fixed time, don't they?

B: There will be three periods every day in the afternoon.

Three periods?

B: Three periods of forty or fifty minutes. That means that we want to keep what was there before in the afternoon, the same principle.

Three periods? Let me see...

C: Three successive classes, Mother.

The school opens at a fixed time, doesn't it? The students must be there at that time. They can't come at just any time.

A: Yes, Mother.

Because "free progress" does not mean indiscipline....

A: No, no, that is understood.

The student should not arrive half an hour late just because he is free, because this kind of freedom is not freedom, it is simply disorderliness. Each one must have a very strict discipline for himself. But a child is not capable of self-discipline, he must be taught the habit of discipline. So he should get up at the same time, get ready at the same time and go to school at the same time. That is indispensable, otherwise it becomes an impossible muddle.

A: At 7.45, Mother.

All right. So the school officially opens at 8 o'clock.

A: 7.45.

No. The school, the building opens at 7.45.

A: No, no... the classes begin at 7.45.

Ah! They begin at 7.45. And they finish?

A: At 11.30.

11.30. (*To B*) So you say that in the afternoon you want...

B: They will come to school at 1.50.

1.50. And when do they leave?

B: At 4 o'clock.

4 o'clock. At what time do they have to be at the Playground?

A: 4.30, Mother, something like that.

B: 4.30 or 5 o'clock.

A: Sometimes 5 o'clock.

When they go there, they eat, they are given something to eat. That's at 4.30. Well, that's possible...

B: They are given something to eat, Mother, from 3.30 to 4.30.

It is possible, if they are very regular. But I would like to understand. "Three periods" means... the same teacher takes three different groups of students, or do the same students go to three different teachers and the teacher teaches each one separately?

B: No, it is a little different, Sweet Mother.

Make yourself clear. How many students do you have in your class?

B: We have nearly one hundred and fifty.

One hundred and fifty! All right. So your one hundred and fifty come. Then what happens?

B: There, for each student, there will be a fixed class to which he has to go.

One hundred and fifty? One hundred and fifty students in one class! Impossible!

B: Not in one class. We divide them into classes, for French and English, into different standards.

Ah! They are not all at the same standard.

B: From five to ten.[3]

Oh, oh, oh! And so how many teachers does that make for those one hundred and fifty students?

---

[3] The reference is to standards, not to the age of the children.

B: *Thirty teachers, almost thirty teachers.*

Thirty teachers. All right. So what is going to happen? How many classes, how many classrooms do you have?

B: *We shall have nearly fifteen or sixteen classrooms.*

And so what do you teach in the afternoon? Look here, do you teach fixed things or is it still the same kind of work?

A: *Mother, allow me... The remaining difference will be that for us the progress is entirely free, while they want to let the fixed classes go on to a certain extent as before.*

Fixed classes?

A: *That is, a fixed standard, with a fixed number of students, with a fixed teacher...*

Ah! And so it is the teacher's method of teaching that will change, but he will teach a particular subject to particular students...

A: *... who will have to come at that time.*

Yes, yes. That is good. That can do. Only this means that you have to... But what do you teach at that time? Languages?

A: *Essentially languages, yes, Mother.*

Ah! It is only for languages.

A: *It is only for languages.*

I understand. And so how many languages will there be for those one hundred and fifty students?

413

*B: In principle, three: English, French, and their mother
tongue.*

Ah! But that makes a lot! There is Bengali, Gujarati, Hindi, and
then Tamil, Telugu. That makes five already.

B: Sanskrit!

That is not... Everyone should learn that. Especially everyone
who works here should learn that... not the Sanskrit of the
scholars... all, all of them, wherever they may have been born.

*A: In principle, Mother, that is what we are thinking of
— next year, to make all the children do Sanskrit, plus
their mother tongue.*

Yes. Not Sanskrit from the point of view of scholarship, but
Sanskrit, a Sanskrit — how to put it? — that opens the door to
all the languages of India. I think that is indispensable. The ideal
would be, in a few years, to have a rejuvenated Sanskrit as the
representative language of India, that is, a Sanskrit spoken in
such a way that — Sanskrit is behind all the languages of India
and it should be that. This was Sri Aurobindo's idea, when we
spoke about it. Because now English is the language of the whole
country, but that is abnormal. It is very helpful for relations
with the rest of the world, but just as each country has its own
language, there should... And so here, as soon as one begins to
want a national language, everyone starts quarrelling. Each one
wants it to be his own, and that is foolish. But no one could
object to Sanskrit. It is a more ancient language than the others
and it contains the sounds, the root-sounds of many words.

This is something I studied with Sri Aurobindo and it is
obviously very interesting. Some of these roots can even be found
in all the languages of the world — sounds, root-sounds which
are found in all those languages. Well, this, this thing, this is

what ought to be learnt and this is what the national language should be. Every child born in India should know it, just as every child born in France has to know French. He does not speak properly, he does not know it thoroughly, but he has to know French a little; and in all the countries of the world it is the same thing. He has to know the national language. And then, when he learns, he learns as many languages as he likes. At the moment, we are still embroiled in quarrels, and this is a very bad atmosphere in which to build anything. But I hope that a day will come when it will be possible.

So I would like to have a simple Sanskrit taught here, as simple as possible, but not "simplified" — simple by going back to its origin... all these sounds, the sounds that are the roots of the words which were formed afterwards. I don't know whether you have anyone here who could do that. In fact, I don't know whether there is anyone in India who could do it. Sri Aurobindo knew. But someone who knows Sanskrit can.... I don't know. Who do you have to teach Sanskrit? V?

B: V, W.

W? But he is never here.

B: He is coming back in February.

A long time ago there was also X.

B: X... and there are some young teachers, Y and Z.

No, we would need someone who knows it rather well. Once I spoke to V. He told me that he was preparing a simplified grammar — I don't know what he has done — for a language that could be universal throughout the country. I don't know. Perhaps, after all, V is the best.

415

So, in the afternoon, which teachers do you have? You say about thirty.

B: For all the classes, for classes five to...

For the whole school?

A: The secondary stage, Mother.

Below that, it is not your concern?

A: Other groups of teachers deal with that.

Yes, of course. And you have thirty teachers for approximately one hundred and fifty students in the secondary stage. And so what do they know when they come? Nothing? In the kindergarten they are supposed to teach them French, eh? They speak to them in French. But I don't know whether it is strict.

A: Not very strict, Mother.

Not very, eh?

D: It used to be strict before. Now most of the time they speak in Hindi.

When children are very small, very young, they tend to amuse themselves, they have... there is nothing crystallised inside and they find it very amusing to learn the various names that various languages give to the same thing. They still have... or they do not yet have any mental rigidity. They still have this flexibility which makes one aware that a thing exists in itself and that the name that is given to it is simply a convention. And so for them, I think that it is like this, that the name which is given is a convention. And so, many children find it amusing to say such and such a thing, for example "yes" or "no". Take these words, "yes" or "no", the sense of affirmation and negation. In French they say it like this, in German they say it like this, in English they say it like this, in Italian they say it like this, in Hindi they say it like this, in Sanskrit they say... This is a very amusing game. If you knew how to make him play, take an object and then say, "There, you see, this is..." Like that. Or a small living dog, or a small living bird, or a small living tree, and then you tell them, "You see, there are all these languages and..." It is quite blank in there, they can learn this very well, and very easily. It is a very amusing game. (*To B*) But that is not your concern, you are already...

All right. So, naturally, with your thirty teachers and your one hundred and fifty students, you should... They go to the various classes, according to the language they want to learn. That is quite natural, that even seems unavoidable, because it is no use having all the teachers together — they will start chattering... and then the students will come and all that will make a... No! That is good.

When one wants to learn French, one goes to this class, when one wants to learn English, one goes there, when...

C: *It's not like that, Mother.*

Then?

B: *It is like that in the morning.*

And so you, what do you teach?

B: *I teach mathematics.*

That has nothing to do with languages!

417

B: And history.

Do you teach mathematics in French? Yes, but then, there the problem becomes more complicated.... What (*laughter*), what is the matter? (*To B*) What do you have to tell me?

A: (To B who is turning towards him) What should we explain?

B: What we want to do exactly.

C: Do you also have oral classes?

B: Oral classes, not only for languages, also for mathematics and science.

A: Mother, they are continuing the fixed classes which the children have to attend for languages, mathematics and science in the afternoon only, the morning being reserved for free work. In the afternoon they are keeping fixed classes for three subjects, whereas we have nothing...

Languages?

A: Languages, mathematics and science... and history too.

Science?

A: And science too, yes, natural science, physics.

Yes, it's a whole world. Then why?... What is left? Literature? And what else? Besides your science which covers everything, there is literature, and then? Arts? Naturally, this...

A: (To B) Are you keeping fixed classes for all subjects?
(To Mother) Mother, to sum up, we can say that, to
a certain extent, in the afternoon, they are keeping an
organisation which is very similar to what was there
before, that is, fixed classes. But in the morning, the
work is relatively free.

Here, I am curious. How is a language taught? Because a teacher
who starts telling everyone the same thing... They come out of
there and they have understood nothing! A language is precisely the thing that should have the most life, the most life!
And in order for it to have some life, the students have to
participate. They should not be ears listening and sitting on
a bench! Otherwise, they come out of there and they have learnt
nothing.

A: Mother, as far as we are concerned, languages
are organised in the following way: for all the writ-
ten work, there is an individual relationship between
teachers and students. For all the oral work, meet-
ings, etc., we offer the children various possibilities
every day and they are free to attend this one or that
one.

Possibilities?

A: For example, there is discussion, conversation, with
various subjects of conversation — some children would
rather take a scientific subject, for example, than a sub-
ject on current affairs, etc. Or there will also be dramatic
improvisation, etc. All this is announced to the chil-
dren on the preceding day or on the day itself; they
have to go to a class, but they can choose where they
want to go... and everything that concerns composition,
grammar, etc., all that.

419

Yes, because these children already know the language. (*To B*) And you?

A: *For him it is the same thing too.*

(*To A*) Yes, like that, it is all right.

(*To B*) But then your afternoon class... How are you going to go about it? Like that? The children sitting on the bench and the teacher giving a lecture? My God, how boring it is! The teacher feels bored, he is the first one to feel bored, so naturally he passes on his boredom to his students.

There could be an organisation like this: you take a subject and the teacher asks questions here and there, to this one, "There, what do you have to say about this? What do you know about this?" And so on, like that. And then, naturally, if the others are listening, they can benefit. A kind of organisation like that, with some life in it — not a boring lecture where everyone falls asleep after five minutes. You ask questions, or else, if there is a blackboard, on the blackboard you write a large question in large letters so that everyone can read, and you say, "Who can answer?" You do that and then you ask questions, here and there, you question those who have asked.... And so when one of them answers, then you say, "Is there anyone who can add to what this one has said?" The teacher must have some life in him.

I understand that — one class for each language, separate groups — that is understood, in the afternoon. But for heaven's sake, none of that... sitting on a bench and, "When is it going to end?" They look at their watches.... Not one teacher out of a hundred is amusing enough to amuse everyone. And to begin with, he is the first one to feel bored. For him, it is... not here, but outside, it is his livelihood, so...

You should have twenty, thirty students, forty students there.... How many at a time? Twenty? About twenty?

420

B: Yes, Mother.

Just: "Ah! We are going to have some fun. Let's see what we can do to have some fun. What game can we play?" And so, naturally, in this way you find, you invent. And he [the teacher] remains living himself, because he has to find something. And the students are there, like that.... When they have a little self-respect, they want to be able to say something, and that creates a living atmosphere. Wouldn't that be more amusing for you than doing... learning at home? If you are honest, you work in the evening for the class you are going to take the next day, you learn very carefully, you take notes and you write, and... You can prepare a subject, prepare, see, so that you are ready to answer every question. It is not always easy. But to prepare your subject well, that is good; to try to receive a little light and inspiration during the night, and then, on the next day to find a living way of living what you know. And not the students and the teacher... no! A group of living beings, some of whom know a little more than the others, that's all.

A: Mother, now there is one question, another important question. You have often told us that it is only in the inner silence that we can find the true answer to a question. What is the best way to make the children discover how this silence is established? Is this how consciousness is substituted for knowledge?

(*Long silence*)

You see, in this system of classes where everyone is sitting down, the teacher is there and they have a limited time in which to do the work, it is not possible. It is only if you have absolute freedom that you can establish the silence when you need to be silent. But when all the students are in class and the teacher is in class... when the teacher is establishing the silence in himself, all the students... then it is not possible.

He can establish the silence at home, at night, the day before, to prepare himself for the next day, but you cannot... It cannot be an immediate rule. Naturally, when you are at the very top of the scale and you are used to keeping your mind absolutely silent, you cannot help it; but you have not reached that point, none of you. So it is better not to speak about it. So I think that during the... Especially with this system, classes with a fixed time, with a fixed number of students, with a fixed teacher, and a fixed subject... you must be active while you are there.

It must be... If the students want to practise meditation, concentration, to try to come into... it is to come into contact with the intuitive plane, it is — instead of receiving a purely mental reply which is like that — to receive a reply from above which is a little luminous and living. But that habit should be acquired at home.

Naturally, someone who has this habit, in the class — when the teacher asks the question, writes this question on the black-board, "Who can answer?" — he can do this (*Mother puts both hands to her forehead*), receive, oh! and then say... But when we reach that point, it will be a great progress.

Otherwise, they bring out of the storeroom everything they have learnt. It is not very interesting, but at least it gives them some mental gymnastics. And the class system is a democratic system, eh? This is because... you must be able in a limited time, in a limited space... you have to teach the greatest pos-sible number of people, so that everyone can benefit. This is the democratic spirit, absolutely. So this requires, this requires a kind of... equalisation. Well... you put them all on the same level and that is deplorable. But in the present state of the world, we can say, "This is still something necessary." Only the children of the rich would be able to afford... obviously, it is not pleasant to think of. No, there will be a primary class problem for the whole population... for Auroville. And that will be an interesting problem: how can we prepare the children, children taken from anywhere, who have no way of learning at home, whose parents are ignorant, who have no possibility of having any means to learn, nothing, nothing, nothing but the raw material, like that — how can we teach them to live? That will be an interesting problem.

> *A: With what we have done for next year, Mother, we shall achieve total respect for the child's personality, you know. Total, at every moment — he alone will count, not the group to which he belongs. Absolutely. And then, concerning the question I was asking you just now, the working conditions in the morning are rather different, since the work will be free. So, in these conditions, perhaps the children will be able to...*

Yes, there, the morning work, like the work they do there, "Vers la Perfection"[4]... They can very well do that: remain silent, concentrated for a moment, silence all that, everything that is noisy inside, like that, and wait. In the morning, they can do that. No, I mean, when you have an hour's class, or three-quarters of an hour's class with... all together with the teacher... you have to keep yourselves busy. It would be amusing if for three-quarters of an hour everyone could stay... (*laughter*).

One thing could be done once, at least once: you set a subject, like that, from the course of subjects, you set it and tell them, "For a quarter of an hour we shall remain silent, silent; no noise, no one should make any noise. We shall remain silent for a quarter of an hour. For a quarter of an hour try to remain completely silent, still and attentive, and then we shall see in a quarter of an hour what comes out of it." You can reduce it to five minutes to begin with, three minutes, two minutes, it doesn't matter. A quarter of an hour

---

[4] The name given by Mother to a group of classes based on the Free Progress System.

is a lot, but you should do... try that... see. Some of them will start to fidget. Very few children, perhaps, know how to keep still; or else they fall asleep — but it doesn't matter if they fall asleep. You could try that at least once, see what happens: "Let's see! Who will answer my question after ten minutes' silence? And not ten minutes which you will spend trying to get hold of everything you may know mentally about the subject, no, no — ten minutes during which you will be just like this, blank, still, silent, attentive... attentive and silent."

Now, if the teacher is a true teacher, during these ten minutes, he brings down from the domain of intuition the knowledge which he spreads over his class. And so you do some interesting work, and you will see the results. Then the teacher himself will begin to progress a little. You can try. Try, you will see!

A: *We have tried that, Mother.*

You see, for those who are sincere, sincere and very — how to put it? — very straight in their aspiration, there is a marvellous help, there is an absolutely living, active consciousness which is ready to... to respond to any attentive silence. You could do six years' work in six months, but there should... there should not be any pretension, there should not be anything which tries to imitate, there should be no wanting to put on airs. There should... you should be truly, absolutely honest, pure, sincere, conscious that... you exist only by what comes from above. Then... then... then you could advance with giant strides.

But don't do it daily, regularly, at a fixed time, because it becomes a habit and a bore. It should be... unexpected! Suddenly you say, "Ah! Supposing we did this"... when you feel a little like that yourself, a little ready. That would be very interesting.

You ask a question, a question that is as intelligent as you

424

can make it, not a dogmatic question, an academic question, no — a question that has a little life in it. That would be interesting.

(*Silence*)

You will see, the more you strive to realise, you will discover in the nature — the lower nature, that is, the lower mind, the lower vital, the physical — how much pretension, sham and ambition there is.... One can use any... The desire to put on airs: all that must be eliminated, absolutely, radically, and replaced by a sincere flame of aspiration, of aspiration for the purity which makes us live only for what the Supreme Consciousness demands of us, which makes us able to do only what it wants, which makes us do only what it wants, when it wants. Then we can be entirely different.... It is a little far along the path, but we try to do that, always, this purification of the whole being which...

Then there is no more school, teachers, students, boredom; there is... life trying to transform itself. There: that is the ideal, this is where we have to go.

Do you have any more questions to ask me?

A: *Mother, will you please give a message to the children for the first day of school, on December 16th?*

If it comes, I shall give it.

E, give me the flowers. There is a vase with red flowers. There. These are for these two. There.

(*To A*) Here, this is for you.

(*To B*) And this is for you. You — you have a whole future before you. You must break the... You know, you are still bound up in old habits of thought. You have not taken sufficient advantage of the fact that you have lived here all the time, you are still too much like that....

So now, you must take that, break everything, break everything, break everything. Live only by the light that comes from above. Liberate, liberate your consciousness. This is important. It is good that you came. You are still very closed, like that, bound up in all the old habits and... and still, there is still something more, there is still the weight of atavism and all that.... It is the same for everyone, but, well, for the moment it is only... I am still liberating you. You are still like that... like that... like that... like that... your old habits of thought, your old habits of learning, your old habits — not very old — old habits of teaching. So all that: break it! Like that... when you go to class, every day, before you go to class, you should say a kind of prayer, make an invocation to the Supreme Consciousness, and ask it to help you to bring all this mass, this mass of living matter under its influence. Then it will become interesting, living. There you see.

Good-bye.

And now, for D, a rose.

(*To D*) Here. Now this, you see, this is more dynamic. You won't be able to see it, but it is more dynamic.

But women, women are in principle the executive power. You must never forget that. And in order to receive the inspiration, you can take support from a masculine consciousness if you feel the need for it. There is the Supreme Consciousness which is more certain, but still, if you need an intermediary... But for the execution, it is you who have the power to carry it out in all the details, with all the power of organisation. I am instilling this into our women Members of Parliament — you know, there are women in Parliament, and I am teaching them that: do not be submissive to men. It is you who have the power of execution. This will have its effect.

(*To A and B*) Oh! This is not to belittle... (*laughter*) The inspiration comes... the execution is... There.

So I have given to you, I have given to you... (*To E*) You — I haven't given to you. Over there!

Here. And this is for C.

There, my children. Good-bye.

(*To A*) And when you need something, you can always write. I don't say that I shall reply immediately, but like that (*Mother puts her hand to her forehead*), I reply immediately. You must learn that, eh? Like that (*writing*), it takes time. But, well, all the same, it is better to keep me informed.

A: Yes, Mother.

Good-bye.

8 February 1973

A: What is the best way of preparing ourselves, until we can establish a new system?

Naturally, it is to widen and illumine your consciousness — but how to do it? Your own consciousness... to widen and illumine it. And if you could find, each one of you, your psychic and unite with it, all the problems would be solved.

The psychic being is the representative of the Divine in the human being. That's it, you see — the Divine is not something remote and inaccessible. The Divine is in you but you are not fully conscious of it. Rather you have... it acts now as an influence rather than as a Presence. It should be a conscious Presence, you should be able at each moment to ask yourself what is... how... how the Divine sees. It is like that: first how the Divine sees, and then how the Divine wills, and then how the Divine acts. And it is not to go away into inaccessible regions, it is right here. Only, for the moment, all the old habits and the general unconsciousness put a kind of covering which prevents us from seeing and feeling. You must... you must lift, you must lift that up.

In fact, you must become conscious instruments... conscious... conscious of the Divine.

Usually this takes a whole lifetime, or sometimes, for some people it is several lifetimes. Here, in the present conditions, you can do it in a few months. For those who are... who have an ardent aspiration, in a few *months* they can do it.

(*Long silence*)

Did you feel anything?

428

Be completely sincere. Say whether you felt anything, or whether there was no difference for you. Completely sincere. Well? Nobody is answering. (*Mother asks each person in turn and each gives his or her reaction.*)

B: *Sweet Mother, may I ask you whether there was a special descent?*

There is no descent. That is another wrong idea: there is no descent. It is something that is always there but which you do not feel. There is no descent: it is a completely wrong idea.

Do you know what the fourth dimension is? Do you know what it is?

B: *We have heard about it....*

Do you have the experience?

B: *No, Sweet Mother.*

Ah! But in fact that is the best approach of modern science: the fourth dimension. The Divine, for us, is the fourth dimension... within the fourth dimension. It is everywhere, you see, everywhere, always. It does not come and go, it is there, always, everywhere. It is we, our stupidity which prevents us from feeling. There is no need to go away, not at all, not at all, not at all.

To be conscious of your psychic being, you must once be capable of feeling the fourth dimension, otherwise you cannot know what it is.

My God! For seventy years I have known what the fourth dimension is... more than seventy years!

(*Silence*)

Indispensable, indispensable! Life begins with that. Otherwise

429

one is in falsehood, in a muddle and in confusion and in darkness. The mind, mind, mind, mind! Otherwise, to be conscious of your own consciousness, you have to mentalise it. It is dreadful, dreadful! There.

A: *The new life, Mother, is not the continuation of the old, is it? It springs up from within.*

Yes, yes...

A: *There is nothing in common between...*

There is, there is, but you are not conscious of it. But you must, you must... It is the mind which prevents you from feeling it. You must be... You mentalise everything, everything.... What you call consciousness is the thinking of things, that is what you call consciousness: the thinking of things. But it is not that at all, that is not consciousness. The consciousness must be capable of being totally lucid and *without words*.

(Silence)

There, everything becomes luminous and warm... *strong*! And peace, the true peace, which is not inertia and which is not immobility.

A: *And Mother, can this be given as an aim to all the children?*

All... no. They are not all of the same age, even when they are of the same age physically. There are children who... who are at an elementary stage. You should... If you were fully conscious of your psychic, you would know the children who have a developed psychic. There are children in whom the psychic is only embryonic. The age of the psychic is not the same, far from it.

Normally the psychic takes several lives to form itself completely, and it is that which passes from one body to another and that is why we are not conscious of our past lives: it is because we are not conscious of our psychic. But sometimes, there is a moment when the psychic has participated in an event; it has become conscious, and that makes a memory. One sometimes has... one sometimes has a fragmentary recollection, the memory of a circumstance or an event, or of a thought or even an act, like that: this is because the psychic was conscious.

You see how it is, now I am nearing a hundred, it's only five years away now. I started making an effort to become conscious at five years old, my child. This is to let you know.... And I go on, and it goes on. Only... Of course, I have come to the point where I am doing the work for the cells of the body, but still, the work began a long time ago.

This is not to discourage you, but... it is to let you know that it does not happen just like that!

The body... the body is made of a substance which is still very heavy, and it is the substance itself which has to change for the Supermind to be able to manifest.

There you are.

14 February 1973

In connection with a question on the need for continuity in organising the work with young children, Mother made the following remarks:

But there is one thing, one thing which is the main difficulty: it is the parents. When the children live with their parents I consider that it is hopeless, because the parents want their child to be educated as they were themselves, and they want them to get good jobs, to earn money — all the things that are contrary to our aspiration.

The children who are with their parents... really, I don't know what to do. The parents have such a great influence on them that in the end they ask to go away to a school somewhere else.

And that, of all the difficulties — *all* of them — that is the greatest: the influence of the parents. And if we try to counteract that influence the parents will begin to detest us and it will be even worse than before, because they will say unpleasant things about us. There.

That is my experience. In ninety-nine cases out of a hundred the children have taken a bad turn because of the parents.

This seems indispensable to me. We should write a circular letter saying: "Parents who want their children to be educated in the ordinary way and learn in order to get a good job, to earn their living and have brilliant careers, should not send them here." There.

We should... And that is very important.

You see, there are many, many parents who send their children here because it is less expensive than anywhere else. And that is worse than anything, worse than anything. We should... we should... we must absolutely tell them: "If you

432

want your children to be educated in order to have a brilliant career, to earn money, do not send them here." There.

> *A: Mother, we shall write a circular letter and I shall read you the text. We shall write something with B and the others.*

There were some children who were doing very well and were very happy. They went to their parents for the holidays and came back completely changed and spoiled. And then if we tell them that, it will be even worse because their parents will tell them, "Oh, these people are bad, they are turning you against us." So it must be... the parents must know that before they send them.

This has been my experience for so many, so many, so many years, so many years! The danger is not the children, it is not laziness, it is not even that the children are rebellious: the danger, the great danger is the parents.

Those who send their children here should do it knowingly, they should do it because it is unlike anywhere else. And there are many who won't come... And those who come only because it is less expensive, well, they will stop sending them.

When the teacher was about to leave, Mother added:

I would like... I would like the attitude of our school to be made known to people before they send their children, because it is a pity when the children are happy and the parents are not; and that creates situations that are ridiculous and sometimes dangerous. This is very important, very important!

18 February 1973

A: Tonight, I am going to read you a letter from X. She gave us a letter about her class. You know that this year she has started working with the young children.

Oh!

A: So this is what she writes: "We would like to make it possible for each child to develop integrally and above all we want his desire to learn to remain spontaneous." (The letter goes on to describe the games suggested to the children, the material prepared for them and various group activities, and continues:) *"But because all the tendencies of the children come into play when they are given enough free scope, several difficulties arise, especially in controlling the noise and movements they make. A few days ago, they began to make swords and pistols out of meccano."*

Oh!

A (continuing to read the letter): "We have tried giving them a play to act in the hope that it will calm down after a while. But what should we do with this desire for violence, this preference for war — or even detective-stories?"

Do you have something to write with?

A: Yes.

Violence is necessary so long as men are dominated by their ego and its desires.... Is that all right?

434

A: Yes, Mother.

But violence should be used only as a means of self-defence if one is attacked. The ideal towards which humanity is moving and which we want to realise, is a state of luminous understanding in which the needs of each one and of the overall harmony are taken into account.

A: Yes, Mother.

The future will have no need of violence, for it will be ruled by the divine Consciousness in which everything harmonises with and completes everything else.
   Is that enough?

A: Yes. I shall read out what you have just said, Mother.
(A reads out the note.)

Is that all right?

A: Yes, Mother. Quite all right.
   So, in a general way, when these things come up, when the children are engaged in this kind of activity, X was asking: "Should we intervene, or wait until the movement dies down and disappears?"

You should... you should question the children and ask them in an off-hand way, "Oh, you have enemies? Who are these enemies?"... That is what you should say.... You should make them talk a little.... It is because they see that... There is a strength and a beauty in the army which children feel strongly. But that should be preserved. Only, armies should be used not to attack and capture but to defend and...

435

A: Protect.

... and protect. That's it.

First she must understand properly: for the moment, we are in a condition where weapons are still necessary. We have to understand that this is a passing condition, not final, but that we must move towards that.

Peace — peace, harmony — should be the natural result of a change of consciousness.

A: And so, she has a second question, Mother. She says — I remind you that she has children aged eight to ten — she says: "As this is the age when the mental approach is beginning to appear in several children, how can we make use of this mental movement and enrich it without hampering the inner spontaneity?"

That depends so much on the case, and the child!

You see, there is this idea of non-violence about India, which has replaced material violence by moral violence — but that is far worse!

You should make them understand this.... You can say this, explain to the children that to replace physical violence, material violence, by moral violence, is no better.

Lying down in front of a train to prevent it from passing is a moral violence which can create more disturbances than physical violence. You... can you hear me?

But it depends on the child, it depends on the case. You must not give any names, say what this or that person has said. We must make them understand ideas and reactions.

You should... That is a good example: you should make them understand that lying down in front of a train to prevent it from passing is as great a violence... even greater than attacking it with weapons. You understand, there are many, many things that could be said. It depends on the case.

I myself encouraged fencing a great deal because it gives a skill, a control of one's movements and a discipline in violence. At one time I encouraged fencing a great deal, and then too, I learned to shoot. I used to shoot with a pistol, I used to shoot with a rifle because that gives you a steadiness and skill and a sure-sightedness that is excellent, and it obliges you to stay calm in the midst of danger. I don't see why all these things... One must not be hopelessly non-violent — that makes characters that are... soft!

If she sees children... What was it? They were making swords?

A: Yes, Mother, they made swords out of meccano.

She should have taken the opportunity to tell them, "Oh, you should learn fencing!"

And a pistol too?

A: Yes, Mother.

And tell them... teach them to shoot... make it into an *art*, into an art and into a training of calm and self-controlled skill. One should never... never raise a hue and cry.... That will not do at all, at all, at all. I am not at all in favour of that. The methods of self-defence should be mastered, and for that they must be practised.

At this point A mentioned archery as it is practised in Flanders in the North of France, but for lack of a precise explanation, Mother thought that he was referring to toy bows and arrows.

They will start killing birds....

A: But we do not have the facilities here, Mother, for archery, and that is the difficulty.

437

They would start damaging things. I am not very... Of course if there is... But when they have thoroughly grasped that it should be a means of self-defence, not anything else....

No, we would have accidents. I don't think that it is prudent. You can teach them fencing and shooting if they show that they are interested, that is, like that, like what I am writing to X.... If she sees a child doing that, she must not... (*Mother raises her arms as if in horror*). She should tell him, she must know how to explain to him, "It gives you control over your muscles, it obliges you to be strong and calm and self-controlled." On the contrary, it is an opportunity to give them a very good lesson. But you must be able to understand yourself, and above all, above all, make them understand... make them understand that moral violence is just as bad as physical violence. It can even be worse; that is, at least physical violence obliges you to become strong, self-controlled, whereas moral violence... You can be like this (*Mother demonstrates an apparent calm*) and yet have a terrible moral violence.

24 February 1973

A: *For this evening I would like to read you a letter from X, which follows on from what you said the other day in reply to her question: "We have noticed that in some children there is a very strong vital movement which follows the physical gesture. For others, it is just a game. There is even one boy who marches up and down the veranda, announcing that he is going to be a soldier in 'Mother's Army'. Have you any precise indication to give us about these various cases?"*

Marches what?

A: *He marches on the veranda.*

Not on the edge?

A: *No, no. And then he makes an about-turn, he stands to attention, saying, "I am going to be a soldier in Mother's Army."*

That's very good.

A: *Shall I go on, Mother?*

Yes, yes.

A: *"As for moral violence, I do not understand very well which elements in the nature may indicate the possibility of it. Is it, for example, the tendency in a child to sulk, to revolt against everything that checks his fancies, or*

*something else? What must be done to turn this in the
right direction so that it can in the end be transformed?"*

I think that you should not give any importance to these little
movements in the children — that only encourages them. You
must not take any notice, don't look as if you attach any importance to them. That is a much better way of getting rid
of them than by giving them importance. You must not... you
must not pay any attention to all these little movements of
self-importance. Don't look as if you have even noticed — that
removes all their psychological support. If a child sulks, you
don't take any notice. That robs his sulking of all effect. You
understand?

A: Yes, Mother.

You must not give any importance to these little movements in
the children... above all, no importance.

*A: Because if they notice that you attach importance to
them, they are tempted to do it again.*

But of course!
    Children instinctively want to attract attention to them-
selves. Like the boy who pretends to be a soldier on the ter-
race... and things like that. You must not give it any importance,
you must let them be. Don't scold them, above all, don't scold
them... and don't take any notice.
    Children are weak creatures, and so they think that by
making themselves awkward they will attract attention to themselves. They must see that it doesn't work.

A: And we shouldn't scold them, should we?

Oh, especially not that! Above all, don't scold them, don't scold
them. The teacher becomes just as bad as the student. When he

scolds he gives the impression that... he loses his temper. That means that he is on the same level as the student. One must know how to keep smiling... always.

A: *That is very important.*

Very, very, very important.

B reads a paragraph from *The Supramental Manifestation Upon Earth* by Sri Aurobindo:

"The Supermind is in its very essence a truth-conscious-ness, a consciousness always free from the Ignorance which is the foundation of our present natural or evo-lutionary existence and from which nature in us is trying to arrive at self-knowledge and world-knowledge and a right consciousness and the right use of our existence in the universe. The Supermind, because it is a truth-consciousness, has this knowledge inherent in it and this power of true existence; its course is straight and can go direct to its aim, its field is wide and can even be made illimitable. This is because its very nature is knowledge: it has not to acquire knowledge but possesses it in its own right; its steps are not from nescience or ignorance into some im-perfect light, but from truth to greater truth, from right perception to deeper perception, from intuition to intuition, from illumination to utter and boundless luminousness, from growing widenesses to the utter vasts and to very infinitude. On its summits it pos-sesses the divine omniscience and omnipotence, but even in an evolutionary movement of its own graded self-manifestation by which it would eventually re-veal its own highest heights it must be in its very nature essentially free from ignorance and error: it

441

starts from truth and light and moves always in truth and light. As its knowledge is always true, so too its will is always true; it does not fumble in its handling of things or stumble in its paces. In the Supermind feeling and emotion do not depart from their truth, make no slips or mistakes, do not swerve from the right and the real, cannot misuse beauty and delight or twist away from a divine rectitude. In the Supermind sense cannot mislead or deviate into the grossnesses which are here its natural imperfections and the cause of reproach, distrust and misuse by our ignorance. Even an incomplete statement made by the Supermind is a truth leading to a further truth, its incomplete action a step towards completeness. All the life and action and leading of the Supermind is guarded in its very nature from the falsehoods and uncertainties that are our lot; it moves in safety towards its perfection. Once the truth-consciousness was established here on its own sure foundation, the evolution of divine life would be a progress in felicity, a march through light to Ananda."[1]

It is very, very, very important. Very important.

All the people who pretend to manifest the Supramental will be quieted down.

(Silence)

B: *That's all for this evening, Sweet Mother.*

That is good. Where is it going to be published?

---

[1] Some Answers from the Mother, Cent. Vol. 16, pp. 41-42.

B: In a book I am preparing for young people.

Ah! It is so good... and so important.

In Auroville there are people who believe that they are already manifesting the Supramental. And when you tell them that it is not so, they don't believe you. They ought to read that. It should be read by everyone.

A: Mother, recently they asked me whether I would go and speak to them about Sri Aurobindo. I shall take the opportunity to read them this passage.

Oh, very good, very good, very good. You must read it slowly, so that they have time to hear it properly.

26 February 1973

A reads out to Mother a series of questions to be answered by the teachers.

A: And now the last question that we have is: "Mother wrote that there should be no difference in the mind of the child between play and work, especially for young children, for whom the joy of learning should come from interest. How do you think things should be so that there is no difference between play and work? Do you have any suggestions to make?"

The most important thing is the parents and their *school... school... going to school.* We could very well not tell them, "You are going to school... You are coming... Today we shall play such and such a game... today we shall play such and such a game...." And so on, like that. But the parents? Those who are here without their parents are...

A: Privileged.

Oh, highly privileged!

A little later, A asked Mother whether she had any questions to ask the teachers. After a long silence, Mother replied, laughing:

My head is blank.

14 March 1973

B reads a letter to Mother from a teacher who expressed the desire "to get away from this agitation and to leave the school for this year." Then the circumstances that determined this decision were explained to Mother.

As for me, I don't understand anything about all these matters. For me they are... What does A have to say about this?

A: I don't know what to tell you, Mother.

Just tell me: what impression do you have? I have the feeling that a spirit of confusion has entered into the school and is making a... They mean the same thing and they use different terms, and so the terms clash. I know that they have a very similar aspiration, but each one speaks his own language and so the languages are not in harmony and they argue about nothing. There, I think that the best thing to do would be for each one to remain quiet for a while. Tell me your solution.

I too, with the people who are... who are with me, I never used to have any difficulty, and now it is as if we were speaking in a different language.

A: And instead of stressing the things that bring us closer, we lay stress on the points of divergence, so...

Yes, they lay stress on that. But for me, it has a strange effect: it makes me feel as if I am ill. There is nothing wrong with me. I am well and that gives me the feeling of being ill, all the time.

A: It is a vibration of disharmony.

Yes, in truth it is the transition from the ordinary mental

consciousness to the supramental consciousness. The mental consciousness is panic-stricken in the presence of the supramental consciousness. I have the feeling — I shall tell you, this is how it comes to me — that at every moment one could die, the vibration is so different. And so it is only when I am very still... the being, the consciousness... the old consciousness — which is not the mental consciousness at all, but still — the old consciousness goes on repeating its mantra. There is a mantra... it goes on repeating its mantra. And so that is like a background, like a point of contact.... It is strange.... And then beyond that, there is something which is full of light and force, but which is so new that it causes almost a panic. So, you understand, if the same thing... I who am... I have a long experience, eh? So if it causes that in me, if something like that occurs in the others, I have the feeling that we shall all go mad! There, that will do.

Does this correspond to something?

A: Yes, Mother.

So I think that we should keep very quiet so as not to lose the...

A (after a short digression on a new approach to biology): But then, to come back to our situation, couldn't we, for example, by laying stress on the things that bring us closer and by trying to realise as rapidly as possible what you were saying the other day, that is, this fusion of the various elements.... I suppose that if each one were bent on finding out how the various aspects of the work could be integrated, well, they would forget the points of divergence and think only about the things that bring them closer.

Yes, yes, but our language... I was about to tell you, "It's a good idea," but I caught hold of myself by the ear just as I was saying it to myself. It is not an idea, you understand, it is our language which has the... it is like a bell-jar covering it up, a mental bell-jar which it does not want to get rid of. Really, it is *a difficult time*. I think that we ought to be *very* quiet, *very* quiet, *very* quiet. I am going to tell you my old mantra; it keeps the outer being very quiet:

OM NAMO BHAGAVATE.

These three words. For me they meant:

OM — I implore the Supreme Lord.

NAMO — Obeisance to Him.

BHAGAVATE — Make me divine.

This is a translation of it, I mean... Did you hear?

A: Yes, Mother.

For me that has the power to calm everything.

Part Three

Dramas

Towards the Future

A one-act play in prose that can be staged in any country, with small changes in the details of the presentation which local custom may require.

PERSONS OF THE DRAMA

SHE
THE POET
THE CLAIRVOYANT
THE PAINTER
THE SCHOOLFRIEND

Towards the Future

As the curtain rises, She and the Schoolfriend are sitting side by side on the sofa.

SHE
How nice of you to come and see me after such a long time... I thought you had forgotten me.

SCHOOLFRIEND
Certainly not. But I had lost trace of you and did not know where to find you. And now that I have found you, what a surprise! You, married... how strange! I can't believe it.

SHE
I too find it hard to believe.

SCHOOLFRIEND
I understand... I remember how ironically you used to refer to marriage as "a co-operative venture in consumption and pro-duction", and how distasteful you used to find everything that displayed human animality, the beast in man. And how you used to say, "Let us not be mammals..."

SHE
Yes, I have always enjoyed making fun of current ideas and social conventions. But in all fairness you must admit that I have never said anything against true love, the love that comes from a deep affinity and is marked by an identity of views and aspirations. I always dreamt of a great love that would be shared, free from all animal activity, something that could physically represent the great love which is at the origin of the worlds. This dream accounts for my marriage. But the experience has not been a very happy one. I have loved deeply, with great sincerity and

intensity, but my love has not met with the response it hoped for...

SCHOOLFRIEND
My poor friend!

SHE
Oh, I am not telling you this to arouse your pity. I am not to be pitied. My dream is practically unrealisable in the world as it is. Human nature would have to change so much for this to become possible. Besides, my husband and I are very good friends, although that does not prevent us both from feeling very isolated. Esteem and mutual concessions create a harmony that makes life more than merely bearable. But is that happiness?

SCHOOLFRIEND
For many people that might be happiness.

SHE
True, but sometimes I feel such an emptiness in my life! It may have been to fill this emptiness that I gave myself entirely and in all sincerity to that marvellous cause which is so dear to me: to relieve suffering humanity, to awaken it to its capacities and its true goal and ultimate transformation.

SCHOOLFRIEND
I can see that something great, something out of the ordinary rules your life. But as I do not know what it is, it seems rather mysterious to me.

SHE
Of course, I owe you an explanation. I must tell you about it in detail, but that will take some time. Would you like me to come and visit you?

SCHOOLFRIEND

What an excellent idea! Nothing could please me more. When will you come? Would you like to come today?

SHE

Yes, I would be very glad to do so. I always find a deep joy in speaking of the marvellous teaching that guides our life and directs our wills. Just now, I have a few things to arrange so that when my husband returns from his walk he will find everything ready. And as soon as he has started his work, I can go out and I shall come and see you.

SCHOOLFRIEND

Very well, then. Goodbye, I shall see you soon.

(*She accompanies her friend to the door behind the screen. Then She returns to the writing table to arrange some papers and books and writing materials. She places some flowers in a vase on the table and looks around her to see that everything is in order. At that moment a key is heard turning in the lock.*)

SHE

Ah, there he is. (*The Poet enters. She approaches him affectionately.*) Did you have a pleasant walk?

POET (*absent-mindedly*)

Yes, thank you. (*He puts his hat down on a chair.*) I have found an ending for my poem. It came while I was walking. A little activity in the open air really does help the inspiration. Yes, I think this will be good: I end with a song of triumph, a hymn of victory in praise of the evolved man who has discovered, together with the consciousness of his origin, the knowledge of all that he is capable of doing and the power to realise it. I describe him advancing in the happy

455

splendour of union towards the conquest of earthly immortality. It will be beautiful and truly universal, don't you think? It is high time that art should stop being a justification for ugliness and defeat... What a happy day it will be when poetry, painting and music express only beauty, victory and joy, leading the way towards the realisation of the future, towards the advent of a world in which falsehood and suffering, ugliness and death will be no more... But meanwhile, how much misery still for man, how much pain and anguish and bitter solitude... It is terrible! Each one has his burden to bear, come what may, whether he wants it or not. (*He stands deep in thought.*)

SHE (*approaching him affectionately and putting her hand on his arm*)
Come, set to work, you know that is the best cure for sadness. I am going to leave you to your inspiration. I promised my friend that I would go and spend the afternoon with her and tell her something about the marvellous teaching that guides our life. We shall probably read together some of those pages that are so full of profound truth. To meditate on these things is a great joy to both of us. That would upset the ideas of many men, wouldn't it? They are convinced that women cannot do anything except talk about clothes. On the whole, they are not entirely wrong. Most women are terribly frivolous, or at least they seem to be. For very often this lightness on the surface hides a heavy heart and veils an unfulfilled life. Poor creatures! I know so many of them who deserve to be pitied.

POET
You are right. Women really deserve to be pitied. Almost all of them lack the protection they need and are like frail craft with no harbour to shelter them from the storm. For most of them do not receive the education that would teach them to protect themselves.

SHE

That is true. Besides, even in the strongest of women, there is a deep need for affection and protection, for an all-powerful strength that leans over her and enfolds her in comforting sweetness. This is what she seeks in love, and when she has the good fortune to find it, it gives her confidence in life and opens up for her the door to every hope. Without that, life for her is like a barren desert that burns and shrivels up the heart.

POET

Oh, how well you say these things! You say them like one who has experienced them very deeply. I shall make a note of them for my next book, which will deal with the education of women. Well then, I shall start my work.

SHE

That's right; I am going. Goodbye, work well. (*She takes a book and goes out.*)

POET (*sitting down at his desk and seeing everything ready for his work*)

Always the same kind and affectionate attentions. She never fails in her care and her sweetness. When I look at her, it is like seeing a light: her intelligence and kindness shine so brightly around her, spreading to all who are near her, whom she guides towards nobler horizons. I admire her, I feel a deep respect for her... But all that is not love... Love! What a dream! Will it ever become a reality? (*A melody sung by a magnificent voice is heard. The poet jumps to his feet and goes to the open window.*) What a wonderful voice! (*He listens in silence until the melody dies away. Sighing, he is about to return to his table when there is a knock at the door.*) Hello, who's there? (*He opens the door. The Painter enters.*)

POET

It's you! Hello, old friend, what good wind brings you here?

457

PAINTER

I had something to tell you. I met your wife and she told me you were in your "sanctum". So I am here.

POET

You did the right thing... So come into the "sanctum" as you call it, and speak. Don't keep me in suspense. Is it about painting?

PAINTER

No, my painting is going well. But I shall tell you about that another time. It is about music. (*The Poet shows interest.*) Yesterday evening, when visiting some friends, I heard a true singer who, I am told, is your neighbour. (*The Poet makes a gesture of surprise and interest.*) Do you know her?

POET

No, but I often hear her singing from here. She has a superb voice, a voice that stirs all the fibres of my being. The very first time it struck my ears, it sounded familiar to me, like an echo from very ancient times. For nearly six months I have been hearing this voice, which forms a kind of pleasant accompaniment to my work. I have very often wished to become acquainted with the owner of such a beautiful voice.

PAINTER

What a wonderful coincidence! Yesterday evening I was introduced to this young lady and she seems to be very charming indeed. We had a long chat together and in the course of the conversation she expressed her admiration for your poetry, which she seems to read with enthusiasm. She also told me that she is all alone in life, that she has to fend for herself and that sometimes she finds it difficult to pull through, and so on. She dreams of becoming a concert-singer. I immediately thought of you and all your connections. Everyone knows how obliging you are. So I volunteered to speak to you about her and to ask you if you could introduce her to a few well-known musicians or composers. That is why I have come.

POET

You did just the right thing. It will be a great pleasure for me to do something for her. So what did the two of you decide?

PAINTER

It was arranged that, if you agreed, I would go and fetch her immediately — it is not very far — and bring her to you so that you may get to know each other.

POET

Perfect. Go and fetch her. I shall wait for you. (*The Painter goes out.*)

POET (*striding restlessly back and forth*)

How strange, how strange... There is no such thing as chance; everything is the effect of causes that are simply beyond our control. The power of affinity — who knows? I am curious to know whether the singer is as beautiful as her voice. Here they are. (*The door which was only pulled to is pushed open from outside.*) Oh, how pretty she is! (*The Clairvoyant enters, smiling, followed by the Painter.*)

PAINTER

Mademoiselle, may I introduce my friend, the well-known poet whom you admire so much.

POET

I am very happy to meet you, mademoiselle, and to be able to tell you how much I admire your beautiful voice, which you use with such artistry.

CLAIRVOYANT

You are very kind, monsieur, and I thank you. You will excuse me, won't you, for coming with so little ceremony. But we are such near neighbours. I knew you even before I was introduced to you. I noticed that you often came to your window to listen to me singing and even, at first, I was not very pleased when you applauded me. I thought you were making fun of me.

POET
How wrong you were! I simply wanted to express my admiration and to thank you for all the aesthetic pleasure you give me.

PAINTER
Now that I have done my duty, I shall leave you. I have an appointment with my art-dealer. Ah, the blackguard! He wants to make me paint absurdities because, he says, it is the current taste. But I am resisting...

POET
Yes, resist, resist valiantly. Do not encourage this degeneracy of modern taste, this lapse into falsehood which seems to have seeped into the consciousness of all our contemporaries, in every field of human creativity.

PAINTER
Very well, my friend, I go, fired with a new courage, to do battle for the truth. Goodbye.

POET AND CLAIRVOYANT
Goodbye.

POET (*indicating the sofa*)
Please sit down, mademoiselle.

CLAIRVOYANT (*sitting*)
So you are willing to introduce me to a few people and let them hear me?

POET

Certainly. One of our foremost conductors is a friend of mine and with a talent like yours all doors will easily open to you.

CLAIRVOYANT

It will be a great help to me. Thank you so much.

POET

No, no, do not thank me. (*He sits by her side.*) If you knew all the joy you have given me... If you knew what a pleasant accompaniment the harmony of your rich voice has been to my daily work. I owe you many good and happy hours; yes, it is I who should be grateful to you.

CLAIRVOYANT

It is very kind of you to tell me all this. (*She looks around her, then turns to the Poet with a smile.*) It is strange how familiar everything seems to me here, perhaps not so much the objects themselves as the air, the atmosphere which envelops them. Excuse my boldness, but I feel as if I were at home, I feel as if I had been coming here always. And I have the feeling that all sorts of wonderful things are going to happen to me now.

POET

I shall be the first person to be glad of it.

CLAIRVOYANT (*after a short silence*)

I must tell you a strange thing. When I came to settle in this town about six months ago, after my mother's death, in the hope of earning my living, I had a choice of several small apartments, each one with its advantages and inconveniences. The one that I rented here in this house is no better than any other, but I was impelled to take it by a kind of intuition that I would be happy here, that good things were in store for me here... It is strange, isn't it?

461

POET (*thoughtfully*)
Strange, yes, very strange... (*Aside*) Is this affinity? Who knows?
(*To the Clairvoyant*) You know, this is strange too, I have felt
much calmer and more contented since I have been hearing your
voice each day, and I had a very great desire to know you.

CLAIRVOYANT
And I knew you only as a writer whose talent I greatly admired
and whom I hardly dared to hope to meet one day. There are
such extraordinary and mysterious things in life... mysterious
perhaps only because we do not know their causes, otherwise
everything would be very simple and natural. And look, at this
moment, I too feel a sensation of calm and well-being, and it
gives me great strength. If only you knew how much I need
strength and encouragement... Life is hard for a helpless and
unprotected orphan who is forced to earn her living all alone
and who knows nobody to support her in her struggle. But now
that I have met you, I feel that all my difficulties will melt away.

POET
Rest assured that I shall do everything in my power to help you.
It is a duty and a very great pleasure to be of use to an artist and
a woman like you.

CLAIRVOYANT (*taking his hand in a spontaneous move-ment*)
Thank you. I feel as if we have always been sitting like this, side
by side, and that we are friends, old friends... We are friends,
aren't we?

POET (*solemnly*)
Yes, from the depths of our hearts.

CLAIRVOYANT
I feel so much at ease here, that I am forgetting all conventions.
And now to crown my impoliteness, I am overcome by an

imperative need to sleep. I have been sleeping so badly at home for such a long time. I feel uneasy, spied on by invisible enemies who wish me harm. I am unable to achieve the calm which would give me a much-needed rest. Whereas here, I have the feeling that something warm and strong enfolds me like a living cloak and little by little I am being overwhelmed by sleep.

POET (*looking at her tenderly*)
Lie down here, on these cushions. Make yourself comfortable; don't let anything bother you. And above all do not think even for a moment of customs and conventions; they are fetters of no real value which seem to have been forged by man for his own misery.

CLAIRVOYANT
I am in great need of sleep. I have a persistent pain in my head which makes me suffer a great deal. I have worked so hard to achieve a result as quickly as possible and my brain is terribly tired.

POET (*eagerly*)
Will you allow me?... I think I can easily give you some relief. (*He passes his hand several times across her forehead, then lays it on her head for a moment. The Clairvoyant, who is lying on the cushions, falls asleep with an expression of joy and well-being.*)

CLAIRVOYANT (*half asleep*)
It is all right now, there is no more pain... And I feel so happy.

POET (*arranging the cushions so that she may lie comfortably and sitting by her side, holding her hand in his; to himself*)
Poor child, so pretty and yet so lonely.

CLAIRVOYANT (*speaking in her sleep*)
Oh, how beautiful!

POET (*softly*)
What is beautiful?

CLAIRVOYANT (*still asleep*)
There, all around you, that violet light... It is like a living and luminous amethyst. It is all around me too, it is giving me strength. It is a protection, a sure protection... Nothing harmful can come near me now. (*Enraptured*) How beautiful is the violet light around you!

POET
Since you are comfortable, sleep quietly now, without seeing anything.

CLAIRVOYANT (*in a far-away voice*)
I am falling asleep, falling asleep. Oh, what calm, what ease.

POET (*looking at her tenderly*)
Yes, sleep, child — a healing sleep. Life has been hard for you and you have great need of rest. (*After a moment's silence*) What is the use of trying to deceive myself? I have to admit it: just as her voice thrilled my whole being, so too her presence fills me with a calm and profound happiness. And now she has fallen asleep, under my protection, her first conscious sleep. Her very trust gives me a responsibility, a responsibility which would be very sweet to me. But my wife! I know that she is strong and brave, I know that long ago she realised that what I feel for her is nothing more than friendly affection. She herself cannot be satisfied with that; the depths of her love remain untouched. Yet I have responsibilities towards her too. How can I tell her that my whole being is concentrated upon another? And yet I cannot conceal my feelings; falsehood is the only evil. Besides, it would be quite useless: a woman like her cannot be deceived. Oh, life is often so cruel!

CLAIRVOYANT (*still sleeping, turning round and laying her hand on his*)
I am happy... happy... (*She rests her head on the Poet's lap in a movement of childlike confidence.*)

POET
Dear child! What can I do? (*He gazes at her, deep in his thoughts. The Clairvoyant sighs, stretches, and wakes.*)

CLAIRVOYANT (*looking around her with some surprise*)
I have slept... How well I have slept, never in my life have I slept so well.

POET
I am so glad.

CLAIRVOYANT (*looking at him affectionately*)
You see, the light that encircled you and covered me too was at once a nourishment and a protection; it was so beautiful, so comforting. Even now that I am awake I can feel it around me.

POET
Yes, it is still around you. Is this the first time you have seen coloured lights like this?

CLAIRVOYANT
I remember having seen lights or a coloured mist around certain people. But I have never seen any as beautiful as yours or any to which I have felt so close. Often, around others, it is like a turbid, unwholesome fog. What is it?

POET
It would take rather long to give a clear reply. But I shall try to explain it to you as best I can in a few words. Stop me if I bore you. We are made up of different states which can be compared to earth, water, air and fire. Do you follow?

465

CLAIRVOYANT
Yes, it is most interesting.

POET
A less dense state penetrates and flows through a denser one, as water evaporates through a porous vessel, with the difference that no loss follows. In the same way, what is more subtle in us forms a kind of sheath around our bodies and we call this subtle sheath the aura.

CLAIRVOYANT
I understand, it is very clear. So then it can be very useful to see auras in this way?

POET
You are right, it is most useful. You can easily understand that the aura is the exact reflection of what is within us, of our feelings and our thoughts. If the thoughts and feelings are calm and harmonious, the aura too will be calm and harmonious; if the feelings are tumultuous and the thoughts disturbed, the aura will express this tumult and disturbance. It will be like the mist which you say you have seen around certain people.

CLAIRVOYANT
Yes, I understand. So these auras are very revealing.

POET
Yes, for those who see auras, deception can no longer exist. For example, however much a man of bad will may try to look like an angel of light, it will be in vain. His aura will reveal that his thoughts and motives are dark.

CLAIRVOYANT (*admiringly*)
Magnificent! What effects this knowledge might have in the world! But where did you learn such beautiful things? For I do not think that many people are aware of them.

POET

No, especially in modern times, in an age like ours in which success and the material satisfactions it brings are the only things that matter. And yet an ever-growing number of dissatisfied people are trying to find the purpose and goal of life. On the other hand, there are those who know and strive to help suffering humanity; they are guardians of the supreme knowledge which has been handed down from generation to generation and which serves as the basis of a method of self-development whose aim is to awaken man to the consciousness of what he truly is and what he can do.

CLAIRVOYANT

How beautiful this teaching must be! You will reveal it to me little by little, won't you? For we are going to see each other often, aren't we? I wish we never had to part again.... While I was asleep I felt that you were everything for me and that I belong to you for ever. And I felt that from now on your protection will always enfold me. And I who was so full of fear, who felt exposed to so many enemies, I am now quiet, calm, confident, for I can tell all who want to harm me: "I fear you no longer, I am effectively protected, by a protection that will never fail me." I am right, am I not?

POET

Yes, yes, you are right.

CLAIRVOYANT

I am so happy to have met you at last. I have waited for you so long! And you, are you happy?

POET

Yes... Just now, while you were asleep, I felt a calm and a quiet happiness which I had never experienced before. (*Thoughtfully*) Yes, this is the true love, which is a force; it is the union that enables new possibilities to be realised... But...

467

CLAIRVOYANT
But what? Since we are so happy together, what could prevent us...?

POET (*rising suddenly*)
Oh, you do not know! (*He stops short at the sight of She, who has been standing behind the screen for some time already.*) Oh! (*She comes forward smiling and very calm.*)

CLAIRVOYANT (*amazed*)
I did not know that you were married!

SHE (*to the Clairvoyant*)
Do not be upset. (*Turning to the Poet*) Nor you. Yes, I heard the end of your conversation. I returned just as Mademoiselle was waking up. I did not want to disturb you and was about to withdraw, but I thought it would be more useful for all of us if I heard. So I stayed. For I was sure, my dear, that you would find yourself in a cruel predicament. I know your straightforwardness, your loyalty, and I knew that you would be painfully divided between two opposite paths. You know what is said in the teaching which for us is the truth: love is the only legitimate bond of union. The absence of love is enough to invalidate any union. Certainly, there are unions without love, based on esteem and mutual concessions, which can be quite tolerable, but I consider that when love comes, everything else should give way to it. My friend, you remember our pact: we promised each other full freedom the moment love would awaken in either of us. That is why I listened, and now I have come to tell you: you are free, be happy.

POET (*deeply moved*)
But you, you? I know you always live at the summit of your consciousness, in a pure and serene light. But solitude

468

is sometimes hard and the hours can be monotonous and sad.

SHE

Oh, I shall not be alone, for I shall go and join those through whom we have found the path, those who possess the eternal wisdom and who have, from a distance, guided our steps until now. Surely they will shelter me. (*She turns towards the Clairvoyant and takes her by the hand.*) Come, do not be upset. Women who are sensitive and sincere have the right to freely choose the person who will be their protector and guide in life. You have acted according to the natural law and all is well. Our way of looking at things and our behaviour may surprise you; they are new to you and you do not know the reasons for them. (*Pointing to the Poet*) He will explain them to you. I am going away, but before I go let me join your hands. (*She places the hand of the Clairvoyant in the hand of the Poet.*) No blessing can ever be equal to the blessing of love. And yet I shall give you mine, knowing that it will be dear to you. And if you permit, I shall add some advice which is almost a request. Do not allow your union to serve as an excuse for the satisfaction of animal appetites or sensual desires. On the contrary, make it a means of mutual support so that you may transcend yourselves in a constant aspiration and an effort for progress towards the growing perfection of your being. May your association be both noble and generous, noble in quality, generous in action. Be an example to the world and show all men of goodwill the true aim of human life.

CLAIRVOYANT (*deeply moved*)

You can be sure that we shall do our utmost to deserve the trust you have shown us and be worthy of your esteem. But I would like to hear from your own lips that my coming to this house and the event that has followed do not mean an irreparable misfortune to you.

469

SHE

Have no fear. I now know for certain that only one love can satisfy my being: it is the love for the Divine, the divine love, for that alone never fails. Perhaps one day I shall find the favourable conditions and the necessary help for the achievement of the supreme realisation, the transformation and divinisation of the physical being which will change the world into a blessed place full of harmony and light, peace and beauty.

(*The Clairvoyant, more and more deeply moved, remains silent, her hands clasped as if in prayer. The Poet bows respectfully to Her, takes her hand and lays his forehead on it as the curtain falls.*)

The Great Secret

Six Monologues and a Conclusion

by

THE MOTHER

in collaboration with

NOLINI (*The Writer*)
PAVITRA (*The Scientist*)
ANDRÉ (*The Industrialist*)
PRANAB (*The Athlete*)

Letter of the Mother concerning *The Great Secret*

My dear André,

I know that you are a very busy man and that you do not have much time to spare. However, I am going to ask you to do something for me and I hope that it will be possible for you to do it.

The thing is this.

For the first of December I am preparing something which does not fall into any category of dramatic art and which certainly cannot be called a play, but, nevertheless, it will be put on the stage and I hope that it will not be without interest. I am putting words into the mouths of men who have had very different lives and careers, and it would be better, naturally, if they did not all speak the same language; I mean that their styles should differ. I have asked several people to put themselves in the shoes of one character or another, and to write down for me what, according to them, this character would say. If afterwards there is any touching up to do, I shall do it.

I am enclosing the introduction, which will be read out before the curtain rises; it will give you some idea of what I want to do and help you to understand what I mean.

Among the characters, you will see that there is an industrialist, a big businessman. I am not very familiar with industrial terms and language and I thought that you could help me to write something true to life. The man tells the story of his life and I want it to be the life of a big magnate (American or other) on the lines of Ford, for example. I am making them speak one after another; they each have a maximum of ten minutes to relate their lives, their great triumphs which, at this critical hour, leave them unsatisfied and yearning for something which they do not know or understand. At the same time I am sending you the conclusion of the industrialist's speech as I conceive it, but of course you can make any changes you find necessary.

I have asked Pavitra to write the account of the scientist, Nolini is dealing with the man of letters, Pranab has already written what the sportsman will say (in English, but I shall put it into French), I have already outlined the statesman, I am taking care of the artist and of course the Unknown Man, since I shall be speaking through him.

Afterwards we shall still have to decide who the actors will be; Debou will play the Unknown Man, Hriday the sportsman, I am trying to persuade Pavitra to embody the scientist, Manoj will play either the artist or the writer. Naturally, the ideal would be for you to come and speak what you have written — but maybe you will regard that as an unrealisable folly... To tell the truth, this is only a feeler; we shall speak about it again later... I hope I have not left out anything important. But if you want any further details, I shall send them to you.

7 July 1954

The Great Secret

Six Monologues and a Conclusion

Six of the world's most famous men have been brought together, apparently by chance, in a life-boat in which they have taken refuge when the ship that was carrying them to a world conference on human progress sank in mid-ocean.

There is also a seventh man in the boat. He looks young or, rather, ageless. He is dressed in a style belonging to no period or country. He sits at the helm, immobile and silent, but listens attentively to what the others are saying. They treat him as a nobody and take no notice of him.

The persons are:
    The Statesman
    The Writer
    The Scientist
    The Artist
    The Industrialist
    The Athlete
    The Unknown Man

Water is running out, provisions have come to an end. Their physical suffering is becoming intolerable. No hope on the horizon: death is approaching. To take their minds off their present miseries, each one of them in turn tells the story of his life.

The curtain rises.

THE STATESMAN

Since you ask me, I will be the first to tell you what my life has been.

Son of a politician, I was familiar from childhood with government affairs and political issues. All that was freely discussed at the dinners which my parents gave for their friends and which I used to attend from the age of twelve onwards. The opinions of the various political parties were no mystery to me and my enthusiastic young mind would find a simple solution to every difficulty.

Naturally, my studies ran along these lines and I became a brilliant student of Political Science.

Later, when the time came to pass from theory to practice, I had to face the first serious difficulties and I began to understand how virtually impossible it is to put one's ideas into practice. I had to resort to compromises and my great ideal gradually crumbled away.

I also noticed that success does not really correspond to a person's worth, but rather to his capacity to adapt himself to circumstances and to make himself agreeable. For that, one must flatter people's weaknesses rather than attempt to correct their imperfections.

No doubt, all of you know about my brilliant career, so I shall not dwell upon it. But I should like to tell you that as soon as I became Prime Minister and my position gave me some real power, I remembered the humanitarian ambitions of my youth and tried to be guided by them. I tried not to be a "party man". I wanted to find a solution to the great conflict between the various political and social trends that are tearing the world apart and all of which, nevertheless, in my opinion, have their advantages and disadvantages. None of them is perfectly good or wholly bad, and a way should be found to adopt what is good in each one in order to form a harmonious and practicable whole. But I was not able to discover the formula of the synthesis that would reconcile these contraries, not to speak of being able to translate it into action.

Thus, I wished for peace, concord, understanding between nations, collaboration for the good of all, and I was compelled by a force greater than mine to wage war and to triumph by unscrupulous means and uncharitable decisions.

And yet I am considered a great statesman, I am overwhelmed with honours and praise and people call me "a friend of humanity".

But I feel my own weakness and I know that I have lacked the true knowledge and power which would have enabled me to fulfil the beautiful hopes of my childhood.

And now that the end is near, I feel that I have done very little and perhaps even very badly, and I shall cross the threshold of death sad and disillusioned.

THE WRITER

With winged words I sought to capture the beauty and the truth that throb in our mortality. This panorama of creation that lies extended before our eyes — men and creatures, beings and things, scenes and happenings — and the other one equally extended in our feelings and perceptions, in our consciousness, they make a mysterious web, a Daedalus' complex. They cast their spell upon me and I heard their voice calling me to know, understand and seize, a voice sweeter and more compelling than any Aegean siren could command. The ring of that voice I sought to give to my words.

I aimed at uttering the mystery of things, I aimed at making the Sphinx speak out. What lies hidden, what lies sealed, what moves from its secrecy suns and stars and hearts, that I endeavoured to unveil and present in the broad light of day. The labour of things, mundane or supra-mundane, is a dumb and even confused pantomime; I offered speech and consciousness to them. Words appeared to me a most marvellous instrument, the instrument *par excellence*. It has just the consistency to embody and to express, neither so fluid as to be vague, nor so concrete as to be opaque. The word pertains to two worlds at once. It is of the material world and therefore can give a form of matter: and it is sufficiently immaterial to be in contact with subtle things, forces and vibrations, principles and ideas. It can materialise the immaterial, embody the disembodied; and above all, it can give the meaning of things, the precise sense enclosed in a form.

In my lyrics I sought to uncover the yearnings of the heart, in man or in nature, what things cry for, what their tears are for. On a larger canvas, through legends and parables, I portrayed the various facets of life's moods and urges, its rare wisdoms and common foolishnesses, gave a pulsating accent and a meaningful concreteness to episodes that constitute history, the history of man's and nature's consciousness. The tragedies and comedies of life I cast in the dramatic form too, and it is not for me to say how pleased you were to see the ancient form serving magnificently the needs and demands of the modern temperament. I moulded in unforgettable individualities figures and characters of living forces. A wider and still more explicit instrument is the novel which is perhaps more agreeable to the scientific and enquiring spirit of the age. For it is both illustrative and explanatory. I have given you the life history of individuals and social aggregates and I have attempted to give you too something of the life history of humanity taken as a whole, the massive aggregate in its circling, coiling, mounting movements. But I knew and I felt that it is not mere extension, largeness — the wide commonalty — that is enough for the human spirit. It needs uplift. It needs the grand style. So I gave you my epic. It was indeed a whole life's labour. Well, many of you do not and did not understand, more were overawed, but all felt its magic vibration. Yes, it was my desperate attempt to tear open the veil.

I have varied the theme and I have varied the manner. Like a consummate scientist I juggled with my words, I knew how to change their constitution and transmute them as it were,

478

make them carry a new sense, a new tone, a new value. I could command something of the Ciceronian swell, something of the Miltonic amplitude, something of the Racinian suavity; I was not incapable of the simplicity of Wordsworth at his best, nor was even the Shakespearean magic quite unknown to me. The sublimity of Valmiki and the nobility of Vyasa were not peaks too high for me to compass.

And yet I have not achieved. I am not satisfied. I am unhappy. For, after all, these are dreams that I have created, "dreams have I sown in the air". I feel I have not touched the true truth of things nor their soul beauty. I have scratched the mere surface, I have caressed the outer robe that Nature puts on herself; but her very body, her own self has escaped me. I have woven a gossamer around creation's limbs, however seemingly true, however apparently delightful. The means, the instrument itself which I once thought in its nature to be faultless and perfect in its capacity to penetrate and reveal and express and embody, I found in the end failing me. A great silence, a sheer dumbness, I thought at last to be nearer the heart of things.

In this unending flux, in this myriad mutability I stretch my helpless arms and cry out like Faustus, "Where, where shall I capture thee, O infinite Nature?" Another great poet was once likened to "an ineffectual angel beating in vain its luminous wings in the void". Our whole tribe is nothing better.

At the end of my life, I ask, in the ignorance of a child, what does all this mean? To which God shall we bow down and make our offering? What is the vision of the Shekinah like? Wherefore to have lived, wherefore to die? What is the sense of this fleeting appearance upon earth, all this effort and struggle, all this success balanced against so much suffering? The marvellous hopes and the triumphant enthusiasms leading but to abysses of inconscience and ignorance that nothing can fill up? And the inevitable finale of it all: disappearance, dissolution, more mysterious than appearance, that gives the impression of something absurd, a bad joke at once gruesome and useless.

479

THE SCIENTIST

Unlike some of you, I did not set out in life with any intention of improving the condition of my fellow-men. In my case, knowledge rather than action was the main attraction — knowledge in its modern guise: Science. I felt that nothing could be more wonderful than to lift a corner of the veil that screens from us the secrets of Nature, to understand a little more of her hidden springs. I assumed, perhaps unconsciously, the postulate that any increase of knowledge must necessarily result in an increase of power, and that any new mastery over Nature must sooner or later bring about an improvement in man's condition, his moral as well as his material well-being. For me, as for all other thinkers who have their roots in the last century, the century of the foundations of science, ignorance was the primary if not the only evil. It was this that held back mankind in its drive towards perfection. We admitted, without any discussion, the endless perfectibility of the human race. Progress might be rapid or slow, but it was nonetheless sure. Having come so far, we knew that we could go further. For us, to know more was automatically to understand more, to become wiser, more just — in short, to become better.

There is another postulate that we also accepted implicitly: that it is possible for us to know the Universe as it really is, to grasp its laws objectively. This seemed so obvious that it was never questioned. The Universe and I — we both exist, the function of the one being to understand the other. Undoubtedly, I am part of the Universe, but in the process of knowing it, I stand apart from it and view it objectively. I admit that what I call the laws of Nature exist independently of me, of my mind; they exist in themselves and they will be the same for any other mind capable of perceiving them.

I started my work inspired by this ideal of pure knowledge. I chose the science of Physics and more particularly the study of the atom, of radioactivity, the field in which Becquerel and the

Curies had mapped out a royal road. It was the period when natural radioactivity was being superseded by artificial radioactivity, when the dreams of the alchemists were coming true. I worked with the great physicists who discovered uranium fission and I saw the birth of the atom bomb: years of hard, dogged and one-pointed labour. It was at this time that I conceived the idea which was to lead me to my first discovery, the one which enables us today to obtain electric power directly from intra-atomic or nuclear energy. As you all know, this discovery resulted in a radical change in the economic condition of the whole world, because it brought energy at a low cost within the reach of all. If this discovery was so sensational, it was because it freed man from the curse of toil, from the need to earn his bread by the sweat of his brow.

So I realised the dream of my youth — a great discovery — and at the same time I saw its importance for humanity — to which, without especially intending to do so, I had brought this great boon.

I had reason enough to be fully satisfied, but if I was, it was not for long. For soon after — I can tell you this because we are now within an inch of death and my secret will probably be buried with me — soon after this, I say, I discovered the way to free atomic energy not only from uranium, thorium and some other rare metals, but from most of the common metals such as copper and aluminium. But then I was faced with a stupendous problem that strained me almost to breaking-point. Should I make known my discovery? To this day, no one knows this secret except me.

All of you know the story of the atom bomb. You know that it has been succeeded by an infinitely more destructive weapon, the hydrogen bomb. You also know as well as I do that humanity is staggering under the impact of these discoveries, which have placed in its hands an unequalled power of destruction. But if I now revealed my new discovery, if I unveiled my secret, I would place a diabolical power in the hands of just anybody.

481

And without any control or restriction... Uranium and thorium were easily monopolised by the governments, first on account of their relative scarcity, but mostly because of the difficulty of activating them in atomic piles. But you can well imagine what would happen if any criminal or crank or fanatic could in any make-shift laboratory put together a weapon capable of blowing up Paris, London or New York! Would that not be the finishing blow for humanity? I too have reeled under the weight of my discovery. I hesitated a long time and have not yet been able to come to any decision which satisfies both my reason and my heart.

Thus the very first postulate with which I set out as a young scientist in quest of Nature's secrets, has fallen to pieces. Even though an increase in knowledge may bring an added power, it does not follow at all that humanity will be automatically bettered. Scientific progress does not necessarily imply moral progress. Scientific and intellectual knowledge is powerless to change human nature, and yet that has become the pressing need. If human greed and passion remain what they are today, almost the same as they were in the Stone Age, then humanity is doomed. We have reached a point where, unless there is a rapid and radical moral change, mankind will destroy itself with the power it has in its own hands.

Now what has happened to the second postulate of my youth? Can I at least have the joy of pure knowledge, can I be certain that I have grasped something of the hidden mechanism of Nature? Can I hope to enjoy the understanding of the true laws that govern Nature? Alas! I fear that here too my ideal has failed me. We men of science have long ago given up the idea that a theory must be either true or false. We now say only that it is convenient, that it fits the facts and gives a working explanation of them. But as for knowing whether it is true, that is to say, whether it conforms to reality — that is quite another thing. And perhaps the question itself is meaningless. Undoubtedly there are, I should say, certainly there are other theories which explain the same facts just as well and are therefore just as valid. After all, what are these theories? They are nothing but symbols. They are certainly useful, since they enable us to predict; they tell us how things happen, but not the why or wherefore. They do not bring us into touch with reality. One always has the impression of circling around the truth, the reality, of approaching it from different angles, from different points of view, without ever being able to discover it or grasp it; nor does it spring forth and reveal itself.

Then again, on the other hand, we ourselves interfere with all the measurements that we take, expecting them to tell us something about the external universe. By the very fact of measuring we disturb, however slightly, the outer phenomena and thus alter the aspect of the world. And so the knowledge that these measurements give us is not at all sure. All that we can deduce from them is a probable state of the world, not a certainty. For phenomena on our own scale, the uncertainty is negligible, but this is not the case with the infinitely small, the world of the atom. Here, it is an essential incapacity, an obstacle that we can never hope to surmount. It is due to the very nature of things and not to the imperfection of our methods of investigation, so that we shall never succeed in casting away the tinted glasses through which we study the universe. All my measurements, all my theories contain me, the human mind, just as much as they contain the universe. They are subjective as well as objective and perhaps, in fact, they exist only in my mind.

On the shores of the Infinite, I discovered a footprint and I sought to reconstruct the being which had left its mark on the sands. I succeeded at last and found that it was myself. This is where I stand — where we all stand — and I see no way out.

....

But after all, perhaps the fact that I do not have any certitudes about the world, only probabilities, leaves a ray of hope — that the fate of humanity is not finally sealed.

THE ARTIST

Born into a thoroughly respectable bourgeois family where art was considered as a pastime rather than a career and artists as rather unreliable people, prone to debauchery and with a dangerous disregard for money, I felt, perhaps out of contrariness, a compelling need to become a painter. My entire consciousness was centred in my eyes and I could express myself more easily by a sketch than in words. I learnt much better by looking at pictures than by reading books, and what I had once seen — landscapes, faces or drawings — I never forgot.

At the age of thirteen, through much effort, I had almost mastered the techniques of drawing, water colour, pastels and oil painting. Then I had the chance to do some small commissions for friends and acquaintances of my parents, and as soon as I earned some money, my family began to take my vocation seriously. I took advantage of this to pursue my studies as far as I could. When I was old enough to be admitted, I joined the School of Fine Arts and almost immediately started taking part in competitions. I was one of the youngest artists ever to win the Prix de Rome and that gave me the opportunity to make a thorough study of Italian art. Later on, travelling scholarships allowed me to visit Spain, Belgium, Holland, England and other countries too. I did not want to be a man of one period or one school, and I studied the art of all countries, in all forms, oriental as well as occidental.

At the same time I went ahead with my own work, trying to find a new formula. Then came success and fame; I won first prizes in exhibitions, I sat on juries, my paintings were shown in the leading museums of the world and snatched up by the art dealers. It meant wealth, titles, honours; even the word "genius" was used... But I am not satisfied. My conception of genius is quite different. We have to create new forms, with new methods and processes, in order to express a new kind of beauty that is higher and purer, truer and nobler. So long as I still feel bound to human animality, I cannot free myself completely from the forms of material Nature. The aspiration was there, but the knowledge, the vision was lacking.

And now that we are about to die, I feel that I have produced nothing of what I wanted to produce, I have created nothing of what I wanted to create. And in spite of all the fame that has been heaped upon me, I feel that I am a failure.

THE INDUSTRIALIST

Since we are all opening our hearts and, moreover, since what I am going to say cannot be used by my competitors or by those who resent my success — my so-called success — I shall tell you the story of my life as I see it and not as it has been so often related.

The facts themselves have been correctly reported. My father was a blacksmith in a small country town. From him I inherited a liking for metal-work; it was he who taught me the joy of a work well done and the satisfaction of giving oneself entirely to one's task. He also instilled into me the desire to do always better — better than others, better than before. The desire for gain was not his chief motive, but he never denied that he was proud of being at the top of his profession and he enjoyed the praise of his fellow-townsmen without any false modesty.

At the beginning of the century, when the internal combustion engine made its first appearance, we small boys were thrilled by the possibilities it opened up, and to build a horseless carriage, or a motor-car as it was beginning to be called, presented itself as a goal worthy of our greatest efforts. For the few models we had already seen were very far from perfect.

The first car, built with my own hands from parts collected here and there and never intended for the use to which I put them, undoubtedly gave me the greatest joy of my whole life. Perched precariously on a somewhat uncomfortable seat, I drove the few hundred yards from my father's workshop to the Town Hall, and nothing seemed more beautiful to me than this odd contraption, wobbling and puffing its way along, scattering the pedestrians and making the dogs bark and the horses rear.

I shall not dwell on the years that followed, on the hostility of those who proclaimed that the horse had been created by God to draw carriages and that it was already quite impious enough to have made railways without going even further and launching these new diabolical inventions upon the roads and in the cities. Even more numerous were those who could see no future in a temperamental machine that could only be handled by experts or single-minded cranks. The few adventurous souls who lent me my first dollars to set up a small workshop, hire a couple of hands and buy some steel, seemed to have the same blind faith as the first gold-seekers who went out in pursuit of a problematical and elusive fortune in a hostile and desolate country.

As for me, I was not seeking fortune but only the satisfaction of manufacturing a motor-car that would be easier to handle and cheaper than the existing models. I felt somehow that this means of transport should be economical because, after all, its driving power would only have to be fed while it was working. If its purchase price could be made low enough, many people would buy it who would shy at the permanent expense of maintaining a team of horses.

Everybody still remembers my first mass-produced model. It was high on its wheels so that it could run on country roads, it was robustly built to stand up to the rough handling of the crudest farm-hand, but somewhat despised by those who still considered the motor-car a luxury for the wealthy. And yet this model, which could be driven easily, almost effortlessly, already foreshadowed the time when motor-cars would be handled even by the most inexperienced drivers.

Still it was not until the First World War that the motor-car won its first great victory over the horse. Ambulances, ammunition transports, everything that had to move fast, everything that was unusually heavy was "motorised". My factory reached a tremendous pitch of activity. The huge quantities ordered by the Army gave me the opportunity to improve my equipment and perfect new methods of manufacture and assembly.

By the end of the War, I had a smooth-running organisation which, however, seemed out of proportion to civilian needs. My assistants got scared. They urged me to reduce the rate of manufacture, to dismiss some of the employees, to cancel orders placed with suppliers and to wait some time to see where the actual demand would stand. This was wise, no doubt; but here was an opportunity, probably unique, to produce the cheapest car in the world. Slowing down the production would mean an increase in costs. So I decided that the problem lay in selling our output rather than in producing what people were willing to buy from us. Within six months, after a brilliant advertising campaign, I had proved my point.

From then onwards my company moved forward almost by itself. More and more I had to leave important decisions to my assistants and to confine myself to laying down the guiding principles. These were, to produce at the lowest cost without sacrificing quality and without reducing wages — actually, my workers should be the highest paid in the world; to sell at the lowest price in order to go on reaching ever new markets — not only should the profit margin be brought down to a minimum without jeopardising the stability of the company, but the advertising should be handled so as to obtain the required turnover without unduly increasing the cost of production; finally, in case normal suppliers demanded too much profit, to have no hesitation in undertaking the manufacture of our own spare parts, semi-finished products and even raw materials.

My business began to grow as if it were a living thing. Whatever I undertook seemed to become successful. This is how I became almost a legendary figure, a demi-god who had created a new way of life, an example to follow, so much so that any trifling word of mine, any act however insignificant was analysed, turned inside out, made into a great principle and presented to the masses as a new gospel.

Is there anything real in all this? My business survives only by getting bigger. Any check to its growth would be fatal. For the general expenses, which do not lag far behind the increasing production, would soon swallow up the profit margin, which is very narrow in comparison with the overall turnover. My business is growing so rapidly that it now looks more like an inflated balloon than a living body moving harmoniously and steadily towards maturity. For instance, some departments have to drive their workers like galley-slaves in order to keep pace with the rest, and as soon as this is corrected at one point by improving the equipment, it reappears at another. I feel helpless in face of this state of affairs, because any disruption in the production line would only result in more hardship for the workers.

And what have I contributed to humanity? Men travel more easily. Do they understand each other any better? Following my example, all sorts of labour-saving gadgets have been mass-produced and made available to an increasing number of customers. How far has this done anything more than to create new needs and a corresponding greed for gain? My workers are well paid but it seems that I have only succeeded in arousing in them the desire to earn always more — and above all more than workers in other factories. I feel that they are dissatisfied, unhappy in fact. Contrary to my hopes, raising their standard of living, assuring their security, has not induced them to develop their human personality. Indeed, the mass of human suffering remains practically unchanged, as formidable as ever, and, it seems, incurable by the means I have used. There is something fundamentally wrong which my actions fail to correct and which I even fail to understand. I feel that there is a secret yet to be discovered; and without this discovery all our efforts are in vain.

THE ATHLETE

I was born in a family of athletes. Both my parents were very good performers in all sorts of games, sports and physical exercises. The speciality of my mother lay in swimming, diving, archery, fencing and dancing. She was well known for her skill in these events and she also held several local championships.

My father was a wonderful fellow. Whatever he touched turned out a success. In his student days he was a renowned footballer, basketball and tennis player. In boxing and cross-country running he was already the best in our district. Then, later, he entered a circus troupe and became famous in the flying trapeze and in horse-riding displays. But his speciality was in body-building and wrestling. He won a wide reputation for these activities.

Naturally these were ideal conditions to be born in and grow into a healthy, strong and capable state of physical fitness. All the physical qualities that were acquired by my parents by ardent practice of the different athletic exercises were easily passed on to me. Moreover, my athlete parents wanted to see their dream fulfilled in me, — they wanted me to be a great and successful athlete. So they brought me up carefully, devoting to me all their knowledge and experience of attaining health, strength, vigour and vitality; and they would let nothing that would help me to achieve this end escape. From my very birth, they fulfilled all the best conditions of health and hygiene, as regards food, clothing, sleep, cleanliness, good habits and so on, that were materially possible. Afterwards, through well-planned physical exercises, they brought out gradually in my body symmetry, proportion, grace, rhythm and harmony. Then they cultivated in me agility, a daring spirit, alertness, accuracy and co-ordination, and finally I was trained to acquire strength and endurance.

I was sent to a boarding school. Naturally the programme of physical education appealed to me the most. I started taking keen interest in it and in a few years I gradually took my place among the good players and athletes of my school. Then my first success came when I won the inter-school boxing championship. How happy and proud my parents were when they saw their dream on the way to fulfilment! I was very much encouraged by my success, and henceforth put all my determination with earnestness, care and hard effort into mastering the technique and acquiring the skills of all the branches of physical education. I was taught to develop all the different capacities of the body by participating in all the sporting activities. I believed that by an all-round physical training one could be highly successful and be master of more than one or even a few activities. That is why I participated in all the sporting items that opportunity offered me. Year after year, in open championship I regularly won the wrestling, boxing, weight-lifting, body-building, swimming, track and field events, tennis, gymnastics and many other activities also.

Now I was eighteen years old. I wanted to compete in the national games championship. As a believer in all-round development I selected the Decathlon event as my item in the national championship. It is the toughest of all events, — it demands a supreme test of speed, strength, endurance, co-ordination and many other qualities. I got down to training and after six months of hard work I took the championship easily, keeping my second man far behind.

Naturally my success made the national organisers of physical education think of sending me to compete in the world Olympics. I got an offer to represent my country in the world Olympiad which was going to be held within the next two years, in the Decathlon event. It is no joke to compete in the world championship, where the cream of the world's best athletes come together. There was not much time to waste.

So I got down to training under my father's coaching and mother's care. I had to do a lot of hard work. Sometimes the progress seemed impossible and everything seemed so difficult.

But I pushed on in my work day after day, month after month, and then finally came the date of the world Olympic sports.

I should not boast, but I did much better than even I had expected. Not only did I become the world champion in the Decathlon event, but I scored so high as had never been done before, nor has again been repeated. Nobody thought it was possible. But so it happened, and the highest ambition both of myself and my parents was fulfilled.

But something strange happened in me. Though I was on the pinnacle of success and glory, I noticed a kind of sadness, a kind of emptiness was slowly approaching me; — as if somebody was saying within me that something was missing, something had to be found out, something had to be established in me. It seemed to be saying: perhaps there is something more for which my physical skill, capacity and energy may be better utilised. But I had not the slightest idea what it could be. Then slowly this condition passed away. Afterwards I joined many important competitions and did very well in all of them. But I noticed this feeling used to possess me after each success.

My reputation caused a batch of young people to gather round me. They asked me to help them in different activities of physical training, which I gladly did. Then I found that there was a great joy in helping others in my favourite occupation, that is, games, sports and physical exercises. I was also doing well as a coach. Many of my students were showing wonderful results in different events of games, sports and physical activities. Seeing my success as a teacher of physical education and because I liked games and sports so much that I did not want to lose touch with them, I thought of taking up this teaching as my life's work. In order to prepare myself in the theoretical side of it, I took my admission in a famous college of physical education and in four years I got my degree in physical education.

Being a master of both practice and theory in the subject of physical education I got down to work. So long as I was an athlete, my sole purpose had been to gain health, strength, skill, physical beauty and to reach a high perfection in my own body. Now I started helping others in order to make them do the same. I organised teachers' training centres all over my country and trained very good instructors and directors of physical education. With the help of them I opened innumerable centres of physical education in every corner of my country. The object of these centres was to spread the popularity and practice of health, physical education and recreation in a scientific way among the general masses of our country. They did their work very well and after several years the general health of my country was very much improved. They showed good results at home and abroad in games and sports. Soon my country got a very high international reputation in the sporting world. I must admit that I was helped and backed by the government of my country and a special portfolio was given to me as the Minister of Physical Education. That is why I could do so much.

Soon my name spread to every part of the world as a great physical educator and organiser, and I was considered an authority on physical education in the international sphere. I was invited to many countries by the authorities to speak on and introduce my system of physical education to their land. Letters were pouring in from every corner of the earth asking me about my method and seeking my advice on their special problems in the field of Physical Education.

But in the midst of my busy hours often I was feeling that all my energy and skill, all my country-wide organisation and the power that was growing from it, all the strong influence that I had in the international sphere, could be used perhaps for some higher, some nobler and loftier purpose and then only all that I did could have some true meaning. But up to now I could not know what it might be.

Even sometimes I have been called "superman"; but I am not a superman. I am still the slave of nature, a man with all his ignorance, his limitations and incapacities, at the mercy of an accident or illness or one of those human passions that empty you of all your energy. I feel that after all I am not above all these things and that there is something else to learn and to realise.

Now, when I am standing face to face with death, I am not afraid in the least to die. The thought of extreme suffering, hunger and thirst does not disturb me. But I am sorry that I could not solve my problems in my lifetime. I achieved a great success in life, got fame, honour, wealth and everything that a man could dream of. But I am not satisfied because I have no answers to my questions: —

"What is it that I miss so badly in the midst of all? What could be the highest use of my physical perfection and ability? For what purpose could the power of my country-wide organisation and my international influence be best utilised?"

Then the voice of the Unknown Man is heard, calm, gentle, clear, full of a serene authority.

THE UNKNOWN MAN

What you want to know, I can tell you.

All of you have had a similar experience, although your activities are so different in their nature and scope. All six of you have come to a similar conclusion in spite of the success that has crowned your efforts. For you have been living in the surface consciousness, seeing only the appearance of things and unaware of the true reality of the universe.

You represent the élite of mankind, each one of you has achieved in his own sphere the utmost of what man is capable of; you are therefore at the summit of the human race. But from this summit you look down into an abyss and you can go no further. None of you are satisfied but at the same time none of you know what to do. None of you know the solution to the twofold problem presented by life and your own goodwill. I say a twofold problem, for in fact it has two aspects, one individual and the other collective: how can one fully realise one's own good and the good of others? None of you have found the solution, for this riddle of life cannot be solved by mental man, however superior he may be. For that, one must be born into a new and higher consciousness, the Truth-Consciousness. For behind these fleeting appearances there is an eternal reality, behind this unconscious and warring multitude there is a single, serene Consciousness, behind these endless and innumerable falsehoods there is a pure, radiant Truth, behind this obscure and obdurate ignorance there is a sovereign knowledge.

And this Reality is here, very near, at the centre of your being as it is at the centre of the universe. You have only to find it and live it and you will be able to solve all your problems, overcome all your difficulties.

This, you may say, is what the religions preach: most of them have spoken of this Reality, calling it God, but they have supplied no satisfactory solution to your problem, no convincing answer to your questions, and they have totally failed in their attempt to provide a remedy to the ills of suffering humanity.

Some of these religions were based on prophetic revelation, others on a philosophical and spiritual ideal, but very soon the revelation changed to rituals and the philosophical ideal to dogmas, and so the truth they contained vanished. Moreover, and most important, all religions, almost without exception, offer man an almost identical other-worldly solution, based on death, not on life. Their solution amounts to this: bear all your miseries without complaining, for this world is irremediably evil, and you shall be rewarded for your meekness after death; or else: renounce all attachment to life and you shall escape forever from the cruel necessity of living. This certainly cannot provide any remedy to the sufferings of humanity on earth nor to the condition of the world in general. On the contrary, if we want to find a true solution to the confusion, chaos and

494

misery of the world, we have to find it in the world itself. And this is in fact where it is to be found. It exists potentially, we have only to discover it; it is neither mystic nor imaginary; it is altogether concrete and disclosed to us by Nature herself, if we know how to observe her. For the movement of Nature is an ascending one; from one form, one species, she brings forth a new one capable of manifesting something more of the universal consciousness. All goes to show that man is not the last step in terrestrial evolution. The human species will necessarily be succeeded by a new one which will be to man what man is to the animal; the present human consciousness will be replaced by a new consciousness, no longer mental but supramental. And this consciousness will give birth to a higher race, superhuman and divine.

The time has come for this possibility, promised and anticipated for so long, to become a living reality upon earth, and that is why you are all unsatisfied and feel that you have been unable to obtain what you wanted from life. Nothing but a radical change of consciousness can deliver the world from its present obscurity. Indeed, this transformation of the consciousness, this manifestation of a higher and truer consciousness, is not only possible but certain; it is the very aim of our existence, the purpose of life upon earth. First the consciousness must be transformed, then life, then forms; it is in this order that the new creation will unfold. All Nature's activity is in fact a progressive return towards the Supreme Reality which is both the origin and the goal of the universe, in its totality as well as in its smallest element. We must become concretely what we are essentially; we must live integrally the truth, the beauty, the power and the perfection that are hidden in the depths of our being, and then all life will become the expression of the sublime, eternal, divine Joy.

There is a silence as the six men exchange glances, showing their approval. Then:

495

The Writer

Your words have a compelling force, a contagious power. Yes, we feel that a new door has opened before us, a new hope is born in our hearts. But it will take time to realise, a long time perhaps. And now death awaits us, the end is near. Alas, it is too late.

The Unknown Man

No, it is not too late, it is never too late.

Let us unite our wills in a great aspiration; let us pray for an intervention of the Grace. A miracle can always happen. Faith has a sovereign power. And if indeed we are to take part in the great work to be done, then an intervention will come and prolong our lives. Let us pray with the humility of the wise and the candid faith of a child; let us invoke with sincerity this new Consciousness, this new Force, Truth and Beauty which must manifest, so that the earth may be transformed and the supramental life realised in the material world.

They all concentrate in silence. The Unknown Man continues:

"O Supreme Reality, grant that we may live integrally the marvellous secret that is now revealed to us."

They all repeat the prayer softly and remain in silent concentration. Suddenly the Artist cries out:

Look! Look!

A ship appears, like a dot on the horizon, and slowly comes closer. Exclamations. The Unknown Man says:

Our prayer is heard.

When the ship becomes clearly visible, the Athlete jumps up onto the gunwale waving a white handkerchief which he pulls from his pocket. The ship comes nearer. The Scientist exclaims:

They have seen us. They are coming!

And the Unknown Man says slowly:

Here is salvation, here is new life!

Curtain.

The Ascent to Truth

A Drama of Life
in a Prologue, Seven Stages
and an Epilogue

PERSONS OF THE DRAMA

THE PHILANTHROPIST
THE PESSIMIST
THE SCIENTIST
THE ARTIST
THREE STUDENTS
TWO LOVERS
THE ASCETIC
TWO ASPIRANTS

Prologue: In the Artist's studio, preliminary meeting.

Seven stages of the ascent, of which the seventh is at the summit.

Epilogue: The new world.

Prologue

In the Artist's studio

Evening, at night-fall; the end of a meeting held by a small group of people united in a common aspiration to find the Truth.

Present:

The man of goodwill, the philanthropist.
The disillusioned man who no longer believes in the possibility of happiness on earth.
The scientist who seeks to solve the problems of Nature.
The artist who dreams of a more beautiful ideal.
A group of three students (two boys and a girl) who have faith in a better life and in themselves.
Two lovers who are seeking for perfection in human love.
The ascetic who is prepared for any austerity in order to discover the Truth.
Two beings brought together by a common aspiration, and who have chosen the Infinite because they have been chosen by the Infinite.

The curtain rises.

ARTIST
My dear friends, our meeting is drawing to an end and before we close and take the final resolution which will unite us in action, I must ask you once again if you have anything to add to the declarations you have already made.

PHILANTHROPIST

Yes, I would like to state once again that I have devoted my whole life to helping humanity; for many years I have tried all known and possible methods, but none has given me satisfactory results and I am now convinced that I must find the Truth if I want to succeed in my endeavour. Yes, unless one has found the true meaning of life, how can one help men effectively? All the remedies we use are mere palliatives, not cures. Only the consciousness of Truth can save humanity.

PESSIMIST

I have suffered too much in life. I have experienced too many disillusionments, borne too much injustice, seen too much misery. I no longer believe in anything, I no longer expect anything from the world or from men. My last remaining hope is to find the Truth — always supposing that it is possible to find it.

FIRST ASPIRANT

You see us together here because a common aspiration has linked our lives; but we are not bound by any carnal or even emotional ties. One single preoccupation dominates our existence: to find the Truth.

ONE OF THE LOVERS (*indicating the Aspirants*)

Unlike our two friends here, we two (*he puts his arm around his beloved*) live only by each other and for each other. Our sole ambition is to realise a perfect union, to become a single being in two bodies, one thought, one will, one breath in two breasts, one beat in two hearts that live only by their love, in their love, for their love. It is the perfect truth of love that we want to discover and live: to that we have dedicated our lives.

ASCETIC

It does not seem to me that the Truth can be reached so easily. The path that leads to it must be difficult, steep, precipitous, full of dangers and risks, of threats and deceptive illusions. An unshakable will and nerves of steel are needed to overcome all these obstacles. I am ready for every sacrifice, every austerity, every renunciation in order to make myself worthy of the sublime goal I have set before me.

ARTIST (*turning to the others*)
You have nothing more to add? No. So we are all agreed: together, by uniting our efforts, we shall climb this sacred mountain that leads to the Truth. It is a difficult and arduous enterprise, but well worth the attempt, for when one reaches the summit, one can look upon the Truth and all problems must necessarily be solved.

So tomorrow we shall all meet at the foot of the mountain and together we shall begin the ascent. Good-bye.

All withdraw after saying good-bye.

Seven Stages of the Ascent

FIRST STAGE

A kind of green plateau from which one has a view of the whole valley. From this plateau, the path which has been easy and wide so far suddenly narrows and winds round the spurs of the massive and rocky mountain rising to the left.

All arrive together, full of energy and enthusiasm. They look down on the valley below. Then the Philanthropist calls them together with a gesture.

PHILANTHROPIST

Friends, I must speak to you. I have something serious to tell you. (*Silence. All listen attentively.*)

Cheerfully, easily, we have climbed the mountain all together as far as this plateau from which we can look at life and better understand its problems and the cause of human suffering. Our knowledge is becoming vaster and deeper and we are nearer to finding the solution I am seeking... (*Silence*)

But here we come to a decisive turning-point. Now the ascent will become steeper and harder and above all, we are going to cross over to the other side of the mountain where we shall no longer be able to see the valley and men. This means that I shall have to give up my work and betray my pledge to help humanity. Do not ask me to stay with you; I must leave you and return to my duty. (*He starts back on the downward path. The others look at one another in surprise and disappointment.*)

ASCETIC

Poor friend! He has gone back, vanquished by his attachment to his work, by the illusion of the outer world and its appearances.

504

But nothing should slow us down; let us continue on our way, without regret, without hesitation.

They set out once more.

SECOND STAGE

A part of the path where the slope becomes steeper and turns at right angles, so that it is impossible to see where it goes. Below, a long, white, very dense cloud completely isolates it from the world.

They all pass by more or less cheerfully except the Pessimist who comes last, dragging his feet, and sinks down on the bank by the roadside. He holds his head in his hands and sits there without moving. The others notice that he is not following them and look back. One of the Students retraces his steps and touches him on the shoulder.

FIRST STUDENT
Well, well, what's the matter with you? Are you tired?

PESSIMIST (*waving him away*)
No, leave me, leave me alone. I have had enough! It's impossible!

FIRST STUDENT
But why? Come on, take heart!

PESSIMIST
No, no, I tell you I am worn out. It's a stupid and impossible venture. (*Pointing to the cloud beneath their feet.*) Just look at that! We are completely cut off from the world and life. Nothing, nothing is left on which we can base our understanding.

(*He looks back towards the point where the path turns at right angles.*) And there! We can't even see where we are going!

505

It is an absurdity or a delusion — perhaps both! After all, there might not even be any Truth to discover. The world and life are only a dead end — a hell in which we are imprisoned. You can go on if you like, but I won't move, I refuse to be taken in!

He buries his head in his hands once more. The Student, losing all hope of convincing him and not wanting to linger, leaves him to his despair and joins the others. They continue their climb.

THIRD STAGE

The Scientist and the Artist arrive together after the others, as if they had dropped behind while talking. They are nearing the end of their conversation.

SCIENTIST

Yes, as I was telling you, I believe we set out on this adventure a little rashly.

ARTIST

It is true that so far our ascent seems to have been rather fruitless. Of course, we have made some very interesting observations, but these observations have not had much result.

SCIENTIST

Yes, I prefer my own methods — they are much more rational. They are based on constant experimentation and I do not take a step forward until I am sure of the validity of the previous one. Let us call our friends — I think I have something to communicate to them. (*He beckons and calls to the others. They draw near and the Scientist addresses them.*)

My dear friends and fellow-travellers, as we move further and further away from the world and its concrete reality, I have the growing feeling that we are behaving like children. It was revealed to us that if we climbed this precipitous mountain whose summit no one has yet been able to scale, we would reach the Truth — and we set out without even bothering to study the way up. How do we know that we have not taken the wrong path? Where is our assurance that the result will conform to our hopes? It seems to me that we have acted with unpardonable imprudence and that our endeavour is not at all scientific. I have therefore decided, although to my great regret, since my friendly feelings towards you all remain intact, that I must stop here in order to study the problem and if possible to form some certainty about the path to follow, the right path, the one which leads to the goal.

(*After a pause*) Besides, I am convinced that if I can find the secret of the composition of the smallest thing in Nature, for example this humble stone on the path, I shall have found the Truth we are seeking. So I shall stay here and bid you *au revoir* — yes, *au revoir*, I hope; for perhaps you will come back to me and to scientific methods. Or else, if I find what I am looking for, I shall come to you to bring you the good news.

ARTIST

I too am thinking of leaving you. My reasons are not the same as those of our friend the scientist, but they are just as compelling.

During this interesting climb of ours, I have had some experiences: new beauties have been revealed to me; or rather, a new sense of beauty has taken birth in me. At the same time, I have been seized with an ardent and imperious need to express my experience in concrete forms, to cast them in Matter, so that they may serve for the education of all and especially so that the physical world may be illumined by them.

I am going to leave you, then, regretfully, and stay here until I can give form to my new impressions. When I have said all that

I have to say, I shall take up the ascent again and rejoin you, wherever you are, in quest of new discoveries.

Good-bye, and good luck!

All the others look at one another in some dismay. The second Student (the girl) cries out:

SECOND STUDENT

What do we care about these defections! Each one follows his destiny and acts according to his own nature. Nothing can turn us away from our endeavour. Let us continue on our way, courageously, boldly, without weakening.

They all go on except the Scientist and the Artist.

FOURTH STAGE

The two Aspirants and the Ascetic pass by together without stopping and continue their ascent at a firm and steady pace.

Behind them, the two lovers, absorbed in each other, walk hand in hand, taking no notice of the others.

Just behind them the three students arrive, visibly tired. They stop.

FIRST STUDENT

Well, my friends! This is what I call a climb! What a path! It goes up and up without a break — there's no time to catch your breath. I am beginning to feel tired.

SECOND STUDENT

What! You too want to give up? That's not very sporting of you!

FIRST STUDENT
No, no, there's no question of giving up. But why don't we rest a while and sit down for a moment to get our breath back? My legs are hurting me. We shall climb much better after relaxing a little. Have a heart, let's sit down for a moment, only for a moment. Afterwards we shall set out with more enthusiasm. You'll see!

THIRD STUDENT
All right! We don't want to leave you here moping all alone. Besides, I feel rather tired too. Let's sit down together and tell each other what we have seen and learnt.

SECOND STUDENT (*after a moment's hesitation, she too sits down*)
Well, it's only because I don't want to part company with you. But we must not stay here long. It is dangerous to linger on the way.

The Lovers look back and seeing them sitting there, continue on their way.

FIFTH STAGE

Much higher up. The path is narrower and overlooks a wide horizon. The valley is still hidden from sight by dense white clouds. To the left, just off the path, stands a small house facing the sky. The first three pass on without stopping. Then the Lovers arrive arm in arm, absorbed in their mutual dream.

GIRL (*noticing that they are alone*)
Look, no one is left... We are alone.

509

What do the others matter! We don't need them — aren't we perfectly happy together?

BOY (*seeing the house on the roadside*)
Look, darling, look at that little house on the hillside, isolated and yet so welcoming, so intimate and yet opening onto infinite space. What more do we need? An ideal place to shelter our union. For we have realised, we two, a perfect, total union, without shadow or cloud. Let us leave the others to their climb towards a problematic Truth — we have found our own, our own truth. That is enough for us.

GIRL
Yes, my love. Let us settle in this house and enjoy our love without a care for anything else.

Still arm in arm, they leave the path and go towards the house.

SIXTH STAGE

The end of the path has become extremely narrow and stops abruptly at the foot of a huge rock whose sheer wall rises towards the sky so that the summit is out of sight. To the left, there is a kind of small plateau at the far end of which a small low hut is visible. The whole scene looks bare and deserted.
The last three climbers arrive together. But the Ascetic stops and halts the others with a gesture.

ASCETIC
I have something important to communicate to you. Will you kindly listen to me, both of you? In the course of our ascent I have discovered my true being, my true Self. I have become one

510

with the Eternal and nothing else exists for me, nothing else is necessary. All that is not That is illusory, worthless. So I consider that I have reached the end of the path. (*He gestures towards the plateau on the left.*) And here is a sublime and solitary spot, a place that is truly favourable to the life I shall lead from now on. I shall live here in perfect contemplation, far from earth and men, free at last from the need to live.

Without another word, without a gesture of farewell, without looking back, he goes straight towards the realisation of his personal goal.

Left to themselves, the two Aspirants look at each other, moved by the greatness of his gesture. But they recover themselves immediately and the girl cries out:

SECOND ASPIRANT

No! That cannot be the Truth, the whole Truth. The universal creation cannot be merely an illusion from which one has to escape. Besides, we have not yet reached the summit of the mountain, we have not yet completed our ascent.

FIRST ASPIRANT (*indicating the end of the path stopping short at the wall of rock that rises almost vertically*)

But here the pathway stops. It seems that no human being has ever gone any further. To climb this sheer rock that rises before us and seems to be inaccessible, we must discover for ourselves the way to go on step by step, by our own efforts, with no other guide or help than our will and our faith. No doubt we shall have to hew our own path.

SECOND ASPIRANT (*eagerly*)

Never mind! Let us go on, ever onwards. We still have something left to find: the creation has a meaning that we have yet to discover.

511

They set out once more.

SEVENTH STAGE

The Summit

The two Aspirants who have valiantly withstood every test, haul themselves up with a supreme effort to the summit, bathed in brilliant light. Everything is light except the little patch of rock on which they stand and which is hardly big enough for their feet.

FIRST ASPIRANT
The summit at last! The shining, dazzling Truth, nothing but the Truth!

SECOND ASPIRANT
Everything else has disappeared. The steps by which we so laboriously climbed to the summit have vanished.

FIRST ASPIRANT
Emptiness behind, in front, everywhere; there is only room for our feet, nothing more.

SECOND ASPIRANT
Where do we go now? What shall we do?

FIRST ASPIRANT
The Truth is here, Truth alone, all around, everywhere.

SECOND ASPIRANT
And yet to realise it we must go further. And for that another secret must be found.

FIRST ASPIRANT
Obviously, all possibility of personal effort ends here. Another power must intervene.

SECOND ASPIRANT
Grace, Grace alone can act. Grace alone can open the way for us, Grace alone can perform the miracle.

FIRST ASPIRANT (*stretching his arm towards the horizon*)
Look, look over there, far away, on the other side of the bottomless abyss, that peak resplendent with brilliant light, those perfect forms, that marvellous harmony, the promised land, the new earth!

SECOND ASPIRANT
Yes, that is where we must go. But how?

FIRST ASPIRANT
Since that is where we must go, the means will be given to us.

SECOND ASPIRANT
Yes, we must have faith, an absolute trust in the Grace, a total surrender to the Divine.

FIRST ASPIRANT
Yes, an absolute self-giving to the Divine Will. And since all visible paths have disappeared, we must leap forward without fear or hesitation, in complete trust.

SECOND ASPIRANT
And we shall be carried to the place where we must go.

They leap forward.

Epilogue

The Realisation

A land of fairy light.

FIRST ASPIRANT
Here we are, borne upon invisible wings, by a miraculous power!

SECOND ASPIRANT (*looking all around*)
What marvellous splendour! Now we have only to learn to live the new life.

Curtain.

Note on the Texts

The texts in this volume were first published together in 1978 under the title *On Education*, Volume 12 of the Collected Works of the Mother (first edition). The texts in this second edition (2003) are the same as those in the first.

Part One. Articles

These fifteen articles were first published in the Ashram quarterly, *Bulletin of Physical Education* (later renamed *Bulletin of Sri Aurobindo International Centre of Education*) between 1950 and 1955. The Mother wrote them in French and translated a few, entirely or in part, into English; these translations have been retained here. Early translations made by others have been revised, or new translations made for publication here.

Part Two. Messages, Letters and Conversations

I. **Sri Aurobindo International Centre of Education.** The material in this section was compiled from correspondences, private papers, public messages and tape-recorded conversations of the Mother. Some entries were first published in various Ashram books and journals; others first came out in this volume. Most of the entries were written or spoken in French and appear here in an English translation. Some of the early translations have been revised.

II. **Sri Aurobindo Ashram Department of Physical Education.** The nine short pieces introducing this section first appeared in the *Bulletin* between 1949 and 1950. The middle two subsections comprise written and tape-recorded messages to the participants in the competitions and the annual demonstrations of physical culture organised by the Department of Physical Education. The next subsection contains general messages, and letters to individuals. The final subsection, "To Women about Their Body", was first published as a pamphlet in September 1960. Most of the material was written or spoken in French and appears here in an English translation. Some of the early translations have been revised.

III **The New Age Association.** This collection of messages and comments is taken from *The New Age: Speeches at the Seminars and the Conferences of the New Age Association*, published in 1977. All of the texts were written in English.

IV. **Glimpses of the Mother's Work in the School.** These letters and notations of the Mother's spoken comments were given to a teacher of the Centre of Education between 1960 and 1972. The complete collection was first published in the original French, with an English translation, in the *Bulletin* issues of April and August 1978. The same translation appears here, with a few minor revisions.

V. **Answers to a Monitress.** Written to a young captain of the Department of Physical Education, the seven "Sutras" introducing this section first came out in the French original, with an English translation, in the *Bulletin* of November 1959; the correspondence following them was first published in its entirety in 1975 in *Réponses de la Mère à une monitrice*. Parts of the correspondence appeared earlier in Ashram journals, including a series in the *Bulletin* of February 1970. The early English translations have been revised for publication here.

VI. **Answers to a Monitor.** This section contains letters specifically about education from the Mother's correspondence with a young captain of physical education. The complete correspondence was brought out in the French original, with an English translation, in the *Bulletin* between April 1973 and November 1975. The same translation is published here, with minor revisions.

VII. **Conversations.** This section includes two conversations of 1967 and six of February – March 1973. All were spoken in French and appear here in an English translation. The conversation of 11 November 1967 first came out in the French original, with an English translation, in the *Bulletin* of April 1978. Some of the 1973 conversations were first published in various Ashram publications; this more comprehensive collection first appeared in the French original, with a new English translation, in the *Bulletin* of August 1978. For all these conversations the *Bulletin* translations have been used here, with a few minor revisions.

Part Three. Dramas

The Mother wrote three plays in French for performance on December 1 at the annual cultural programme of the Centre of Education. *Towards the Future* was produced in 1949, *The Great Secret* in 1954 and *The Ascent to Truth* in 1957. Each play was issued as a booklet immediately after its performance, with the text in both the French original and an English translation. (In *The Great Secret*, however, the parts of the Writer and the Athlete were written in English.) In this volume, the original English translations of the French texts have been revised.